Beautiful Easy Herbs

Rodale Press, Inc.
Emmaus, Pennsylvania

Beautiful
Easy
HERBS

How to Get the Most from Herbs—
In Your Garden and in Your Home

Laurence Sombke

**Library of Congress
Cataloging-in-Publication Data**

Sombke, Laurence.
    Beautiful easy herbs / Laurence Sombke.
        p.   cm.
    Includes bibliographical references and index.
    ISBN 0–87596–771–X (hardcover : acid-free
paper).
    1. Herb gardening. 2. Herbs. 3. Cookery
(Herbs). I. Title.
SB351.H5S67 1997
635'.7—dc21   97–4901
                                              CIP

Distributed in the book trade
by St. Martin's Press

2 4 6 8 10 9 7 5 3 1   hardcover

Editor: Nancy J. Ondra
Cover and Interior Book Designer: Tanya L. Lipinski
Design Assistants: Karen Lomax, Dale Mack,
  Jen Miller
Interior Illustrators: Mia Bosna, Jean Emmons,
  Jeff George, Dale Mack, Christopher Rhoads
Cover Photographer: Alison Miksch
Photography Editors: James A. Gallucci,
  Heidi A. Stonehill
Copy Editors: Nancy N. Bailey, Sara Cox
Editorial Assistance: Susan L. Nickol, Jodi Rehl,
  Lori Schaffer, Alison Stubits
Manufacturing Coordinator: Patrick T. Smith
Indexer: Lina B. Burton

RODALE HOME AND GARDEN BOOKS

Vice President and Editorial Director:
  Margaret J. Lydic
Managing Editor, Garden Books: Ellen Phillips
Art Director: Paula Jaworski
Associate Art Director: Mary Ellen Fanelli
Studio Manager: Leslie M. Keefe
Copy Director: Dolores Plikaitis
Office Manager: Karen Earl-Braymer

We're happy to hear from you.

For questions or comments concerning the
editorial content of this book, please write to:

**Rodale Press, Inc.
Book Readers' Service
33 East Minor Street
Emmaus, PA 18098**

For more information about Rodale Press and
the books and magazines we publish, visit our
World Wide Web site at:

http://www.rodalepress.com

On the cover: A collage of beautiful easy herbs,
including (*clockwise from top right*) nasturtiums,
parsley, garlic chives, chives, mints, calendulas,
sage, bay, basil, and lemon thyme

To my wife and gardening buddy, Cathy Herman; to my children Henry and Kit; and to the hundreds of wonderful gardeners who have freely given me the benefit of their vast experience and good wishes. They have enriched my life on many levels.

Contents

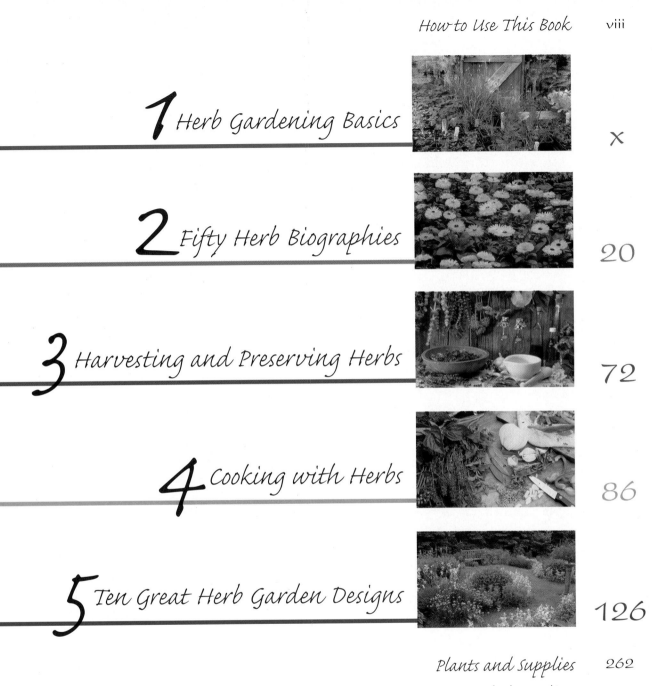

How to Use This Book

From preparing soil for planting to preparing delicious herbal dishes, **Beautiful Easy Herbs** *is your guide to the wonderful world of growing and using herbs. I've included all the basics you need to get your herb garden off to a great start, plus ten garden designs and detailed growing guidelines for 50 beautiful and dependable herbs. You'll also find easy-to-follow pointers for harvesting and preserving your herbal bounty, along with 50 simple but superb herb recipes. The sample pages below show you how each chapter looks, so you'll know just where to go for the information you need to create and enjoy your beautiful easy herb garden!*

1 Herb Gardening Basics

This section covers the nitty-gritty of planning and planting a successful herb garden, from choosing a site and preparing the soil to buying and planting your herbs. You'll also find tips on mulching, watering, and other aspects of garden care, plus pointers on propagating herbs by seed, division, cuttings, and other easy techniques.

2 Fifty Herb Biographies

Want to know how deep to sow savory or the best time to harvest basil? Turn to this chapter to find all the details on growing and harvesting 50 favorite annual and perennial herbs. Each entry offers a photograph and description of the herb, along with tips on how to grow it and how to use it. There's a quick-pick feature, too: Under the photograph, you'll find a quick-reference box that shows you the herb's height, light needs, and moisture preferences at a glance.

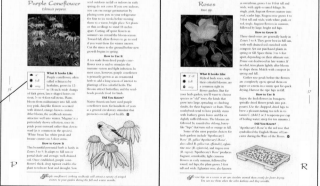

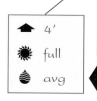

Find out each plant's height, sun or shade preferences, and moisture needs at a glance with this handy key.

viii

3 Harvesting and Preserving Herbs

You've chosen and grown your herbs; now it's time to gather them for use in cooking and crafts. This chapter covers the basics of when and how to harvest for peak flavor and color. You'll also find guidelines on easy preservation techniques, including air, oven, and microwave drying; freezing; and making herbal oils and vinegars.

4 Cooking with Herbs

Even if you never cook, you'll be inspired to try these easy-to-follow recipes with your homegrown herbs. With everything from soups and salads to meat, vegetables, pasta, breads, and desserts, you are sure to find at least one favorite new dish!

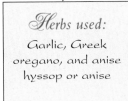

Herbs used:

Garlic, Greek oregano, and anise hyssop or anise

You'll know which herbs you'll need at a glance with this convenient box.

5 Ten Great Garden Designs

In this chapter, you'll find everything you need to create ten beautiful easy herb gardens, including an Early American herb garden; a potpourri garden; a kitchen herb garden; a flowering herb border; an herbal tea garden; a container herb planting; and an herb garden for birds, bees, and butterflies. Each garden includes a plan and illustration of the garden, along with tips on planting and growing each herb. The seasonal guides walk you through the first year for each garden, from planting and care through getting the garden ready for winter.

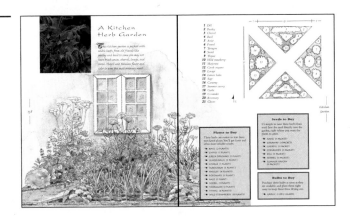

Herb
Gardening
Basics

Chapter 1

Herb Gardening Basics

There's something magical about herbs. Just mentioning their names—chamomile, peppermint, rosemary, thyme—brings to mind delicious dinners, soothing teas, and sweetly scented potpourris and soaps. What is it that makes these plants so special? By definition, herbs are plants that are useful for food, flavoring, medicine, dye, or fragrance. Hundreds or even thousands of plants, including trees, shrubs, grasses, roses, and perennials—have been categorized as herbs because people have found them useful.

But herbs aren't all work and no play. Many herbs can easily hold their own in any flower garden—just think of lavender's spiky blooms, the bright red mopheads of bee balm, or the flat-topped flower clusters of yarrow. Herbs are a natural addition to the vegetable garden as well, giving you one-stop shopping for your dinner fixings plus the pest-fighting benefits of companion planting. (Aromatic herbs also attract pollinators for bigger veggie crops.) Of course, it's also fun to give your herbs a special spot of their own. Grow them in the garden or plant them in pots, keep them outside or bring them indoors—these beautiful easy plants will bring you pleasure anywhere you grow them!

Planning
Your Garden

One of the things I enjoy most about growing herbs is deciding what kind of garden I want. It's fun to plan herb gardens by theme, like an herb tea garden, or by shape, like a wagon-wheel garden. I enjoy period gardens, too, like an Early American garden. What kind of garden *you* plant will depend on how you plan to use your herbs and what style of garden you prefer.

Herbs for Special Uses

Another great thing about an herb garden is that the plants are practical as well as beautiful. If you like to cook, you could have a kitchen garden filled with dozens of sweet and spicy herbs grown for their flavorful leaves, flowers, or seeds. You can specialize and grow a dozen kinds of mint or basil. Or grow herbs with unusually colorful foliage—

Visiting herb gardens is a great way to get ideas. For instance, if you like the look of brick but don't want to be too formal, use curved edges, as this garden does.

If you enjoy drinking tea, consider planting a garden of chamomile, mint, and other beautiful easy tea herbs.

like purple-leaved basil or tricolor sage—to make your dishes as beautiful as they are delicious. If salads are your specialty, you could create a garden of mesclun, basil, and other herbs and greens to provide plenty of fresh fixings for your summer salads. A planting of tasty tea herbs, including chamomile, lemon balm, peppermint, and spearmint, also makes a delightful theme for a garden.

Of course, cooking is only one way to enjoy your beautiful easy herbs. If you enjoy making crafts, consider planting a potpourri garden filled with fragrant and colorful herbs and old-fashioned roses for drying. Many of these same herbs also look great in bouquets and dried wreaths and arrangements. Or how about a colonial herb garden of traditional herbs for old-time home remedies?

Even if you don't have a special use in mind for your herbs, you can still enjoy

the beauty and fragrance of these easy-care plants outdoors. Plant them in containers to brighten a porch or patio. Combine colorful flowering herbs into a pretty perennial border. Or group nectar-rich herbs to create a garden for hummingbirds and butterflies.

To get you started, I've included designs for ten beautiful easy herb gardens, starting on page 126. You can copy these gardens exactly or adjust the plant selections to include your particular favorites.

Formal or Informal?

The mention of herb gardens often brings to mind brick paths, clipped edges, and symmetrical, geometric beds. That's because many herbs *do* lend themselves to this formal look. Others work just as well in informal plantings. Which would work best for you?

If you like the look of straight paths, symmetrical beds, and restrained color schemes, you'll probably enjoy a more formal herb garden. Formal gardens are often a good choice close to a house or deck, where they can complement the colors and lines of the house.

Informal herb gardens have a more casual, cottage-garden feel. They usually have curving lines, and the beds can be any shape. They also can include a wide range of colors and heights—whatever appeals to you.

The ten beautiful easy designs starting on page 126 include both formal and informal herb gardens. If you're not sure which style would work best for you, try visiting other herb gardens in your area to see which you enjoy most.

Choosing
the Right Site

Once you've decided which type of herb garden appeals to you, you need to decide where to put it. Choosing the right site for your herb garden is a critical step in ensuring success. The two main factors to consider are the amount of sun and the drainage of the soil. If you have a property with different sun and soil conditions, you can grow the widest variety of herbs. If your space is limited, you still have plenty of options; you just need to be sure to match the plants you choose with the growing conditions your site has to offer.

Let There Be Light

Almost all herbs thrive in full sun. This means they need at least six hours of sun a day—and ideally more—during the main part of the growing season (roughly from June through mid-September). There are some that can take partial shade (about four hours of sun a day) and a few that can get by on even less sun. To find out the particular light needs of herbs you'd like to grow, look them up in "Fifty Herb Biographies," starting on page 20.

When choosing a site for your herb garden, don't forget to look for buildings or trees that might cast shade at other times of the year. A site that receives full sun in spring may be shaded by summertime if it is under deciduous trees.

Consider the Soil

Herbs have pretty much the same soil needs as other common garden plants. They grow best in a soil that holds some water but is loose enough to let excess water drain freely. They also appreciate a moderate amount of nutrients and organic matter in the soil.

If your other garden plants are thriving, chances are your soil will be fine for a wide range of herbs. If you want to be sure—or if you suspect that your soil is too heavy, wet, or lacking in nutrients—there are a few easy tests you can do.

Testing Soil Texture: A simple squeeze test will tell you a lot about your soil. Just scoop up a handful of moist garden soil and squeeze it. If the ball of soil crumbles when you touch it lightly, it is on the sandy or loamy side—ideal for most herbs. If the soil ball stays in a tight lump when you tap it, your soil is high in clay. Clay soil tends to hold too much water when wet and packs into tight clods when dry.

If you have clay soil, you can still grow herbs. You'll just need to do a little extra work when you prepare the site for planting. One option is to work lots of compost into the soil to loosen up the clay. Digging a 2- to 3-inch layer of compost into the top 8 inches of soil should do the trick for most herbs.

If you have clay soil and plan to grow herbs that require very loose soil, such as lavender, rosemary, and rue, it's worth going the extra step of building raised beds. Raised beds are 4- to 8-inch-deep frames of boards or rocks filled with a mixture of well-drained topsoil and compost. Raising the planting area over the normal soil level will give your herbs extra room for healthy root growth.

*R*aised beds look great and provide the excellent drainage many herbs need to thrive.

Determining Drainage: Soil drainage is often closely related to soil texture. Clay soils tend to be on the soggy side, while loamy and sandy soils are usually well drained. But sometimes even loose surface soil can stay wet if water is coming up from below or if there's a compacted layer just under the surface.

To check the drainage, dig a hole about 1 foot deep and 6 inches across. Fill the hole with water. Let all the water drain out, then fill it again. If it takes more than six hours for the water to drain completely, consider building raised beds, as discussed in "Testing Soil Texture" on the opposite page.

Herbs that are native to the Mediterranean, including oregano, rosemary, and thyme, need excellent drainage. Standing water can kill them. But large-leaved herbs like basil and bee balm can often thrive with more moisture. And some herbs, including pennyroyal, sorrel, and some mints, actually like wet feet.

Checking Soil Fertility: Two other soil considerations are nutrient content and pH (the measure of the soil's acidity or alkalinity). Just like other plants, herbs need a balanced supply of nitrogen, phosphorus, potassium, and other nutrients for healthy, vigorous growth. They also thrive with a pH near neutral—somewhere between 6.5 and 7.2.

If your other garden plants are growing well with little or no extra fertilizer (besides a mulch of compost), the pH and fertility of your soil are probably fine for herbs. If you want to make sure, you can buy simple home test kits at your local garden center. Or for a more detailed analysis, have a sample of your soil analyzed by a soil-testing lab. Check with your county's Cooperative Extension Service for information on your state's soil-testing service, or look in the phone book for private testing labs.

Planning for Planting

Once you've selected the right site for your herbs, you can think about preparing the site for planting. You can work the soil just about any time it isn't frozen, although spring and fall are ideal, since they are also good planting times.

Check Soil Moisture

Before you grab your spade or tiller, make sure your soil is somewhat moist, but not wet. If you dig when the soil is too wet, the soil will stick to your tools, making digging harder than necessary, and it may dry into clumps that are hard to break apart. Digging soil that is too dry also takes extra work, and tilling at this stage can break the good soil crumbs into a powder-fine dust.

To check the moisture content, squeeze a handful of soil from the spot you want to cultivate. If the soil stays in a firm ball when you open your hand, it's too wet to work. If it falls apart, it's too dry. If it holds together until you tap it lightly, it's just right.

Get Rid of the Grass

Unless you're planting herbs in an existing garden, you'll need to get rid of some lawn grass to make your new garden. In small areas, a spade is usually the most practical tool for the job. If you have a large area to prepare, consider renting a sod cutter to remove the grass.

Start by outlining the area you want to clear with a sprinkling of garden lime or flour. If you are using a sod-cutting machine, follow the operating instructions to strip off the turf with just ¼ to ½ inch of soil.

To remove sod with a spade, first hold the blade at a right angle to the surface, and cut around the outside of the area. Then insert the tip of the blade into one of the cut edges and pull the handle back toward you, until it's at a 45- to 60-degree angle to the soil surface. (You want the blade to be nearly parallel with the soil surface.) Then push the blade under the grass plants to sever the tops from the roots. As you loosen flaps of turf, pull them up. Gather them in a wheelbarrow, then dump them on your compost pile.

Removing the sod does take some work, but it's worth your time to do the job right. Please don't be tempted to just work the grass into the soil with a rotary tiller. You'll just chop the grass plants into many smaller pieces that will quickly resprout after you plant your garden. The time and effort you'll spend pulling out all those grass plants from between your herbs will make you wish you'd done the job right!

Cultivating the Soil

Most herbs will do just fine if you loosen the top 8 inches of soil before

CONTROLLING
SPREADING HERBS

Some herbs, including horseradish and mints, can actually grow too well, crowding out other plants. Control them by planting in bottomless pots or buckets that are sunk into the soil, or give them a separate area where they can spread freely.

Cut out the bottom of a plastic or metal container to keep herbs' wandering roots and stems in check. Make sure the container has room for your herb plant to grow!

You'll save yourself a lot of weeding next year if you deadhead herbs before they set seed.

Growing herbs in a patio will keep them from spreading by creeping stems or invasive roots.

A container is a great way to confine invasive herbs like mint.

planting. You can cultivate the site with your own energy or use a power-driven rotary tiller.

Digging by Hand: Digging your garden by hand is very satisfying as well as good exercise. It's also the most practical option if you're digging small areas or if you're preparing odd-shaped beds, such as circles or triangles.

Most gardeners have a favorite digging tool. Some like to use a flat-bladed spade or a curved-bladed shovel; others prefer to use a four-tine spading fork. If you don't already have a favorite, try them out and pick whichever tool you feel most comfortable using.

Don't neglect the faithful trowel when you're thinking about hand tools. For planting a few herbs or inter-planting herbs in existing flower or vegetable beds, a trowel is ideal. It's also great for planting in tight spaces—among tree or shrub roots, for example. If you don't already have a favorite trowel, try out the wide selection at your garden center and pick the most comfortable one.

To prepare a bed for planting, hold the handle of the fork, spade, or shovel straight up and down, and push the blade or tines all the way into the soil. Bend at the waist and knees to slide the blade or tines under a scoop of soil, then straighten up to lift the load. Tilt the handle to drop the soil back into the hole. If needed, use the side of the blade or the tines to break up large lumps before moving to the next spot.

Always start digging along one side of the garden and work backward over the site as you dig. That way you won't step on already-loosened soil.

Using a Rotary Tiller: Tillers can be handy for soil preparation when you're digging a big area or when your time and energy are limited. Unless you plan to put in many new gardens, it's much more practical to rent a tiller for a day or weekend than it is to buy one. Ask which model would be most comfortable for you. Following the operating instructions, set the tines to loosen the top 6 to 8 inches of soil.

Adding Soil Amendments: After the first digging or tilling, spread a 1- to 2-inch layer of compost over the site. If you don't have a compost pile— yet!—you can buy bagged compost or collect it for free from your local yard waste recycling center. But compost is so easy to make that it's a shame not to have your own pile. Just toss on grass clippings, leaves, vegetable scraps, coffee grounds, tea bags, shredded newspaper, even eggshells, and voilà—you're on the way to rich, crumbly compost.

If your soil test results showed that you need to add fertilizer, lime, sulfur, or other amendments, this is a good time to apply them as well. Dig or till the site again to work the compost and other amendments into the top 5 to 6 inches of soil. Then rake the site to break up any remaining clumps, and smooth the surface. Remember that more is not better when it comes to soil amendments for herb gardens. Most herbs prefer an average soil, not rich soil like vegetables or flowers. So follow your soil test recommendations closely.

Buying and Planting Herbs

One of the most fun parts of starting any garden is gathering the plants and seeds you need. Sow or set them out into the soil you've prepared, and your garden is ready to get growing!

Get Your Plants and Seeds

Most garden centers and nurseries sell a reasonable selection of common herbs in spring. For your first herb garden, you might be content with whatever is available locally. But if you are looking for uncommon herbs (like cardoon or 'Apothecary's Rose') or for more unusual kinds of ordinary herbs (such as chocolate mint or caraway thyme), you'll probably need to try mail-order sources.

Some mail-order companies specialize in herbs. You'll love poring over their mouthwatering lists of varieties. Companies that specialize in either flowers or vegetables usually also carry a selection of herbs. You may need to order from a few different sources to get all the plants and seeds you need.

If you have friends with herb gardens, you may be able to get pieces of their plants when they divide their herbs. Anyone with bee balm, horseradish, lemon balm, mints, sweet woodruff, and other vigorous herbs is generally happy to share a clump. And you'll enjoy them more because of their source.

Plant at the Right Time

The ideal time to plant your garden depends on which herbs you're growing. In this case, whether the herb can tolerate frost is more important than whether it's an annual or perennial.

Planting Tender Herbs: Herbs that are sensitive to cold or frost—including basil, rosemary, and scented geraniums—are classified as tender herbs. The general benchmark for sowing or setting out tender herbs is around your last frost date. This refers to the average date of the last spring frost in your area. If you don't know your last frost date, ask gardening friends in your neighborhood or check with your local garden center.

Planting Hardy Herbs: Hardy herbs can withstand cold temperatures. Some of the many common hardy herbs include bee balm, calendula, chives, parsley, and purple coneflower. You can sow seed or set out transplants of hardy herbs as soon as you've prepared the soil for planting. If you purchase plants that were grown in a greenhouse or if you start your own herb seedlings indoors, you'll need to expose them gradually to outdoor conditions, a process called "hardening off." For complete details, see "Handling Hardening Off" on page 10.

HANDLING HARDENING OFF

When you buy herbs from a greenhouse or grow them yourself indoors, they will need some special care to adjust to life in the garden. About a week before planting herbs outside, set them outdoors for an hour or two in a shady, sheltered spot, then bring them back inside. Each day, leave them out for a few more hours, in brighter and more open locations. Bring them in at night if frost is predicted. Water as needed to prevent your herbs from wilting, but don't keep them wet. They'll adapt better to transplanting if they're used to being on the dry side.

Once your herbs have been outside around the clock, you can set them out in the garden. If frost threatens after planting, cover your herbs at night.

Sow the Seeds

Many herbs are easy to grow from seed, either started indoors or sown directly in the garden. Starting seed is fun, and it's a great way to save money if you need lots of herbs to fill a new garden.

Sowing Seed Outdoors: Sowing directly in the garden is the easiest method of starting many herbs, including calendulas, nasturtiums, and summer savory, just to name a few. It's also the best way to start deep-rooted herbs, such as caraway, dill, and fennel. (Transplanting can damage their long, tapering main root, leading to stunted growth in the garden.)

To start seed outdoors, prepare the soil as you normally would for planting, then rake carefully to create a fine, crumbly seedbed free of rocks and debris. Scatter fine seed as evenly as possible over the soil so they're about 1 or 2 inches apart. Place large seeds, like nasturtiums, individually with your fingers. For the sowing depth, follow the recommendations on the seed packet or in the individual entries in "Fifty Herb Biographies," starting on page 20.

After planting, water thoroughly to moisten the seedbed. Use a watering can or a hose with a fine spray to water gently so you don't wash the seeds away. Water frequently—as often as every day, if it doesn't rain—to keep the seedbed moist until your seedlings appear.

When the seedlings are a few inches tall, thin them to the recommended spacings. Use scissors to snip off extra seedlings at ground level; pulling them out could injure the remaining seedlings.

Sowing Seed Indoors: If you like the idea of growing your own herb plants, you can start many of them indoors from seed. Anise hyssop, basil, cardoon, chives, feverfew, horehound, and summer savory are some of the easiest herbs to start inside.

Start your seeds indoors in early to midspring. Buy a bag of seed-starting mix, dump most of it into a large bucket, and add about a quart of warm water. Work the water into the mix with your hands, then squeeze a handful of the mix. If it falls apart when you open your hand, add more water. If water runs out of your hand when you squeeze the mix, add more dry mix. You want the mix to hold together in a ball that crumbles when you tap it.

Now, gather your containers. Plastic, 3- to 4-inch pots are ideal for starting herbs. If you've purchased plants before, you probably have some of these pots sitting around. (Knock out any clinging soil before reusing them.) Otherwise, you can buy them for a few cents each at your local garden center. Fill the pots with moist seed-starting mix to within ⅓ inch of the rim. Smooth the surface of the mix with your fingers.

Scatter the seeds as evenly as possible over the surface of the mix. If the seeds need to be covered (the seed packet should tell you the recommended sowing depth), sprinkle moist mix over the seed. Otherwise, just press the seed lightly into the mix with your fingers.

Set each seed pot into a large plastic bag, blow some air into the bag, and close the top with a rubber band or twist tie. Set the covered pots in a spot

Many herbs, including rosemary, adapt well to life in containers, either indoors or out. Grow them in well-drained potting soil—I like to use a cactus mix.

with bright but indirect light. Leave the bags on until you see sprouts appearing. Then gradually open the bags a little at a time over a few days—maybe an hour the first day, two hours the next, then a half day—then remove it completely.

Move the pots of seedlings to a sunny windowsill, or grow them under fluorescent shop lights. (Hang the lights 4 to 6 inches over the tops of the seedlings.) When the top of the mix dries out—it will usually turn a light brown color—set the pots in a shallow pan filled with 1 inch of water. Let them soak for a few hours, until the surface of the mix looks moist. Remove them from the pan. When seedlings are a few inches tall, start feeding them with fish emulsion, according to label directions.

If your seedlings start to look crowded, remove the whole clump from the pot. Use your fingers or a fork to separate the big clump into four to eight smaller sections. Plant each section in a 3- to 4-inch pot of moist potting soil.

Move your seedlings outdoors at the proper planting time for each herb (as explained on the seed packet or in the individual entries in "Fifty Herb Biographies," starting on page 20). Follow the directions in "Handling Hardening Off" on page 10 to help your seedlings adjust to life outdoors before planting them in the garden.

Time to Plant

If possible, choose a cool, cloudy day to plant your herbs; they'll settle into their new home more quickly if they aren't stressed by hot sun right away.

The night or morning before transplanting, water all of your herbs thoroughly. When you are ready to plant, set the pots out on top of the prepared soil. Adjust the arrangement and spacing of the herbs as needed, until they look good to you. If you are planting according to a plan, don't be tempted to space the plants more closely than the plan calls for. Your herbs will grow quickly and fill their allotted space within a season or two. (If you think the garden looks too sparse the first year, tuck in plants of parsley, basil, or cheerful marigolds as fillers for the first year or two.)

When your arrangement looks good and you're ready to plant, work with one herb at a time. Carefully slide the herb out of its pot. Use your fingers to "comb" the sides of the rootball to loosen any tangled or circling roots. With a trowel, dig a hole big enough to hold the whole rootball, with at least 1 or 2 inches of space around the sides. Adjust the depth of the hole as needed so that the crown of the herb (the point where the roots join the stems) is at the same level that it was when the plant was in the pot.

When the hole is the right depth, hold the herb in place with one hand, and use your other hand to scoop the soil back around the roots. Use your fingers to gently firm the soil around the base of the herb. Water thoroughly to settle the soil around the roots.

Repeat the process with each herb until you've planted them all. If the soil is somewhat dry, water the whole bed again after planting.

In the garden, plant each herb so that the top of the rootball is even with or just slightly above the soil surface.

Keeping
Herbs Healthy

Herbs are tough, easy-to-grow plants that will thrive without a lot of fussing from you. Just a little basic care will help keep them looking—and tasting!—their best.

Add Mulch

Mulch will go a long way toward reducing your garden's maintenance needs. A 1- to 2-inch layer of organic mulch, such as chopped leaves or shredded bark, will help to keep the soil evenly moist, so that you'll water less often. It will also prevent light from reaching the soil, so that weed seeds on the soil surface will be less likely to sprout. Any weeds that do pop up through the mulch layer will be easier to pull out.

If you put down a 1-inch layer of compost before adding the top mulch, you'll be feeding your herbs at the same time you're mulching them. As the compost breaks down, it will release a slow but steady supply of nutrients.

It's good to wait until late spring or early summer to mulch, so your soil has a chance to warm up. (Mulching earlier will keep the soil cold and wet, and your herbs may rot.) If the weather has been dry, water before mulching. And weed thoroughly: Mulch will not smother weeds that are already growing.

When you spread mulch, make sure you keep it 1 or 2 inches away from the base of herb stems. Otherwise, the mulch may hold moisture against the stems and encourage rot. Renew the compost-and-bark or compost-and-leaf mulch each year.

Keep two cautions in mind when using mulch. First, if you live in a rainy or cool climate, keep your total mulch layer only ½ to 1 inch deep, and wait until midsummer to mulch. This will keep the soil from staying too wet and give it more chance to warm up. Second, if you notice that slugs or snails are seriously damaging your herbs— chewing large holes in the leaves or devouring whole plants—immediately rake off the mulch. (Moist mulch provides an ideal hiding place for slugs and snails.) Try replacing some or all of the mulch in a few weeks, when things have dried out. If damage occurs again, rake off the mulch and don't apply any more.

Water Wisely

While some herbs have a reputation for thriving in dry soil, most grow just fine with the same amount of moisture as other garden plants. But if you've added compost to the soil before planting and mulched after planting, your herbs probably won't need much supplemental watering.

If you don't get any rain for a week or two, brush aside some of the mulch and look at the soil. If the surface still looks dark and moist, replace the mulch and check again in a few days. When the soil surface looks dry, use a trowel to dig a small hole a few inches deep. When the top 2 to 3 inches are dry, it's time to water.

If you only have to water a few times a year, you can get by with a handheld hose for watering. Make sure you water long enough to soak the top few inches of soil. It may take several watering sessions (watering for 15 minutes, letting it soak in for 15 minutes, then repeating the process) to apply this much water.

If you normally have to water your other gardens during the summer, it's smart to plan ahead and install a soaker hose right after planting your herbs in spring. Soaker hoses (also known as leaky pipes) look like regular hoses, but their sides have many tiny pores that ooze water into the soil. Simply snake the hose between your plants, leaving about 12 inches between the "rows" of hose. Leave the open end of the hose at one edge of the garden, so you can reach it easily. Apply mulch right over the hose.

When you need to water, just connect the end of your garden hose to the soaker hose, turn on the water, and let it run for a few hours to soak the top 4 to 6 inches of soil.

Groom for Good Growth

A little pinching here and there will help keep your herbs bushy and productive. On herbs that you're growing for their leaves, such as basil, burnet, mint, and sorrel, pinching off the flower buds as soon as you spot them will promote more leafy growth.

On other herbs, you'll want to pinch off the flowers *after* they bloom. This technique, called deadheading, will encourage some plants to keep producing more flowers. It's a good trick for extending the bloom season on bee balm, calendula, feverfew, hyssop, purple coneflower, and yarrow.

Deadheading can also save you weeding time. Angelica, anise hyssop, chives, dill, fennel, feverfew, and lovage are a few of the herbs that produce large amounts of seed. If you let these herbs ripen and drop all their seed, you'll have a big job pulling out all the unwanted

The small flowers of herbs like dill and fennel are rich in pollen and nectar, so they attract pest-eating beneficial insects to your garden.

14

seedlings next year. If you don't plan to collect the seed for cooking or crafts, pinch off all the flowers or flower clusters as soon as they fade. (Or, if you'd like a few seedlings, allow just a few flowers to mature, and pinch or cut off the rest.)

Control Pests and Diseases Organically

When you give your herbs the sun and soil conditions they prefer, they will naturally be vigorous and less prone to problems. Many flowering herbs also attract lady beetles, lacewings, and other beneficial insects that will keep pest problems to a minimum.

To help your herbs stay healthy, pinch or cut off any discolored or spotted leaves and insect-infested stalks as soon as you spot them. A forceful spray from a hose can knock small pests like aphids off leaves and stems. Hand-pick larger pests (wear gloves if you're squeamish!), and drop them into a can of soapy water.

To avoid spreading diseases, stay out of your garden when the plants are wet. To encourage good air circulation around the stems and leaves—and therefore faster drying—cut out some of the stems of crowded clumps, or divide large clumps to reduce their size.

In general, you should avoid spraying any pesticides or fungicides around your herbs, especially if you plan to eat them! Sprays can harm beneficial creatures as well as the bad guys, so pest problems can actually be worse after spraying than before. If you always have a problem with a particular herb, consider moving the plant to another part of the garden or replacing it with another herb.

Meanwhile, try these safe, organic methods when a pest or disease problem breaks out. They work!

Aphids: Aphids are small ($\frac{1}{5}$- to $\frac{1}{12}$-inch), winged or wingless pests that may be green, gray, black, or pink. They tend to cluster on shoot tips and flower buds, but you may also find them on leaves and stems. Their feeding causes yellowing and distorted growth. You may also notice a sticky or black coating on leaves due to the sugary sap the aphids excrete as they feed.

If there are just a few aphids, you can squash them with your fingers. Hose off larger aphid clusters. Pinch or cut off seriously infested plant parts.

Spider Mites: These tiny, spiderlike, pale or reddish brown pests usually congregate on the undersides of plant leaves. Their feeding causes a silvery or yellowish stippling pattern on leaf surfaces. You may also notice tiny webs between the leaves and the stems. Spider mites are often a problem on herbs growing indoors in winter.

A strong spray of water from a hose or shower can knock these pests off your plants. (If your herb is in a pot, cover the soil to keep the water from washing it out of the pot.) Keep rinsing every day or two until the pests disappear.

Whiteflies: These small ($\frac{1}{12}$-inch), white flying insects feed on the undersides of plant leaves, causing distorted growth and discoloration on leaf surfaces. You'll see these pests fly up when you brush against the plant. (They look like a small white cloud!) Whiteflies are most common on herbs grown indoors or purchased from a greenhouse, but they may also feed on outdoor herbs.

If whiteflies are numerous, pinch off infested leaves to remove the eggs. To control the adults, try sucking them off the plant with a portable, handheld vacuum cleaner.

Powdery Mildew: This fungal disease produces powdery gray or white patches on leaves and stems. It is a common problem on bee balm.

Pinch off infected leaves as soon as you see them. To minimize problems, thin out crowded clumps by pinching or cutting out one-third to one-half of the stems at ground level in midspring. If powdery mildew attacks every year, re-place the affected herb with a cultivar that is naturally mildew-resistant (such as 'Marshall's Delight' bee balm).

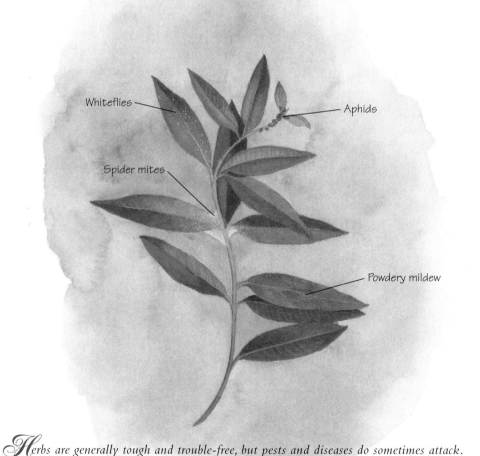

Herbs are generally tough and trouble-free, but pests and diseases do sometimes attack. Pinching off affected parts is a quick and effective control measure.

Making More Herbs

nce you've started your first herb garden, you'll want to grow more and more herbs. Fortunately, there are some simple techniques you can use to add to your herb garden without spending a fortune buying new plants.

Divide to Multiply

Division is a fast and easy way to propagate clump-forming perennial herbs, including bee balm, chives, mint, sorrel, sweet woodruff, tansy, tarragon, yarrow, and many others. Regular division—every three years or so—will also help to keep these herbs vigorous and productive.

Early spring and fall are both good times to divide herbs. Dig up the clump you want to divide by cutting around it with a trowel, spade, or shovel. Lift the clump and set it on the ground. Decide how many pieces you want to get from the clump. A clump about the size of your hand will generally yield two to four sections. Larger clumps can usually give you six to eight new pieces. Each new piece should be big enough to have at least one stem (ideally two or more) as well as some roots.

Divide small clumps with your hands or a trowel. For larger clumps, you may need a knife or hatchet to cut the sections apart. Discard any old, woody growth in the center of the clump.

If the plant has any topgrowth, cut it back to within 1 inch of the roots.

Replant the divisions in the garden immediately. (Add some fresh soil and compost to the hole before replanting in the original spot.) Or plant them in pots of potting soil, and set them in a shady place until you decide what to do with them. Either way, water thoroughly after planting.

Take Cuttings

Many herbs are also easy to propagate by cuttings (sections of stems you remove from a plant and expose to certain conditions to encourage rooting). This technique allows you to make dozens of new plants from just one herb. Bee balm, catnip, hyssop, lemon balm, mints, oregano, scented geraniums, thymes, and wormwood are just a few herbs that grow easily from cuttings. Make sure you take extra cuttings for gifts!

Spring and early fall are good times to take cuttings, since plants are usually growing strongly then. Select vigorous, healthy-looking shoots, ideally without flowers. Use sharp scissors or shears to snip off the top 3 to 5 inches of the shoot tip. Cut just above a leaf or leaf pair.

Snip off the bottom stub of the cutting, just below a leaf or leaf pair. Pull or cut off the leaves on the bottom half of the cutting, and remove any flower buds. Insert the leafless part of the stem into a pot of moist perlite or vermiculite (available at garden centers). You can

Gardening Basics

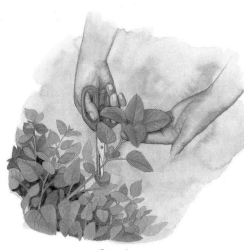

Step 1

Step 2

Step 3

It's easy to start herbs from cuttings! Just follow these three simple steps:

Step 1. *Snip off a 3- to 5-inch section from a vigorous shoot tip.*

Step 2. *Trim the base of the cutting just below a leaf or leaf pair. Remove the bottom leaves.*

Step 3. *Stick the cutting halfway into moist perlite or vermiculite. Cover with a plastic bag, and set in bright but indirect light for four to six weeks.*

usually fit two to four cuttings in a 4-inch pot; just make sure you space them so that their leaves don't touch.

When the pot is full, water to firm the medium around the stems. Cover the cuttings with an upside-down clear jar or plastic bag. (If needed, insert a small stake or a piece of wire bent in a U-shape in the pot to keep the cover from resting directly on the cuttings.)

Set the planted cuttings in a spot with bright but indirect light. Within four to six weeks, your cuttings should start producing new growth. To check for rooting, remove the cover and tug lightly on the stems. If you feel some

18

resistance, roots are forming. Once the cuttings have rooted, remove the cover permanently, and move them to a brighter spot. Within a week or two, your plants will be ready to plant outdoors or into individual pots.

Layer Long Stems

Layering is the easiest way to propagate plants. It's almost trouble-free! Unfortunately, it doesn't work for all plants. But layering is a good way to propagate herbs that have long, flexible stems, such as rosemary, sage, tarragon, and thyme. In spring or summer, select a long stem and gently bend it to the ground. Use a piece of wire bent into a U-shape to pin the stem to the ground. Cover the pin and stem with ½ to 1 inch of soil. Water as needed to keep the soil moist around the stem. New roots will form in four to six weeks. (Check by tugging very gently if you're not sure that the layer has rooted.) When the shoot starts growing again, dig it up with a trowel, separate it from the parent stem, and move it to its new spot.

Some herbs are so easy to layer that you can just scrape a little bare patch in the soil under the stem, bend the stem to the soil, and weight it down with a rock. Check the following season to see if your new plant is ready to separate from its parent. If a layered stem seems reluctant to root, make a small slit on the underside of the stem—the side that's touching the soil—and wedge it open with a toothpick. Roots should

Mound layering works well for propagating thymes. Simply pile sandy soil over and around the plant. The buried parts of the stems will form roots within a few weeks.

form quickly at the site of the cut.

A technique similar to stem layering, called mound or stool layering, works especially well on bushy plants, such as sage and thyme. Simply mound some sandy soil over and around the base of established plants, leaving the shoot tips exposed. After four to six weeks, the buried part of each stem will produce roots. Dig up each rooted section with a trowel, and transplant to a new location.

That's all you need to know to plant and grow beautiful healthy herbs. Pretty simple, right? Now it's time to meet my favorite herbs and find some new (and old) friends of your own. Just turn to "Fifty Herb Biographies" on page 20, and dig in! 🌀

Fifty Herb Biographies

Chapter 2

Fifty Herb Biographies

Herbs are some of the most friendly and interesting plants you can grow. Just like people, they have individual histories, personalities—even neighborhoods (the places they come from). Getting to know your herbs will make your herb garden even more interesting and fun to grow.

In this chapter, you'll find the biographies of 50 herbs—some widely grown, some not as well known as they deserve to be. You'll find out what each herb looks like, where it likes to grow, where it came from, and how to grow it. Read on for how to use each herb in the garden and the kitchen. You'll also learn about some of these herbs' lesser-known relatives as well as some tidbits from their colorful histories. Get ready to make friends with these 50 beautiful easy herbs!

Angelica
Angelica archangelica

8'
full
moist

What It Looks Like
Angelica is likely the largest herb you will ever grow. In its first year, it forms 2- to 3-foot-wide clumps of deeply cut, long-stemmed leaves. In the second year, its hollow, pinkish green stems rise up to 8 feet tall. In spring and early summer, these stems are adorned with domed flower clusters that look much like those of a huge Queen-Anne's-lace. The clusters are made of many small, greenish white, slightly fragrant flowers. The stems and seedheads turn a dusty brown in late fall.

How to Grow It
Angelica is a biennial or short-lived perennial hardy in Zones 4 to 9. It prefers a cool climate and fairly moist soil enriched with compost. It performs well in sun but can also grow in light shade.

Sow seeds in the garden in spring or early fall. (The seeds germinate poorly after about a year, so you'll get the best results from fresh seeds.) Do not cover; the seeds need light to germinate. Just press into the soil and keep moist until sprouts appear. Thin so plants stand 3 feet apart, then mulch heavily.

Let angelica grow as a bushy clump of foliage the first year; it will die back to the ground after frost. In the second year, it will send up new shoots that you can harvest in early spring. Leave a few shoots to mature and flower. If you allow the seedheads to develop, the plant will die after the seed ripens, but the self-sown seedlings will provide all the replacements you can use. Or you can remove the flowerheads before the seeds start to form; this will prevent self-sowing and extend the life of the plant for a few more years.

How to Use It
Cook angelica's second-year stems like celery; they are slightly sweet and are good as a side dish or in stews. You can also candy the stems and use them to garnish cakes and desserts. But the best use of angelica is for its visual impact; grow it at the back of the herb garden for structure and vertical interest.

Did You Know?
Legend has it that during the Middle Ages, the Archangel Michael appeared in a dream and informed a monk that angelica could be used to cure the plague. Angelica was also reputed to ward off the evil spirits of witchcraft.

A

Anise

Pimpinella anisum

🔺	18"
☀	full
💧	avg

What It Looks Like

Anise, also known as aniseed, is a graceful, tender annual that forms 12- to 18-inch-wide clumps of small, delicate, licorice-scented leaves. The leaves are somewhat rounded and toothed when young, but they become much more finely cut and feathery as the plant matures. Flattened clusters of tiny, white, starlike flowers appear on 12- to 18-inch stalks in late summer. The lacy bloom clusters will attract many beneficial insects to your garden.

How to Grow It

Choose a well-drained planting site in full sun. A spot protected from strong wind is ideal to keep the thin stems from getting blown over. Anise prefers slightly alkaline soil, so add a little lime if your soil is on the acid side. This taprooted herb transplants poorly, so it's best to sow seed directly into the garden. Plant in late spring after all danger of frost has passed. Thin plants to stand about 18 inches apart. Be sure to keep weeds under control, at least until the seedlings have several leaves; established plants are trouble-free. Anise will self-sow if you allow a few seeds to drop at harvesting time.

Pick tender, young leaves as needed for fresh use. Harvest, dry, and store the seeds when they ripen in late summer or early fall. The plant dies in fall with frost.

How to Use It

Anise's sweet-tasting leaves add zip to salads. They also make an attractive and unusual garnish. But the main reason to grow anise is for its aromatic seeds; add them whole or crushed to breads, cakes, and pastries. The crushed seeds are also a fragrant addition to potpourri.

Did You Know?

Anise is native to Europe and the Mediterranean. The Egyptians began cultivating anise around 1500 B.C. The Romans included anise seeds in dessert cakes as a digestive aid. Anise is used to flavor liqueurs, including anisette, ouzo, and Pernod. 🔆

A

Anise seeds mature and drop quickly, so keep a close eye on them. Clip off the seedheads into a large paper bag as soon as the seeds turn brown.

Anise Hyssop

Agastache foeniculum

3'

full

avg

What It Looks Like

Anise hyssop is a bushy, perennial herb with sturdy, square stems clad in pointed, green leaves. The stems rise up to 3 feet tall and are topped with 3- to 6-inch spikes of lavender-blue flowers in mid- to late summer. You will see a lot of bees and butterflies buzzing around this beauty, seeking its rich nectar. The leaves and flowers have a slight licorice-like scent and flavor. If you prefer white flowers, look for the cultivar 'Alabaster'.

How to Grow It

Anise hyssop is hardy in Zones 4 to 9. Give it a site with full sun and average, well-drained soil. Buy young plants, or start the seeds indoors in late winter. (Sow them ⅛ inch deep.) Set plants out 2 feet apart in spring around the last frost date. Even though anise hyssop is a perennial, the seedlings usually are vigorous enough to reach blooming size

the first year. They do tend to be short-lived, however, so divide the clumps every year or two in spring to keep them vigorous. Or simply let the parent plants die out; if you have allowed their flowers to set seed, you will end up with plenty of replacement seedlings. Anise hyssop dies back to ground level after a hard frost and is very slow to emerge in the spring.

Pick leaves and flowers as needed for fresh use in summer, or dry them for winter use.

How to Use It

Anise hyssop is an excellent addition to gardens to attract bees and butterflies. It is so pretty that it deserves a place in the perennial border as well as in the herb garden. The fresh or dried leaves add a licorice flavor to hot or cold tea, and the fresh flowers are attractive in salads. The dried leaves and flowers are a fragrant addition to potpourri.

Did You Know?

Anise hyssop is native to North America and was used by Native Americans in cough syrup.

24

A

Harvest anise hyssop by cutting plants to the ground and hanging them upside down in a dark, airy place. Strip off the dried leaves and flowers.

Arugula
Eruca vesicaria subsp. sativa

↑	16″
☀	full
💧	avg

What It Looks Like
Arugula, also known as rocket, roquette, or rugula, grows in rosettes of lobed, lance-shaped, green leaves that look somewhat like dandelion leaves. It produces elongated clusters of yellowish white, dark-veined flowers in summer. This salad herb grows 12 to 16 inches tall and about 10 inches wide.

How to Grow It
Arugula is a half-hardy annual that you grow from seed. It thrives in compost-enriched soil in full sun but appreciates afternoon shade on hot summer days. Sow the seed in early spring, as soon as you can work the soil. Scatter the seeds over a well-prepared bed, cover with ¼ inch of fine soil, and water as needed to keep the soil moist until seedlings appear. Thin seedlings to leave 6 to 10 inches between plants. Make several more small plantings two or three weeks apart in spring and then again in late summer for a continuous crop. The plants will withstand light frost. This easy garden crop also grows well in containers and windowboxes.

Arugula is a cut-and-come-again herb. Regular harvesting will encourage the plant to keep producing new growth. You can start harvesting within four to six weeks after sowing. Pick the leaves as needed when they are 4 to 6 inches long. For best flavor, harvest the tender, young leaves before the flower-stalk appears. When warm weather arrives and plants begin to bloom, you can harvest the stems and flowers. If you allow a few plants to flower and set seed, you can collect the seeds for next year's crop or simply let them self-sow.

How to Use It
The tangy leaves taste a lot like peppery watercress. They have a thick, delicious meaty texture. Use arugula fresh in salads, or add the chopped leaves to stir-fries, pasta dishes, and chicken soup.

Did You Know?
This Mediterranean native has been grown and eaten by Roman, Italian, and Provençal people for centuries. It has recently become more widely grown as a gourmet salad green. 🍥

A

Basil

Ocimum basilicum

▲ 2'
☀ full
♦ avg

What It Looks Like

Beginning herb gardeners are most familiar with sweet basil, a vigorous, bushy herb that grows 18 to 24 inches tall and wide and has smooth, bright green leaves. 'Mammoth' is a selection with exceptionally large, smooth green leaves, ideal for wrapping fillings for hors d'oeuvres. At the other extreme is 'Spicy Globe', with 6- to 10-inch, dense mounds of tiny but flavorful foliage. Add extra color to your herb garden with purple-leaved basils, such as the smooth-leaved 'Red Rubin' and attractively crimped 'Purple Ruffles'.

How to Grow It

In the garden, basil needs full sun and average, well-drained soil. All basils are tender annuals that are quickly killed by frost. In cooler northern states, start seeds indoors about six weeks before your last frost date; transplant to the garden after all danger of frost, when the soil temperature is at least 50°F. In warmer southern states, sow seed directly in warmed garden soil in late spring or early summer. Indoors or out, sow seed about ⅛ inch deep. Making additional sowings every two or three weeks until midsummer can help extend your harvest.

Set or thin small-leaved basils to stand 6 to 8 inches apart; allow 12 to 18 inches between large-leaved types. Water during dry spells. Pinch off the flower spikes as they form.

Regular harvesting will promote bushy growth. You can start picking as soon as plants have several pairs of leaves.

How to Use It

Basil's rich, spicy flavor blends well with many meats and vegetables. Add fresh, frozen, or dried basil to pasta dishes, Mediterranean and Thai foods and fresh or frozen basil to pesto. Add a few sprigs to a bottle of olive oil or white wine vinegar for a flavorful salad dressing.

Did You Know?

Basil is a holy plant in the Greek Orthodox Church because it was said to be growing at the door of Christ's tomb. ⊛

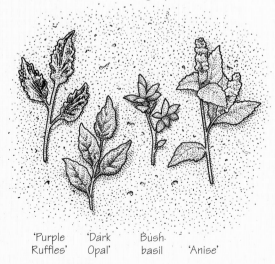

'Purple Ruffles'   'Dark Opal'   Bush basil   'Anise'

B

Fragrant and flavorful, basils make excellent culinary herbs. Their range of leaf colors, shapes, and growth habits makes them attractive garden plants, too.

Bee Balm
Monarda didyma

▲	3'
☀	full
💧	avg

What It Looks Like
Bee balm, also commonly called bergamot or Oswego tea, is an upright, 2- to 3-foot-tall perennial herb with green, pointed, sweet-smelling leaves. Plants grow in spreading clumps that can gradually reach 2 to 3 feet wide. The red midsummer flowers are held in whorls at the tops of the stems. 'Gardenview Scarlet' has bright scarlet-red flowers and tends to be resistant to powdery mildew, a fungal disease that causes gray patches on leaves and stems. 'Marshall's Delight' is a partic-ularly good selection with bright pink flowers and mildew-resistant foliage.

How to Grow It
Bee balm is a long-lived perennial hardy in Zones 4 to 9. Give it an open, sunny site and well-drained, compost-enriched soil. You can grow your own plants from seed (sow indoors in early spring, and barely cover them with soil), although it will take plants two or three years to reach blooming size, and you may not get the colors you want. For faster and more predictable results, buy plants and set them out in spring. Once established, bee balm can spread vigorously. Keep plants at their best by dividing the clumps in spring or fall. Water during dry spells, and thin out crowded stems to improve air circulation around leaves. If mildew appears, cut the plants to the ground and new growth will appear.

Pick leaves as needed for fresh use or for drying. Gather the flowers soon after they open. After bloom, cut the whole plant back by one-half to two-thirds to encourage regrowth and possibly another flush of flowers.

How to Use It
Bee balm deserves a place in the garden for its flowers alone. Besides being beautiful, they are attractive to bees, butterflies, and hummingbirds. The flowers are colorful in salads (when fresh) and potpourri (when dried). You can also use the dried leaves to add fragrance to potpourri or a citrus favor to tea blends.

Did You Know?
During the period of the Boston Tea Party, American colonists enjoyed tea made from bee balm leaves as an alternative to black tea. 🌀

B

Borage
Borago officinalis

want the plants to grow, in a sunny location with well-drained soil. It adapts to a range of conditions but thrives with extra moisture. Plant seeds ½ inch deep. Thin seedlings to stand 18 to 24 inches apart. Mulching with compost will promote vigorous growth. Borage self-sows freely. If you want to move the seedlings, dig them up gently while they are still small to avoid damaging the roots.

To harvest, pick the leaves and stems as needed for fresh use. The leaves are best when young and tender. Pick open flowers for fresh use or for drying.

How to Use It

Chop fresh young leaves into salads, or mince and add them to cottage cheese or cream cheese. Toss fresh flowers into salads or punch bowls, candy them for a unique dessert decoration, or dry them to add color to potpourri. In the garden, pair borage with calendulas for an eye-catching, blue-and-orange combination.

Did You Know?

Crusaders drank beverages that had borage flowers floating on the surface to give them courage.

▲ 3'
☀ full
◈ avg

What It Looks Like

Borage is a bushy, somewhat sprawling plant with rough, hairy, gray-green leaves that smell and taste like cucumber. Clumps grow 2 to 3 feet tall and about 18 inches wide. Clusters of five-petaled, star-shaped, heavenly blue flowers top the plant from midsummer until fall.

How to Grow It

Borage is a half-hardy annual. It grows best from seed sown directly where you

B

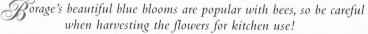

Borage's beautiful blue blooms are popular with bees, so be careful when harvesting the flowers for kitchen use!

Burnet
Poterium sanguisorba

1'
full
moist

What It Looks Like
Burnet, also known as salad burnet, is an attractive, compact herb that is 1 foot tall and wide. This perennial plant produces ferny, pale green foliage that is semievergreen during mild winters. Burnet's aromatic leaves have a mild cucumber flavor. It produces pinkish flowers in summer, making it a very useful edging plant. The curious flowerheads bear male flowers at the base, female flowers at the tip, and flowers with both male and female parts in the middle.

How to Grow It
This easy-to-grow perennial is hardy in Zones 4 to 9. Sow seeds in early spring or early fall in well-drained, evenly moist garden soil. Burnet prefers sun but can adapt to partial shade. Thin the seedlings to stand 12 to 18 inches apart. Pinching off the flowerstalks will promote more leafy growth, but you may want to allow a few flowers to mature to get self-sown seedlings. If you wish to transplant seedlings, move them while they are still small to minimize root disturbance.

Pick the young leaves as needed for fresh use; older leaves may be somewhat bitter. Burnet does not dry well.

How to Use It
Add young burnet leaves to salads, salad dressings, or herb butters, or mince them into cream soups.

Did You Know?
Burnet is native to Europe and Asia. During the days of King Henry VIII, burnet was planted along walkways with mint and thyme to perfume the air. 🌀

29

B

Burnet's lacy leaves and mounding habit make it an attractive addition to any garden. As a plus, it also grows well in containers.

Calendula
Calendula officinalis

↑ 2'

☀ full

💧 avg

What It Looks Like
Calendula, also known as pot marigold, produces bushy, many-stemmed plants that grow 1 to 2 feet tall and 8 to 12 inches wide. The stems are topped with orange or yellow, daisylike flowers all summer long. 'Pacific Beauty' produces long-stemmed, double flowers in a range of yellows and oranges. Flowers in the 'Touch of Red' series have maroon centers and a deep red edging to some of the petals. Plants in the 'Bon Bon' series are particularly compact, uniform, and long-blooming, producing flowers up to 3 inches wide on 12-inch stems. You can buy a mix of yellow, orange, and apricot or get them as separate colors.

How to Grow It
Calendula is a hardy, easy-to-grow annual herb that thrives in full sun and average, well-drained soil. Sow seed directly into the garden in early spring as soon as you can work the soil, or start indoors four to six weeks before the last frost date. Plant seed ¼ inch deep. Around the last frost date, set out transplants or thin direct-sown seedlings to stand 12 to 18 inches apart. Plants grow best in cool weather and often stop blooming during hot spells. Sow again in June to get new plants for fall, or try cutting back tired plants to about 3 inches above the soil; they may produce new growth and flowers when cooler weather returns. Plants will self-sow if you let a few flowers mature on the plants.

Pick newly opened flowers as needed for fresh use or for drying; simply pinch or cut the flowerhead from the stem. Frequent harvesting will encourage plants to produce more flowers.

To dry calendula petals for storage, pick them off the flowerheads and scatter them thinly onto a sheet of paper. Set them in a shady spot.

How to Use It
Use dried, ground calendula petals as a substitute for the much more expensive saffron; they give saffron's orange-yellow color (although not its flavor) to rice dishes, soups, breads, and other foods. Toss fresh petals into salads and dried petals into potpourri to add color. The strong-stemmed blooms also make excellent cut flowers.

Did You Know?
Native to the Mediterranean and Persia, calendula was used in ancient Egypt, Greece, and India as food and as garlands. The ancient Romans used calendula to treat scorpion bites. American doctors used calendula leaves to treat wounds during the Civil War.

C

Caraway

Carum carvi

↟	2'
☀	full
💧	avg

What It Looks Like

Caraway usually grows as a biennial, making only leaves the first year and then flowering and dying the second year. Occasionally it acts like an annual, producing leaves and flowers during the same growing season. Either way, it grows as 6- to 8-inch-wide clumps of feathery, bright green leaves that closely resemble carrot foliage. Lacy, flat-topped clusters of tiny white to pale pink flowers bloom atop 1- to 2-foot stems in spring or early summer.

How to Grow It

Caraway grows best in well-drained, garden soil in a sunny location. It grows from a long taproot that makes transplanting difficult. For best results, sow seeds directly where you want plants to grow. Sow seeds in early spring, or in fall for an earlier harvest the following year. Plant them about ¼ inch deep, and keep the soil evenly moist to encourage good germination. Once they come up, caraway plants need little care. They will readily self-sow if you let a few seed-heads mature in the garden.

Pick young, tender leaves as needed before flowering for fresh use. As the flowers fade in mid- to late summer, watch the developing seeds carefully. When they start to turn brown, clip the seedheads before the seeds loosen and drop off. Hang the seedheads over a screen or upside down in a paper bag to gather the mature seeds. Then dry the seeds on a tray in a shady, warm, well-ventilated area, and store them in a jar with a tight lid.

How to Use It

Plant caraway around fruit trees to attract beneficial insects—they'll help you with organic pest control. Toss the fresh young leaves into soups and green or fruit salads, or use them as a garnish. Add whole or ground seeds to breads, cakes, potatoes, cabbage, and sauerkraut dishes for a licorice-like tang. Caraway seeds are the traditional flavoring for rye bread, and they're delicious in egg and cheese dishes as well. Caraway is said to aid digestion, and it certainly adds a special flavor to many foods. Long cooking can cause the seeds to turn bitter, so if possible, add them during the last 15 minutes of cooking.

Did You Know?

Native to southern Europe, Asia, and India, caraway has been used to flavor food for at least 5,000 years. It is said to ward off witches and to help lovers stay together and never part.

According to the famous 17th century herbalist Nicholas Culpeper, a poultice made from powdered caraway seeds would make bruises disappear. 🌀

C

Cardoon

Cynara cardunculus

🔺 6'

☀ full

💧 avg

What It Looks Like

A relative of the artichoke, cardoon is a dramatic 4- to 6-foot-tall herb. It looks something like a thistle, forming 3- to 4-foot-wide clumps of flat, downy, grayish green leaves on long, fleshy stalks. In summer, 4- to 6-foot-tall stalks rise from the center of the plant and are topped with huge, lavender-blue, thistlelike flowers.

C

How to Grow It

Cardoon thrives in deeply dug, compost-rich soil in a sunny, open location; good drainage is critical. It is usually hardy in Zones 5 to 9, but it may not survive the winter where the soil stays soggy. Fortunately, you can even enjoy this beautiful herb as an annual, since you grow it for the leaf stalks. Start indoors four to six weeks before your last frost date, or sow seed ¼ inch deep directly into the garden one or two weeks before your last frost date. Thin seedlings to stand 2 feet apart. Mulch with straw or evergreen boughs in late fall to protect plants from winter cold.

Harvest the young leaf stalks as needed for fresh use. To increase your harvest of tender stems, you can blanch the leaf stalks by tying them together and wrapping them with cardboard or heavy paper. Blanched stems will be ready to harvest three or four weeks after wrapping.

How to Use It

Add fresh, chopped leaf stalks (cut off the flat, leafy parts first) to soups and stews, puree them for dips, or steam and marinate them for antipasto salad. Cardoon's clumps of deeply cut, gray-green leaves also make a showy accent for the back of the herb garden. Its gray-green color is beautifully accented by bright greens and dusky purples; try underplanting it with purple sage or purple basil. The flowers make an eye-catching addition to arrangements.

Did You Know?

The name *Cynara* comes from the Greek word "kuon," or dog's teeth, referring to the jagged edges of the foliage. 🌀

Wrapping cardoon plants with cardboard about a month before the first fall frost will exclude light, making the stems more tender.

Catnip

Nepeta cataria

⬆	3'
☀	full
💧	avg

What It Looks Like

Catnip is a hardy, 2- to 3-foot-tall perennial with jagged-edge, fuzzy, green leaves. The clumps can reach 2 or more feet wide. In summer, the plants are topped with dense spikes of small, whitish to pale pink flowers.

There are other, more ornamental species of this genus; these are commonly referred to as catmints. *N. mussinii* is a 1-foot-tall, mat-forming perennial with lavender-blue, early summer flowers. *N. × faassenii* is a bushy 2-foot-tall perennial adorned with sky blue flowers well into summer.

How to Grow It

Catnip is hardy in Zones 3 to 8. Give it full sun or light shade and average, well-drained soil. Sow seed indoors in late winter, six to eight weeks before your last frost date, or directly in the garden around the last frost date. Just barely cover the tiny seeds, or simply press them into the soil. Keep the seedbed moist to encourage germination. An easier way to start catnip is with a purchased plant or with a division from a friend's patch. However, keep in mind the proverb "If you set it, the cats will eat it; if you sow it, the cats don't know it." Brushing the leaves as you set out transplants can release the fragrance and attract nearby cats, who may chew or roll on plants, so protect transplants with some kind of cover. Thin or space plants to stand 18 inches apart. Divide plants in spring to control their spread.

Pick leaves anytime for fresh use. To harvest for drying, cut stems in mid- to late summer, when plant is in full bloom.

How to Use It

Share a few sprigs of fresh or dried catnip with your cat for fun and frolic. Make longer-lasting cat toys by stuffing small fabric pouches with dried catnip. The fresh or dried leaves make a soothing, pleasant-tasting tea for people.

Did You Know?

Catnip may have gotten its botanical name from the Roman town of Nepeti, where catnip grew wild. 🐾

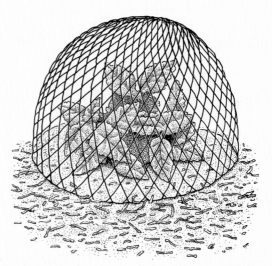

C

Keep kitty at bay by covering catnip transplants with a chicken-wire cage for two or three weeks after transplanting.

Chamomile, Roman
Chamaemelum nobile

6"
full
avg

What It Looks Like
Roman chamomile is a low-growing, perennial herb with lacy, bright green, sweetly scented leaves. Plants only reach 4 to 6 inches tall, but they can spread to 1 foot or more. In summer, the creeping foliage is nearly covered with small, white, daisy-like flowers with bright yellow centers.

German chamomile (*Matricaria recutita*) is an annual cousin to Roman chamomile. It grows in bushy, branching clumps up to 2 feet tall and 8 to 12 inches wide, with finely divided foliage and small, white, daisylike, summer flowers with dark yellow centers. Both the leaves and flowers are aromatic.

How to Grow It
Roman chamomile is hardy in Zones 3 to 8. It grows well in full sun or light shade with average to moist but well-drained soil. It is easiest to start from purchased transplants; set them out 6 to 8 inches apart in spring. Grow annual German chamomile from seed; sow directly into a sunny, well-drained spot in the garden in fall or early spring. Rake the soil to create a fine seedbed, and press the small seeds lightly into the surface. Both kinds of chamomile will self-sow if you leave a few flowers to go to seed. Shearing Roman chamomile plants in half once or twice during the growing season can encourage branching and lower, spreading growth.

Harvest open flowers in summer for fresh use or for drying. Dry the flower-heads on screens or on sheets of paper.

How to Use It
The flowers of either kind of chamomile can make a pleasant-tasting, soothing tea. (If you are sensitive to the pollen of ragweed, chrysanthemums, or other daisy relatives, however, use caution when drinking chamomile tea; it may cause an allergic reaction.) Used as a hair rinse, chamomile tea can bring golden highlights to brown hair. (Let the tea cool, then pour it over your hair after shampooing.) Add dried chamomile flowers to potpourri for their color and scent. In the garden, grow Roman chamomile along paths or between stepping stones to enjoy the fragrance when you walk on or brush against the foliage.

Did You Know?
A cup of chamomile tea was the treatment of choice for Beatrix Potter's famous character Peter Rabbit when he overindulged in Mr. MacGregor's garden.

In medieval England, chamomile's delightful apple fragrance made it fashionable as a strewing herb to place in bed clothes and linens and add to the floor rushes. This apple scent is one reason it's popular in potpourri today.

34

C

Chervil

Anthriscus cerefolium

sowing the seed directly in the garden. Press the seeds into the soil surface, and keep the seedbed moist until seedlings appear, usually in one or two weeks. Make the first sowing in early spring. To extend your harvest, plant again every two or three weeks until hot weather arrives; sow again in late summer for a fall crop. Chervil will self-sow if you allow a few flowers to go to seed in the fall. Thin seedlings to 10 inches apart.

You can start harvesting chervil six weeks after sowing. Snip leaves and stems as needed for fresh use; they lose much of their flavor when dried.

How to Use It

Chervil's flavor is somewhere between anise and parsley. Add the fresh leaves to potato salad, green salad, or cold soups. Chervil also blends well with fresh cooked summer vegetables. It loses flavor quickly when heated, so add it during the last few minutes of cooking.

Did You Know?

Chervil is one of the classic "fines herbes" used in French cooking, along with parsley, tarragon, and thyme.

2'
part
avg

What It Looks Like

This easy-to-grow herb produces ferny mounds of finely cut, bright green leaves in clumps about 1 foot wide. In midsummer, clusters of tiny white flowers bloom atop slender, leafy stems up to 2 feet tall.

How to Grow It

A half-hardy annual, chervil grows best in partial shade and well-drained, compost-enriched soil. It transplants poorly, so you'll get the best results from

For the best flavor, harvest chervil leaves from the center of the plant. These young leaves will be the most tender.

C

Chicory

Cichorium intybus

2'
full
avg

What It Looks Like
Common chicory is a
rather spindly-looking,
1- to 2-foot-tall weed
that grows along road-
sides and farm fields. It has 3- to 4-inch-
long, narrow green leaves and upright
stems topped with lovely sky blue,
summer flowers.

Some types of chicory have been
selected for their pleasantly bitter-tasting
green or red leaves. Cutting, or leaf,
chicories form loose clusters of foliage;
heading chicories, also called radicchio,
grow in dense clusters called heads.
Witloof chicory, also known as Belgian
endive, produces thick roots that are
"forced" to produce sweet, tender leaves.

How to Grow It
All the chicories are perennials hardy in
Zones 3 to 9, although they are commonly grown as an annual crop. They
thrive in full sun and average to moist,
well-drained soil. After the last frost
date, sow seeds directly in the garden,
¼ inch deep, or set out transplants. Thin
or set plants to stand 8 to 12 inches apart.
Mulch to keep the soil evenly moist.

Harvest leaves of cutting chicory as
needed for fresh use. Gather head-
forming types when the heads feel firm.
To force witloof chicory, dig up the roots
in fall, before a hard frost, and cut off the
tops 2 inches above the roots. Store roots
in a cool, dry place. When you are ready
to force them, trim the roots to 8 inches,
and bury them upright in a large bucket
of damp sand or peat moss with the root
tops level with the surface. Cover with
an upside-down pot, and set the bucket
in a cool place (50° to 60°F). When the
pale sprouts reach 4 to 6 inches tall, cut
them off at the base.

How to Use It
Toss or chop leaf and heading chicories
into salads, stir-fries, and pasta dishes, or
marinate the leaves for antipasto.

Did You Know?
Legend says that the blue flowers of
chicory were the eyes of a lass weeping
for her lover's return. 🌀

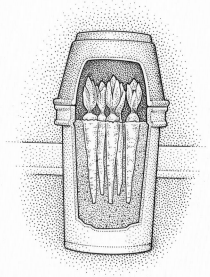

*To force witloof chicory for salads, harvest the roots in fall, replant in
damp sand, and keep them covered for three to four weeks.*

36

C

Chives

Allium schoenoprasum

14"

full

avg

What It Looks Like

Chives produces slender, cylindrical green leaves in dense clumps usually 8 to 12 inches wide. In late spring, 12- to 14-inch-tall stems are topped with clusters of pink flowers.

Garlic chives (*Allium tuberosum*), also known as Chinese chives, forms flattened, rather than rounded, leaves. It blooms in mid- or late summer with white flowers.

How to Grow It

Both common and garlic chives are perennials hardy in Zones 3 to 9. Grow them in a sunny spot with average, well-drained soil. Start seeds indoors in late winter; sow ¼ inch deep. Handling the seedlings in clumps, set them out in the garden in late spring, spaced 8 to 12 inches apart. Divide established clumps every three years in early spring. Cut leaves back to ground level after flowering to promote new growth. Cutting off the spent flowers can also prevent plants from dropping large quantities of seed. For fresh chives all winter long, leave potted chives outdoors for at least six to eight weeks after the first frost. Then bring the pot indoors, and set it on a sunny windowsill. New growth will sprout within a few weeks.

Start harvesting leaves as needed when plants reach 6 inches tall. Cut off the leaf tips at least 2 inches above the soil. The flavor of both the leaves and flowers is best when fresh. Commercially available freeze-dried chives retain their flavor, but home-dried chives are often disappointing.

How to Use It

Just before serving, sprinkle chopped, fresh or dried chives onto baked potatoes, scrambled eggs, salads, and soups for a mild, oniony flavor. The flowers have a similar flavor and add a colorful touch to salads (separate them into individual florets first). Garlic chives adds a zesty garlic flavor to salads and stir-fries.

Did You Know?

Marco Polo helped introduce chives to Europe from the Chinese, who had been growing chives since 3,000 B.C. 🌀

With its grassy clumps of green leaves and clusters of rose-scented white flowers, garlic chives is an attractive addition to both flower and herb gardens.

37

C

Coriander

Coriandrum sativum

3'
full
avg

What It Looks Like

Also known as cilantro and Chinese parsley, coriander has bright green leaves that are somewhat rounded and lobed near the base of the plant and deeply divided along the upper parts. Plants grow in clumps 8 to 10 inches across. In summer, clusters of tiny white to pinkish flowers bloom atop slender, 2- to 3-foot-tall stems.

How to Grow It

Coriander prefers to grow in light, well-drained soil in a sunny location. Sow seeds of this annual outdoors in late spring, around the last frost date, and cover with ¼ inch of soil. Keep the seedbed moist to encourage good germination. Thin seedlings to stand 6 to 8 inches apart. To extend your harvest of leaves, sow again every two weeks until hot weather arrives; sow again in late summer for a fall harvest.

Harvest the leaves as you need them for fresh use; the rounded lower leaves of the plant are more tasty than the finer upper leaves. Coriander foliage loses much of its flavor when dried. To gather seeds, cut or pull out plants in mid- to late summer, when the plants have turned brown but before they drop their seeds. Hang plants upside down over a screen or in a paper bag to catch the ripe seeds as they fall.

How to Use It

Coriander foliage has a bold, sagelike flavor with a citrus tang. Add fresh minced leaves to Mexican salsa, Indian curry dishes, and Thai, Chinese, and Southeast Asian dishes. The dried seeds are an essential ingredient in curry powder and chutney. The ground seeds also add flavor to baked goods, such as gingerbread and banana bread. The seeds are pleasantly scented when ripe, and they become more fragrant as they age; mix them into potpourri.

Did You Know?

The Egyptians grew coriander, and the Israelites ate it as they wandered in the wilderness. It is still often included as one of the bitter herbs of Passover. ✹

Create a zesty dip for chips or vegetables by chopping coriander leaves—better known as cilantro—into a bowl of diced fresh tomatoes, onions, and peppers.

C

Dill

Anethum graveolens

3'

full

moist

What It Looks Like

Dill forms 6- to 10-inch-wide clumps of aromatic, finely cut, blue-green leaves. In summer, the clumps send up 2- to 3-foot-tall, hollow stems topped with broad, flattened clusters of tiny yellow flowers. 'Dukat' produces more leaves than regular dill before flowering and setting seed. 'Fernleaf' is a compact selection, growing to 18 inches tall.

How to Grow It

This annual herb can adapt to a range of conditions but grows best in full sun and moist but well-drained soil. Dill grows from a slender taproot and may not adapt well to transplanting, so it's best to sow seed directly into the garden in early to midspring. Cover the seed with a sprinkling of soil, or just press it into the surface. Water as needed to keep the seedbed moist until seedlings appear. Thin seedlings to stand 6 to 8 inches apart. Dill goes to seed quickly; making one or two additional sowings two or three weeks apart will extend your leafy harvest. You can even sow in fall for an earlier harvest the following year. If you allow a few flowers to mature, dill will readily self-sow. Stake tall plants.

Pick leaves as needed for fresh use, freezing, or drying, starting about eight weeks after sowing. After flowering, check the developing seedheads frequently. When you notice the seeds turning light brown, snip off the seedheads; hang them upside down over a screen or in a paper bag to collect the seeds.

How to Use It

Add fresh, frozen, or dried dill leaves (often referred to as dill weed) or dried seeds to soups, cucumber and tomato salads, creamy dips, and fish dishes, especially poached, grilled, or marinated salmon. Chop the fresh foliage into salads, or use it as a garnish. Dill is, of course, a key flavoring for pickles as well. The flowers attract a wide variety of beneficial insects to the garden, and they make great fillers for flower arrangements.

Did You Know?

Dill was cultivated and used by Egyptians as long as 5,000 years ago. Medieval Europeans believed dill could protect people from witchcraft.

D

Fennel

Foeniculum vulgare

- 5'
- full
- avg

What It Looks Like

Fennel grows in feathery, 8- to 12-inch-wide clumps of finely cut green leaves on 3- to 5-foot-tall stalks. Flat-topped clusters of tiny yellow flowers bloom atop the stalks in mid- to late summer. Bronze fennel (*F. vulgare* 'Purpureum') has chocolate brown leaves and stems. Florence fennel (*F. vulgare* var. *azoricum*) produces a large, tender "bulb" that is prized as a vegetable.

How to Grow It

Common fennel is a perennial hardy in Zones 5 to 9. Give it a sunny site with loose, well-drained soil. Sow the seed directly into the garden in spring or fall. Just barely cover the seeds with soil. Thin seedlings to stand 6 to 12 inches apart. Cut off the spent flowerheads unless you want the seeds for cooking; otherwise, they will self-sow prolifically. Florence fennel is usually grown as an annual. Sow seed directly in the garden in early to midsummer for a fall harvest.

Snip leaves and stems as needed before flowering for fresh use or freezing. Collect the seedheads when the seeds turn brown, but before they start to drop. Harvest Florence fennel bulbs by cutting just below the swollen area.

How to Use It

Use the fresh leaves in salads or as a garnish; eat the tender stems like celery. Fennel seed is also popular in desserts, breads, cakes, and cookies. Chop Florence fennel into salads or soups.

Did You Know?

Gladiators were said to wear wreaths made from fennel leaves for strength.

Grow Florence fennel for its fleshy, bulblike leaf base. It has a crunchy texture and a sweet flavor somewhere between celery and licorice.

F

Feverfew
Tanacetum parthenium

2'

full

avg

What It Looks Like
Feverfew is a 1-foot-wide, spreading plant with lobed, light green, sharp-scented leaves that resemble those of garden chrysanthemums. The 18- to 24-inch stems produce a cloud of 1-inch, daisylike, white blossoms from early summer to early fall. You may find it listed in catalogs under its previous botanical name,

Chrysanthemum parthenium. 'White Wonder' has small, double, white blooms. Golden feverfew (*T. parthenium* 'Aureum') forms mounds of yellow leaves accented with yellow-centered white flowers. 'Golden Moss' is similar but reaches only 6 inches tall in bloom. 'Golden Ball' has green leaves and yellow flowers.

How to Grow It
This perennial herb is hardy in Zones 4 to 9. It thrives in a sunny location with average, well-drained soil; it can also tolerate partial shade. To start plants from seed, sow indoors in early spring or directly in the garden in spring or fall. Just barely cover the seed. Thin seedlings or set transplants to stand 9 to 12 inches apart. Pinch off individual spent flowers to extend the bloom season and minimize self-sown seedlings. Or cut whole stems to the ground after the first wave of bloom for a flush of fresh new foliage and more flowers. For propagation, divide plants in fall or spring, or take cuttings from the new shoots in spring.

Harvest flowering stems when they are in full bloom for fresh arrangements or for drying.

How to Use It
Feverfew is a lovely ornamental plant for the middle to back of an herb garden. The compact selections are wonderful in windowboxes and planters. The fresh flowers make lovely summer bouquets or arrangements; they also dry well.

Did You Know?
Since the 1970s, feverfew has received scientific attention for its medicinal properties, particularly in providing relief from migraine headaches.

F

For a colorful combination, try pairing golden feverfew with purple sage. Tuck in a few plants of green thyme as a groundcover.

Garlic
Allium sativum

↑	2'
☀	full
◆	avg

What It Looks Like
Aboveground, garlic forms clumps of long, narrow leaves with a pungent aroma. The 2-foot-tall, slender stalks are topped with clusters of white flowers late in the summer. Underground, garlic produces dense, fleshy bulbs composed of many individual cloves.

How to Grow It
While garlic is a perennial hardy in Zones 5 to 9, it is most commonly grown as an annual or biennial. It thrives in full sun but can take light shade; good drainage is important. Separate bulbs into cloves just before planting. In most areas, October planting is best; early spring is second best. Push the cloves, with the root end down, 1 to 2 inches into the soil, about 6 inches apart. Don't worry about fall topgrowth being killed by winter freezes; new leaves will appear in spring. Mulching with compost in spring will promote good growth. For the largest bulbs, prune off the flower-stalks that appear in midsummer.

Fall-planted garlic will be ready for harvest in midsummer; spring plantings mature in fall. Dig up the bulbs when about three-quarters of the topgrowth is brown. Use them fresh, or cure them for storage by hanging the plants in loose bunches in a warm, dry, dark, airy place for a few weeks. Store cured bulbs in open-mesh bags at room temperature, or peel the cloves and place them in a container to freeze them. (Save a few of your largest bulbs for planting next year's crop.) You can also snip the green leaves as needed for fresh use. Save the cutoff flowerstalks for the kitchen, too.

How to Use It
Chop garlic cloves into soups, stews, pasta dishes, salad dressings, stir-fries—just about any dish but desserts. Or roast unpeeled cloves in your oven (about 15 minutes at 350°F), then peel and mash them to enjoy the mild, nutty flavor. Try spreading roasted garlic on crusty bread in place of butter.

Did You Know?
Garlic is one of our oldest herbs. Roman soldiers and the pyramid-building slaves of Egypt were given garlic as part of their daily ration. 🌀

Horehound
Marrubium vulgare

▲	2'
☀	full
◐	dry

What It Looks Like
Horehound is a bushy, perennial herb that forms 12- to 18-inch-wide clumps of woolly, gray-green, heart-shaped, aromatic leaves. In midsummer, small white flowers bloom in whorls along the upper stems.

How to Grow It
Horehound is hardy in Zones 4 to 9. Grow it in full sun and poor, well-drained soil. Sow seeds ⅛ inch deep in early spring, either indoors or directly in the garden. Set or thin plants to stand about 18 inches apart. Prune the stems to the ground in early winter. Divide plants in spring every few years to control growth and renew vigor. Plants will self-sow if you do not harvest the tops before flowering.

In the first year, harvest up to a third of the leaves and stems as needed for fresh use or drying. In following years, cut tops down to a few inches above the ground as soon as the flower buds form; a fresh crop of leaves will follow.

How to Use It
Use the fresh or dried leaves to make a tea to soothe coughs, colds, and sore throats; add honey to mask the somewhat bitter flavor. Horehound is also used to make throat-soothing lozenges. It grows well in containers, and its soft, silvery foliage complements both colorful flowers and dark green leaves in the garden.

Did You Know?
The name horehound comes from the Old English term "har hune," a name for a downy plant. ☯

H

Harvest the tops of established horehound plants in early to midsummer, cutting stems a few inches above the ground.

Horseradish

Armoracia rusticana

3'

full

avg

What It Looks Like

Aboveground, horse-radish produces fast-spreading clumps of broad green leaves. In late spring or early summer, the plants send up 2- to 3-foot-tall stalks bearing clouds of small white flowers. Underground, horseradish forms its thick, fleshy, brown-skinned, white-fleshed roots. 'Variegata' is a selection with ornamental white-splashed leaves.

How to Grow It

This perennial herb is hardy in Zones 5 to 9. It thrives in ordinary, deeply dug garden soil in full sun. Horseradish spreads quickly and can become invasive; either give it a site where it won't crowd out other plants, or plant it in a bottomless plastic container filled with soil and sunk at least 2 feet into the soil. Buy potted plants or dormant root cuttings in early spring or fall. Set root cuttings about 1 foot deep. One plant is enough for most families, but if you want to grow more than one, space them 1 to 2 feet apart.

Harvest roots in fall or spring. Break off what you need, and replant a few of the roots. Brush off the soil. Store roots in your refrigerator or in dry sand in a cool cellar for up to three months. Pick leaves from the center of the clump as needed.

How to Use It

Add peeled and grated roots to mustard, or mix them with vinegar to make horseradish sauce. Its hot flavor adds a tangy touch to cocktail sauce, gefilte fish, roast beef, and cream sauces for veal. Freshly ground horseradish is served at Passover as one of the bitter herbs. Spice up salads of mild-tasting greens with a few young, tender horseradish leaves. Or add a little bite to a bland sandwich by mixing a little horseradish sauce into your sandwich topping. Horseradish is a popular ingredient in dips, and horseradish-flavored cheeses are readily available.

Did You Know?

Horseradish is native to Europe but has naturalized itself in most parts of North America. It originally was thought to have medicinal properties but is now used only as a flavoring. ✿

44

H

Hyssop
Hyssopus officinalis

⬆	3'
☀	full
🌢	avg

What It Looks Like

Hyssop grows in shrub-like, semievergreen clumps that reach 2½ to 3 feet tall and 2 feet wide. The somewhat woody stems carry narrow, lance-shaped, dark green, fragrant leaves and are topped with spikes of blue flowers from summer to early autumn. Its blooms are very attractive to bees and butterflies. 'Alba' has white flowers; 'Rosea' blooms pink.

How to Grow It

Hyssop is a perennial herb hardy in Zones 3 to 9. It can adapt to sun or partial shade and grows fine in average to dry, well-drained soil. Sow seed ¼ inch deep indoors in late winter or directly in the garden in late spring. Set or thin plants to stand 1 foot apart. Clipping off spent flowers can help to extend the bloom and promotes bushier growth. Prune to stand 8 inches tall in spring before new growth begins. Plants may die out unexpectedly after a few seasons, so plan on replacing them every three or four years. For propagation, take stem cuttings in summer or divide clumps in spring or fall. Plants may self-sow.

Pick individual leaves and flowers as needed for fresh use. For drying, cut the stems just before the flowers open (or wait until just after they open, if you want the blooms, too).

How to Use It

Hyssop is a charming ornamental herb that is just now being rediscovered. Use the fresh young leaves to add a minty taste to salads. Mix fresh or dried leaves into herbal tea blends. Dry the flowers and leafy stems for bouquets, or toss them into potpourri. In the garden, hyssop seems to thrive on frequent trimming. Try shaping it into a low hedge to edge paths and walkways or garden beds. Hyssop also makes a good container plant.

Did You Know?

Native to the Mediterranean, hyssop has become naturalized in many parts of North America. Benedictine monks brought hyssop to Europe and used it in making their herbal liquors including Benedictine and Chartreuse, both of which were originally considered to be medicinal. 🟢

H

Joe-Pye Weed

Eupatorium purpureum

8'

full

moist

What It Looks Like
The glory of the late summer garden, Joe-Pye weed forms 2- to 3-foot-wide, multistemmed clumps of long stalks with whorls of pointed green leaves. The 6- to 8-foot-tall stems are topped with domed clusters of rosy pink or light purple, sweetly scented flowers in late summer and early fall. Two other species, E. fistulosum and E. maculatum, are very similar, although their flowers tend to be more reddish pink. Many of the cultivars available may be hybrids of these species.

'Atropurpureum' has deep purple-red stems and purple-pink flowers. The cultivars 'Album' and 'Bartered Bride' have white flowers.

How to Grow It
Joe-Pye weed is hardy in Zones 3 to 8. A native American wildflower, it is often seen growing in sunny marshlands or wet meadows across eastern North America. In the garden, choose a site in full sun to partial shade with evenly moist, compost-enriched soil. You can grow Joe-Pye weed from seed (sow outdoors in fall or indoors in late winter, and barely cover), although seedlings may take two or three years to reach flowering size. For a more immediate effect, set out purchased plants 2 to 3 feet apart in spring. Cut the dead stalks to the ground in early winter. It's smart to mark the clump with a label; the shoots are slow to emerge in the spring. It's easy to damage them if you start digging around them to plant other things in what looks like an empty spot!

How to Use It
Joe-Pye weed is a large, showy, ornamental herb that adds color and height to the late summer garden. Be sure to plant it at the back of the border; it will tower over almost all other herbs! The beautiful blooms will attract butterflies to your garden. Cut the flowers for use in fresh arrangements.

Did You Know?
The name "Joe-Pye weed" commemorates a colonial-era Native American medicine man, who was said to have cured a New England town of typhus using this plant.

Lavenders

Lavandula spp.

↟	10"–36"
☀	full
💧	dry

What It Looks Like

Lavenders are bushy, semievergreen herbs with narrow, silvery or grayish green leaves. Both their leaves and flowers are highly aromatic. Common or English lavender (*L. angustifolia*) produces deep purple flowers on 3-foot stems in summer. 'Hidcote' grows 12 to 18 inches tall with dark purple-blue flowers. 'Lady' produces light purple flowers on compact, 8- to 10-inch plants that bloom the first year from seed. 'Munstead' reaches 18 inches tall with purple flowers.

French and Spanish lavenders (*L. dentata* and *L. stoechas*) are also quite ornamental, but they are not cold hardy in most parts of North America. They do, however, make lovely container plants, so it's easy to bring them indoors for the winter. French lavender has finely toothed, gray-green leaves and pale purple flowers. Spanish lavender has narrow, silvery foliage and plump, dark purple flower spikes topped with elongated petals.

How to Grow It

Common lavender is generally hardy in Zones 5 to 8; French and Spanish lavender may not overwinter outdoors north of Zone 9. All lavenders prefer a sunny location in sandy, well-drained soil. Most are difficult to grow from seed, although you can get good results from 'Lady'. Sow ⅛ inch deep indoors in early spring. Your best bet for other types is to buy potted plants. Set them out in spring or fall, spaced 10 to 24 inches apart, depending on their ultimate size. Trim tops back by one-third in early spring to promote bushier growth. Propagate by removing 3- to 4-inch sideshoots in summer. The cuttings may root better if you leave a small "heel" of older wood at the base of the sideshoots when you snap them off.

To harvest for drying, clip off the flowerstalks just as the blooms open.

How to Use It

Use the highly aromatic, dried flowers in sachets and potpourri. Lay or hang bunches of dried lavender in closets and dresser drawers to perfume the area and deter moths. As an ornamental, lavender makes an excellent small hedge or edging plant for a rock garden or herb bed. It's a beautiful and fragrant addition to the perennial border. It also grows well in a container, indoors or out.

Did You Know?

Native to the Mediterranean, lavender is grown extensively on farms in the south of France and in Spain for the commercial perfume business. Lavender was used in the famous "smelling salts" that were so popular in Victorian times when tight corsets led to frequent fainting spells. 🌀

Lemon Balm

Melissa officinalis

2'

full

avg

What It Looks Like

Lemon balm grows in bushy, 18-inch-wide clumps of green, oval to heart-shaped leaves that release a strong lemon aroma when crushed. Small white flowers bloom in clusters along the 1- to 2-foot stems in summer. 'Variegata', also sold as 'Aurea', has green-and-yellow leaves. The foliage of 'All Gold' is bright yellow when young and yellow-green when mature.

How to Grow It

This easy-to-grow perennial herb is hardy in Zones 5 to 9. It grows well in average, well-drained soil in sun or partial shade. Sow seed indoors or outdoors in spring; just press into the soil and keep the seedbed moist until seedlings appear. Or buy a potted plant and set it out in the garden in spring. Space plants or thin seedlings to stand 18 inches apart. When plants begin to bloom, cut off tops 1 to 2 inches above the ground to promote a flush of new growth. Cut stems to the ground in late fall. Divide clumps in spring or fall for propagation or to control their spread.

Pick leaves as needed for fresh use. For drying, cut stems close to the ground before flowering. Lay the leafy stems on screens, rather than bunching them, and set in a hot but shady spot to dry quickly; slow drying may cause leaves to turn black. Fresh lemon balm has the most flavor; much of the fragrance is lost in the drying process.

How to Use It

Use the fresh or dried leaves alone to make a mild, lemony tea, or blend them with mint and/or black tea for a more intense flavor. Toss whole or chopped fresh leaves into green salads, fruit salads, and punch bowls. Add the dried leaves to potpourri. In the garden, lemon balm is excellent for attracting bees. The cultivars with more colorful leaves make attractive ornamentals for flower gardens or for container plantings.

Did You Know?

Native to the Mediterranean and Central Asia, lemon balm was used by the ancient Greeks to honor the goddess Diana. Medieval maidens carried lemon balm as a charm for good luck in love. It was also planted near empty bee hives to attract bees to the hive. 🌀

Lovage
Levisticum officinale

↑	6'
☀	full
💧	moist

What It Looks Like

Lovage is a large, bushy herb with long-stalked, compound, green leaves in clumps up to 3 feet across. In mid- to late summer, the hollow, 5- to 6-foot-tall stems bear flat-topped clusters of tiny yellow flowers.

How to Grow It

A perennial hardy in Zones 3 to 8, lovage prefers full sun or partial shade and evenly moist, compost-enriched soil. If you want many plants and you have the room, sow fresh seed directly in the garden in late summer or early fall; just barely cover. Thin seedlings to stand 2 to 3 feet apart. In most cases, though, one plant will provide all you need; simply set out one potted plant in spring. If you aren't growing lovage for its seeds, cut off the flowers before they bloom to encourage leafy growth and to prevent self-sowing. Cut the topgrowth to the ground in late fall. Mulch with compost each spring to replenish soil nutrients.

You can harvest lightly from lovage the first year, but don't take more than one-third of the topgrowth. Once plants are established, harvest the leaves and stems as needed for fresh use. For drying, cut leaves and stems before bloom and hang in bunches. You can also freeze the leaves. Gather the seeds when they turn brown but before they drop. Hang the seedheads upside down over a screen or in a paper bag to catch the seeds as they drop.

How to Use It

Use lovage as you would celery; it's just as tasty and much easier to grow. Add the flavorful leaves, stems, or seeds to soups and stews, toss the fresh leaves into green or potato salad, or blanch and marinate the stems for an unusual vegetable side dish.

Did You Know?

Medieval travelers put lovage in their shoes to soothe their aching feet. It was also reputed to be an aphrodisiac. 🌀

The celery flavor of lovage's leaves and stems is a welcome addition to soups and stews, and the bushy plants ensure that you'll have plenty for cutting.

Marsh Mallow

Althaea officinalis

How to Grow It

Marsh mallow is hardy in Zones 3 to 8. It grows best in full sun and evenly moist, compost-enriched soil. Unlike many herbs, marsh mallow will also thrive in wet soil. Sow seed directly in the garden in spring or fall (just barely cover with soil) or set out potted plants. Space transplants or thin seedlings to stand 2 feet apart.

Pick young, tender leaves as needed for fresh use. Dig roots in fall from plants that are at least two years old. (This is also a good time to divide clumps.)

How to Use It

Marshmallow candy was originally made from the roots of this pretty herb; now, marsh mallow is grown primarily for its flowers. Its blooms will attract butterflies to the herb garden. Toss a few fresh leaves into spring salads. Or make a tea from the roots to soothe a scratchy throat. (Gently boil $\frac{1}{2}$ to 1 teaspoon of chopped or crushed root per cup of water for 15 minutes.)

Did You Know?

Marsh mallow was widely used by the ancients as a healing herb.

What It Looks Like

Related to hibiscus and hollyhocks, marsh mallow is an upright perennial herb. It forms 2-foot-wide clumps of velvety, gray-green, oval to heart-shaped, 1-to-3-inch-long leaves that can be three- to five-lobed and toothed. The 3- to 4-foot-tall stems carry hibiscus-like, pink or white flowers in mid- to late summer. The flowers are followed by circular seedpods that ripen to brown.

4' / full / moist

M

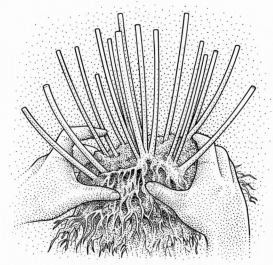

Propagate marsh mallow plants by dividing clumps in fall. Replant a few sections; harvest the roots of the rest or share them with friends.

Meadowsweet
Filipendula ulmaria

4'

full

moist

What It Looks Like
Also commonly called queen-of-the-meadow, this graceful herb grows in 1- to 2-foot-wide, creeping clumps with large, wrinkled leaves that are dark green on top and gray-green underneath. Clusters of almond-scented, creamy white flowers bloom atop the 3- to 4-foot-tall stems in midsummer. 'Flore Pleno' has showy, double, white flowers. 'Variegata' has yellow markings on the leaves. The foliage of 'Aurea' is bright yellow in spring, fading to a yellowish green by midsummer. Both 'Variegata' and 'Aurea' tend to be less vigorous than the species, often reaching only 12 to 24 inches tall.

Queen-of-the-prairie (*F. rubra*) is a native American wildflower that grows 6 to 8 feet tall with astilbe-like clusters of pink flowers in midsummer.

How to Grow It
Native to Europe and naturalized in the United States, meadowsweet is a perennial hardy in Zones 3 to 9. Plant in a sunny to partly shady location with evenly moist, compost-enriched soil. If you can get fresh seeds, sow them outdoors in fall in an out-of-the-way spot. Scatter them thickly and cover lightly. Transplant seedlings to their permanent position in fall or the following spring. For a more immediate effect, buy potted plants and set them out in the garden. Space plants 18 inches apart.

If your meadowsweet's foliage looks tattered by midsummer, cut it to the ground for a new flush of leaves. Cut back the dead topgrowth in late fall. Divide clumps in spring or fall for propagation or to control their spread.

How to Use It
Meadowsweet is a beautiful ornamental plant for the back of the herb border. Its flowers are good for cutting, especially those of 'Flore Pleno'.

Did You Know?
A chemical in meadowsweet is the same as the one used to make aspirin. In fact, aspirin is named after meadowsweet's former botanical name, *Spiraea*.

M

Mints

Mentha spp.

 1'–3'
full
avg

What It Looks Like
Mints are creeping, 1- to 3-foot-tall herbs, with highly aromatic leaves and spikes of pale purple to white, summer flowers. Peppermint (*M.* × *piperita*) and spearmint (*M. spicata*) are the two most commonly grown mints. Peppermint bears smooth, green, strongly scented leaves on 2-foot, purple stems. Spearmint has a milder scent and flavor, with bright green leaves on 18- to 24-inch stems.

There are also many other wonderful mints to try, such as the velvety-leaved apple mint (*M. suaveolens*) and its relative, pineapple mint (*M. suaveolens* 'Variegata'), with showy white edges or splashes on each leaf. Corsican mint (*M. requienii*) grows in creeping mats, with tiny, green leaves that release a powerful scent when you brush against them.

How to Grow It
Most mints are hardy in Zones 5 to 9. They adapt to sun or partial shade and average to moist, well-drained soil. To keep your mints from crowding out less vigorous plants, give them a spot by themselves or grow them in pots. Seedlings tend to be variable in flavor and fragrance, so it's better to buy a few different kinds as potted plants. Set plants out 12 to 18 inches apart. Divide clumps in fall every year or two for propagation or to control their spread. Mint also grows easily from cuttings during the growing season.

Snip shoots for fresh use; regular picking encourages more leafy growth. For drying, cut stems a few inches above the ground just before bloom.

How to Use It
Use fresh or dried mint leaves in teas, or add them to vegetables and Middle Eastern dishes. The fresh foliage makes a refreshing addition to beverages. Include the dried leaves in potpourri.

Did You Know?
Mint is a symbol of hospitality, and a mint bed grows by the back door of many southern households. 🌀

M

It's easy to propagate mints. Just dig up and transplant rooted sections any time during the growing season.

Nasturtium

Tropaeolum majus

1'
full
avg

What It Looks Like

Nasturtiums may grow in low, bushy mounds or produce long, vining or trailing stems. Bushy types usually grow 10 to 12 inches tall and as wide. The stems of vining types can grow up to 6 feet long. Both kinds bear rounded green leaves and dazzling red, yellow, orange, or white flowers from midsummer to frost. 'Alaska' has green leaves prominently splashed with cream and red, orange, or yellow flowers. 'Jewel of Africa' is similar but has a trailing habit. 'Empress of India' forms clumps of blue-green leaves and dark crimson flowers. The blooms of 'Whirlybird' nasturtiums are held well above the mounded foliage, making them more visible than usual. They are available as individual colors or as a mix.

How to Grow It

This easy annual grows best in full sun and average to poor soil. Overly rich soil can cause plants to produce more leaves than flowers. Sow seed ½ inch deep directly in the garden in late spring, after all danger of frost has passed. Thin seedlings to stand 6 to 9 inches apart.

How to Use It

Nasturtium is a colorful ornamental that brightens any garden. Use the bushy types to edge beds and borders. Give vining types a trellis, a fence, or wires to climb, or allow them to sprawl over a slope. Nasturtiums grow well in containers and look great in windowboxes and hanging baskets. In the kitchen, add the fresh leaves and flowers to salads, or use the leaves for dipping in place of potato chips. Both the foliage and flowers have a peppery favor similar to watercress. The flowers also make a very decorative garnish.

Did You Know?

Native to Peru and Bolivia, nasturtiums are now cultivated all over the world. They were brought to Europe by the Spanish conquerors.

53

Spruce up a green salad with a sprinkling of colorful, peppery-flavored nasturtium flowers.

N

Oreganos
Origanum spp.

▲	1'–2'
☀	full
◉	dry

What It Looks Like

Common oregano (*O. vulgare*), also known as wild marjoram, produces bushy, 12- to 18-inch-wide plants with attractive clusters of pink summer flowers atop 2-foot stems. Unfortunately, its fuzzy green foliage is often rather bland. If you want to grow oregano for its flavor, look for Greek oregano (usually listed as either *O. heracleoticum* or *O. vulgare* subsp. *hirtum*). It looks much like common oregano but has whitish flowers. But even if the plants aren't flowering, you can tell the two kinds apart: Greek oregano has a much stronger, pungent aroma.

Sweet marjoram (*O. majorana*) is closely related to the oreganos but has a milder flavor. This tender perennial herb grows in bushy, 8- to 12-inch-wide mounds of oval, gray-green, fuzzy leaves on 1-foot stems. Its tiny, white or pink flowers bloom in clusters along the tops of the stems in late summer.

How to Grow It

Common and Greek oregano are hardy in Zones 5 to 9; sweet marjoram is usually grown as an annual. They all grow best in full sun and average to dry, well-drained soil. You can grow them from seed (sow indoors six to eight weeks before your last frost date, and do not cover), although oregano seedlings will be variable in form and flavor. Your best bet is to set out potted oregano plants. Space or thin plants to stand 8 to 12 inches apart. To keep plants bushy, shear stems close to the ground before or just as the flowers open. For propagation, divide plants in spring or take stem cuttings in spring or fall.

For fresh use, snip leaves as needed through the summer. For drying, cut stems close to the ground just as the flowers begin to open.

How to Use It

The fresh or dried leaves are a perfect complement to tomato-based dishes and are practically indispensable for spaghetti and pizza sauces. They also add a tasty touch when sprinkled on roasting meat or chicken. In the garden, oregano and marjoram will attract bees and butterflies. They also grow well in containers.

Did You Know?

Oregano grows wild on rocky hillsides in much of the Mediterranean Sea area. 🔯

Parsley
Petroselinum crispum

18"

full

moist

What It Looks Like
Parsley grows in dense, 8- to 12-inch-wide mounds of ferny green leaves. If you leave plants in the garden over winter, they will bloom the second year, with airy clusters of greenish yellow flowers on 12- to 18-inch-tall stems in early summer. Curly parsley (*P. crispum* var. *crispum*) produces the frilly leaves you commonly see used as a garnish. Flat-leaved parsley (*P. crispum* var. *neapolitanum*), also known as Italian parsley, bears dark green, flat foliage that looks much like celery leaves. It is less interesting to look at, but gourmet gardeners often prefer its flavor to that of curly parsley.

How to Grow It
This biennial herb can overwinter outdoors in Zones 5 to 9, although you'll probably grow it as an annual for the most generous crop of leaves. Parsley thrives in evenly moist, compost-enriched soil in a sunny to partially shaded location. Sow seed 1/4 inch deep, either indoors six to eight weeks before your last frost date or directly into the garden in mid- to late spring. Keep the seedbed evenly moist until seedlings appear (which could take four to six weeks). Or, for faster results, buy a pack of parsley plants and set them out in spring. Parsley grows from a thick, carrotlike taproot, so you'll have the best luck transplanting seedlings when they have just a few leaves. Set or thin plants to stand 8 to 10 inches apart. Cutting back the flowerstalks as they appear can extend your harvest into the second year, however, you'll get better results by sowing or setting out new plants each year.

Once plants reach at least 6 inches tall, pick leaves as needed for fresh use or drying. Flat-leaved parsley has a stronger flavor than curly parsley, so it's better for drying. Both kinds also freeze well.

How to Use It
Parsley complements almost any dish, except desserts. Mince fresh, frozen, or dried leaves into sauces, soups, stews, and egg dishes. For a natural breath freshener, chew on a fresh leaf or two. In the garden, the dense mounds of foliage make an excellent edging for beds and borders. Parsley is also an excellent choice for outdoor container plantings and windowboxes as well as for indoor herb gardens.

Did You Know?
The ancient Greeks fed parsley to their horses to give their steeds the stamina to win races. It is a very good source of vitamin C as well as a variety of other vitamins and minerals. Parsley may attract colorful caterpillars that become gorgeous swallowtail butterflies.

P

Purple Coneflower
Echinacea purpurea

4'
full
avg

What It Looks Like
Purple coneflower, often called echinacea by herbalists, grows in 12- to 18-inch-wide clumps of dark green, lance-shaped leaves on stout, 3- to 4-foot-tall stems. Plants bloom from midsummer into fall, with rosy pink, daisylike flowers accented with domed, orange-brown centers. After bloom, the seedheads remain attractive well into winter. 'Magnus' is a particularly showy selection, since its petals point outward rather than downward (as is common in the species). 'White Swan' has white petals and bronze centers on 3-foot stems.

How to Grow It
This beautiful perennial herb is hardy in Zones 3 to 9. It adapts to full sun or partial shade and average, well-drained soil. Once established, purple coneflower's thick, deep taproot enables the plant to tolerate heat and drought. Sow seed outdoors in fall or indoors in early spring; do not cover. If you sow indoors, you can encourage germination by placing sown pots in your refrigerator for four to six weeks before moving them to a warm, bright place. Set plants or thin seedlings to stand 18 inches apart. Cutting off spent flowers in summer can extend the bloom season. Toward fall, allow flowers to go to seed if you want them for winter interest. Cut the stems to the ground before new growth begins in spring.

How to Use It
A tea made from dried purple coneflower root is said to stimulate the immune system and fight infection. In most cases, however, purple coneflower is primarily grown as an ornamental herb to add a long season of interest to plantings of less colorful herbs. The blooms attract butterflies, and the seedheads provide food for birds.

Did You Know?
Native Americans have used purple coneflower roots for hundreds of years as a general circulatory stimulant that promotes overall good health.

P

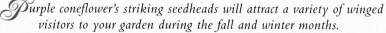
Purple coneflower's striking seedheads will attract a variety of winged visitors to your garden during the fall and winter months.

Roses

Rosa spp.

▲	3'-8'
☀	full
💧	avg

What It Looks Like

Hybrid bush roses, with their colorful blooms, are a common sight in flower gardens. But for your herb garden, you'll want to choose species or "old" roses, the kinds that grow into large, spreading or climbing shrubs, for their fragrance or fruits. These nonhybrids tend to have prickly stems with leathery green leaves and flat or slightly ruffled flowers. The blooms are followed by rounded to oblong, berry-like "hips" that turn red or orange in fall.

Some of the most popular choices for herb gardens include 'Apothecary's Rose' (*R. gallica* 'Apothecary's Rose', also called *R. gallica* var. *officinalis*), eglantine rose (*R. eglanteria*), and rugosa rose (*R. rugosa*). 'Apothecary's Rose' produces fragrant, semidouble, light crimson flowers in early summer, followed by round, red hips; the plant grows 3 feet tall and wide. Eglantine rose, also known as sweetbriar, grows 6 to 8 feet tall and wide, with apple-scented foliage. Its single, pink, fragrant flowers mature into oval, scarlet hips. Rugosa rose grows 4 to 5 feet tall and wide, with white, pink, or red, single, fragrant flowers in summer, followed by large, bright red hips.

How to Grow It

These shrub roses are generally hardy in Zones 3 to 8. They grow best in full sun, with well-drained soil enriched with compost. Set out purchased plants in spring or fall. Space them 3 to 6 feet apart, depending on their ultimate size. Prune out deadwood in late winter. If needed, trim plants lightly after bloom to shape them. Mulch with compost in spring and fall.

Gather rose petals before the flowers are completely open; spread them on paper or screens in a sunny spot for quick drying. Harvest the ripe hips in fall.

How to Use It

Enjoy the fresh flowers in bouquets; sprinkle dried flower petals into pot-pourri. Use the chopped, dried hips to brew a pleasant-tasting tea rich in vitamin C. (Add 2 or 3 teaspoons per cup of boiling water; steep for ten minutes.)

Did You Know?

'Apothecary's Rose' is the red rose that symbolized the English House of Lancaster during the Wars of the Roses. 🌀

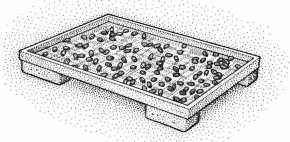

R

Set rose hips on a screen so air can circulate around them evenly for faster drying. You can use them when the color darkens and they wrinkle.

Rosemary
Rosmarinus officinalis

▲ 6'
☀ full
💧 dry

What It Looks Like
Common rosemary grows in shrubby clumps of branching stems with fragrant, needlelike, green leaves. Plants can reach 5 to 6 feet tall and wide where they grow outdoors; container plants are usually 1 to 3 feet in height and spread. Pale blue flowers bloom along the stems, usually from late winter through spring. Prostrate rose-

mary (*R. officinalis* 'Prostratus') has a low, trailing habit.

How to Grow It
Rosemary is generally hardy only in Zones 8 to 10, but you can grow it in colder climates, too, either as an annual or as a container plant. This aromatic herb grows best in well-drained, sandy or gravelly soil in a sunny but protected spot. You can raise rosemary from seed (sow fresh seed indoors in spring, and just cover), although seedlings tend to grow slowly. For faster results, start with purchased plants; set them out after all danger of frost has passed. In Zones 8 to 10, space plants 4 feet apart; elsewhere, space them 1 to 2 feet apart. Trim the stems back by one-third after flowering. Propagate by stem cuttings in spring or early summer. North of Zone 8, bring potted plants indoors for the winter, and give them a sunny, cool, and humid spot.

Snip leaves or shoot tips as needed for fresh use, freezing, or drying.

How to Use It
Rosemary's warm, pungent flavor complements a variety of foods, from roasted lamb, beef, or chicken to egg, cheese, or tomato dishes. Crush or mince the dried or fresh leaves before adding them to foods. Sprinkle fresh rosemary flowers on salads as a garnish. The dried leaves and flowers are also wonderful in potpourri.

Did You Know?
Legend has it that when Jesus, Mary, and Joseph fled to Egypt, Mary spread her blue cloak over a rosemary bush to hide from the Roman soldiers. When she removed the cloak, the shrub's white flowers had turned blue. 🌀

58

R

The trailing stems of prostrate rosemary show off best when cascading over a wall or out of a pot or hanging basket.

Rue
Ruta graveolens

⬆	2'
☀	full
💧	avg

What It Looks Like

This pungently scented, semievergreen herb forms shrubby, rounded mounds to 2 feet tall and wide. The blue-green leaves are deeply divided and sometimes have a light, powdery white coating. In mid- to late summer, the mounds are topped with clusters of bright yellow-green flowers followed by interesting brown seedpods. 'Jackman's Blue' is a compact selection with blue-gray leaves. The leaves of 'Variegata' have striking creamy-colored splashes, particularly on the spring growth.

How to Grow It

Rue is perennial in Zones 5 to 9. Give it a sunny spot in average to poor soil. Good drainage is critical; plants may not survive the winter in a spot where the soil stays damp. Sow seeds indoors in late winter or in the garden in late spring; just cover with soil. Thin or transplant seedlings to stand 18 to 24 inches apart. Prune off dead stems in spring, and trim the remaining top-growth as needed to shape the plants. For propagation, take cuttings in late summer.

How to Use It

Grow rue in your herb or flower garden for its attractive foliage and flowers. Its beautiful blue-green leaves are a perfect complement to white or pastel-colored flowers. Try planting it in a row to create an unusual low hedge. Or combine it with 'Autumn Joy' sedum for a contrasting texture. Rue also makes a great container plant. Harvest the seedheads (with 6 to 8 inches of stem) to add interest to dried arrangements.

Did You Know?

In the 1500s and 1600s, pots of rue were placed in courtrooms to protect the magistrates from the prisoners' pests and fever. Also known as "herb of grace," rue was believed to keep witches and the devil at bay in medieval times. It was also used to ward off plague. 🌀

R

It's smart to wear gloves as you work around rue, since some people experience reddening or blistering skin after touching the leaves.

Saffron Crocus
Crocus sativus

↑	8"
☀	full
💧	avg

What It Looks Like
Saffron crocus looks much like an ordinary spring-blooming crocus. Its small, bulblike corms produce sheaves of thin, grasslike leaves that emerge in late summer to early fall and usually grow 6 to 8 inches tall. Stemless, purplish pink flowers rise from the ground in early fall. Inside each flower, you'll see three thin, red, branching structures, called stigmata or threads. These bear the female parts of the flower, and they are what you harvest for cooking.

How to Grow It
Hardy in Zones 6 to 9, saffron crocus grows in average, well-drained soil in full sun to light shade. Plant the corms as soon as they are available (usually in fall); set them 3 to 4 inches deep and 4 to 6 inches apart. To propagate saffron crocus, dig, divide, and replant clumps after the foliage dies back to the ground.

To harvest, remove the red stigmata from the flowers. (You can pick the whole flower first, or get down on your knees to harvest in the garden; that way, you can still enjoy the blooms outdoors.) Lay the individual threads on a sheet of paper to dry. The threads are tiny and light, so once you've picked them, keep them out of the wind.

How to Use It
Dried saffron threads are a traditional ingredient in Spanish paella, French bouillabaisse, and pastries. Their rich flavor complements cheeses, eggs, rice, and vegetable dishes, and they impart a golden yellow color to breads, cakes, and pastries. Try a pinch in your favorite soup or stew; a little bit goes a long way. Saffron's colorful flowers add interest to the fall garden. Grow it in a low groundcover (such as creeping thyme), or mulch them with gravel to keep soil from splashing onto the flowers.

Did You Know?
Saffron has been valued as a flavoring and as a dye herb for thousands of years. It is one of the world's most expensive seasonings.

S

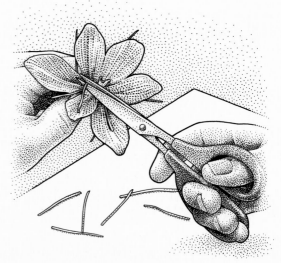

To harvest your saffron, use scissors to snip off the threadlike red anthers from the center of the fall flowers.

Sage
Salvia officinalis

▲	2'
☀	full
💧	avg

What It Looks Like
Culinary sage, the kind commonly used for cooking, grows in shrubby, 1- to 2-foot-wide clumps with aromatic, oblong, gray-green leaves that have a pebbly texture. The mid- to late summer, purple-blue flowers bloom in whorls along the tips of the 1- to 2-foot-tall stems. 'Berggarten' has broad, almost oval, gray leaves. Purple sage (*S. officinalis* 'Purpurea') has grayish to greenish purple foliage. 'Icterina' has green leaves with a showy yellow edge. 'Tricolor' also has green leaves, but with prominent cream and purple-pink splashes.

Besides the traditional culinary sages, there is an amazing variety of other edible and ornamental sages. Pineapple sage (*S. elegans*) is a tender perennial popular for its sweet, pineapple-like scent as well as for its bright red flowers. Annual clary sage (*S. viridis,* also sold as *S. horminium*) has colorful, petal-like bracts in shades of pink, purple-blue, or white veined with green.

How to Grow It
Culinary sage is generally hardy in Zones 4 to 9, although the colored-leaf cultivars are somewhat less cold-tolerant. Pineapple sage survives winters outdoors in Zones 8 to 10; elsewhere, treat it as an annual or bring it indoors for the winter. Sages thrive in full sun and average, well-drained soil. Sow culinary sage seed indoors in late winter or outdoors in late spring; do not cover. Thin or space plants to stand 12 to 18 inches apart. Trim topgrowth back by one-half to two-thirds in midspring. Buy a potted plant of pineapple sage, and plant it in the garden or in a container. Take stem cuttings in late summer to grow the rooted cuttings on a sunny windowsill over winter. Sow clary sage seed in early to midspring where plants are to grow; do not cover. Thin to 8 inches apart. Pinch off spent flowers to prolong bloom.

Pick leaves of culinary and pineapple sage as needed for fresh use. Culinary sage also dries well; harvest leafy shoots before the flowers open. Cut clary sage spikes through the summer for fresh use or for drying.

How to Use It
Culinary sage is the classic Thanksgiving turkey seasoning and the distinctive flavor of American breakfast sausage. Fresh or dried, it also tastes great in soups, stews, and creamy pasta dishes. Add fresh pineapple sage leaves to teas or fruit salad. Dry the flowers of any sage for use in wreaths and potpourri. Sages are also very ornamental garden plants.

Did You Know?
Sage has long been associated with longevity; an old saying asks "Why should a person die, when sage grows in his garden?" 🌀

S

Savories

Satureja spp.

🔺 12"–18"

☀ full

💧 avg

What It Looks Like
Both winter savory (*S. montana*) and summer savory (*S. hortensis*) are bushy, 10- to 12-inch-wide plants with narrow, aromatic, green leaves. The stems of winter savory tend to be woody at the base and have a somewhat spreading habit. They grow 6 to 12 inches tall, topped with white or pale purple flowers from midsummer to early fall. Summer savory blooms from midsummer to frost, with white or light pink flowers along the tops of the soft, 12- to 18-inch-tall stems.

How to Grow It
Winter savory is a perennial hardy in Zones 5 to 9. Summer savory is an annual. Both need full sun and grow well in average, well-drained soil. Summer savory appreciates some extra compost in the soil as well as regular watering. To start either herb from seed, sow indoors four to six weeks before your last frost date or in the garden around the last frost date. Do not cover the seed; just press it into the soil surface and keep moist until sprouts appear. Thin seedlings or space transplants of winter savory 10 to 12 inches apart; allow 6 to 8 inches between summer savory plants. Propagate winter savory by division in spring or fall or by stem cuttings in summer. Summer savory may self-sow.

Once plants are 6 inches tall, snip off shoots as needed for fresh use, or cut them just before flowering and lay them on screens to dry.

How to Use It
Savory is often called the "bean herb" because it tastes so good added to cooked beans. Winter savory tends to be stronger than its cousin, so use it a bit more sparingly until you become familiar with its flavor. Mince fresh or dried leaves into soups and vegetable dishes; they are also good in potato salad, herb butters, and salad dressings.

Did You Know?
In the past, summer savory had a reputation as an aphrodisiac; winter savory was thought to decrease desire. 🌀

Good drainage is critical for success with winter savory. If your soil tends to be damp or clayey, grow this herb in a container in well-drained potting soil.

Scented Geraniums
Pelargonium spp.

⬆	2'
☀	full
💧	avg

What It Looks Like
Scented geraniums look much like their flower-garden relatives, forming 12- to 18-inch-wide, bushy plants with branching stems to about 2 feet tall. But while flowering geraniums are prized for their blooms, scented geraniums are beloved primarily for their fragrant foliage. Rose geranium (*P. graveolens*) has deeply cut, lobed leaves with an old-rose fragrance. If you enjoy a fresh citrus scent, try lemon geranium (*P. crispum*). Peppermint geranium (*P. tomentosum*) bears broad, fuzzy leaves with a refreshing mint fragrance.

How to Grow It
Native to South Africa, scented geraniums are hardy evergreen perennials in the tropical or subtropical Zone 10 regions. In other parts of the country, treat them as annuals, or bring them indoors for the winter; they make excellent houseplants for a sunny window. A few scented geraniums will grow from seed, but it's easiest to buy already-growing plants. Set them out after all danger of frost has passed, in a sunny spot with average to dry, well-drained soil. Space plants about 18 inches apart.

Pick leaves and flowers as needed for fresh use. For drying, harvest leafy shoots just as the flowers start to open.

How to Use It
In the garden, grow scented geraniums along paths and next to benches, where you can easily reach the leaves to rub them and enjoy their fragrance. They also look great in windowboxes and planters. Indoors, add the leaves and flowers to fresh and dried bouquets or potpourri. Make rose geranium sugar by layering 8 to 12 bruised leaves in 1 pound of sugar. After three or four weeks, pick out the leaves. Use the flavored sugar in cake or cookie recipes, or add it to tea.

Did You Know?
Scented geraniums were popular houseplants in Victorian times. 🌀

63

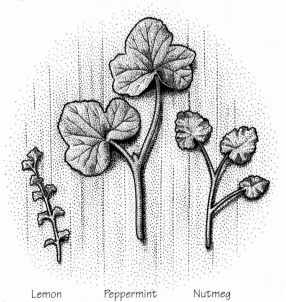

Lemon   Peppermint   Nutmeg

It's hard to grow just one scented geranium when there are so many to choose from. Rub the leaves before you buy to find the scents you like best.

S

Sorrel

Rumex acetosa

30"

full

moist

What It Looks Like

Garden sorrel grows in 18-inch-wide clumps of large, oblong, spinachlike, green leaves. In mid-summer, the clumps send up thin, 24- to 30-inch-tall stems topped with clusters of tiny, reddish brown flowers.

French sorrel (*R. scutatus*) is similar in size to garden sorrel, but its leaves are broader and shaped more like arrow-heads. French sorrel also tends to have a milder flavor. 'Silver Shield' is a particu-larly ornamental selection with blue-gray foliage attractively veined with silver.

How to Grow It

Both of these perennial herbs are hardy in Zones 5 to 9. They thrive in sun to partial shade, in moist, compost-enriched, acidic soil. Buy a potted plant or sow seed ¼ inch deep, either indoors or in the garden, two to four weeks before your last frost date. Set transplants or thin seedlings to stand 12 to 18 inches apart. (Use the thinnings in salads.) Pinch off flower stems as they appear to keep plants bushy. Mulch with compost in fall or spring to encourage vigorous growth.

Harvest the leaves as needed for fresh use. Plants are most productive in spring and fall. Sorrel does not dry well, but you can puree and freeze the leaves for winter cooking.

How to Use It

To enjoy sorrel's tart, citrusy flavor, toss a few tender, young leaves into green salads or stir-fries. Add fresh leaves or frozen leaf puree to hot or cold soups. This tangy herb also livens up herb but-ters and mixed herb sauces for cooked fish. Sorrel's sharp flavor can be an acquired taste, so use it sparingly at first; add a little at a time until you find the flavor you are comfortable with. Heat causes the leaves to fade quickly, so add them at the end of cooking to keep the bright green color. If you allow your plants to flower, harvest and dry the flower spikes for dried arrangements.

Did You Know?

Sorrel is native to North America and Europe. It is one of the few herbs that browsing deer will eat. French sorrel has long been a staple of European cuisine, especially soups.

S

Sweet Woodruff

Galium odoratum

8"

part

moist

What It Looks Like

Sweet woodruff grows in low, spreading carpets to about 8 inches tall. Narrow, lance-shaped, rough-edged leaves grow in whorls or "ruffs" around the slender, brittle stems. In late spring to early summer, the leafy carpet is sprinkled with loose clusters of small, bright white, fragrant flowers.

How to Grow It

This perennial herb is hardy in Zones 4 to 8. It thrives in partial shade and evenly moist, compost-enriched soil, although it can adapt to less than ideal conditions, such as the deeper, drier shade under trees and shrubs. Sweet woodruff seed is very slow to germinate, so buy already-started plants. Set them out in spring, spaced 8 inches apart. Once they settle in, sweet woodruff plants will spread quickly; divide in early spring or fall as needed to keep them under control. If the foliage starts to turn brown (a common problem during very humid weather), mow or cut down all stems to about 2 inches above the ground. Fresh new growth will soon emerge.

Harvest foliage any time during the growing season. Cut stems about 2 inches above the ground, bundle them, and hang in a warm, airy place to dry.

How to Use It

Sweet woodruff is an easy-to-grow groundcover for moist to slightly dry, shady spots. The dried foliage releases a fresh, sweet scent that is wonderful in wreaths and potpourri. Sweet woodruff is an ingredient of May wine, a traditional German beverage that's used to celebrate the return of spring. To make your own May wine, add 10 to 12 sprigs of sweet woodruff to 1 gallon of Rhine wine, and let sit at least overnight. To serve, pour into a punch bowl, and add fresh or frozen strawberries.

Did You Know?

Sweet woodruff has been used to stuff pillows and to add fragrance to linens since the Middle Ages. 🌀

S

It's easy to expand your sweet woodruff plantings. Just dig up rooted sections in spring or fall and move them to the desired spot.

Tansy

Tanacetum vulgare

3'

full

avg

What It Looks Like

Tansy forms lush, leafy, fast-spreading clumps of ferny, bright green, strongly scented leaves. Clusters of buttonlike, yellow flowers bloom atop the 3-foot-tall stems in late summer. Fernleaf tansy (*T. vulgare* var. *crispum*) produces very lacy, finely cut green leaves. It reaches only 2 feet tall and is a handsome foliage plant.

How to Grow It

This ornamental, perennial herb is hardy in Zones 4 to 9. Give it a site in full sun or partial shade, with average, well-drained soil. Tansy can be a very rampant grower. Choose a spot where it can spread freely without smothering other herbs, plant it in a bottomless bucket sunk into the soil, or divide clumps yearly to control their spread. Planting next to a wall or fence will keep winds from knocking over the tall stems. Start with a purchased plant, or sow seed ⅛ inch deep indoors in late winter. Set plants outside 2 to 3 feet apart after the last frost date. If the foliage looks tattered by midsummer, cut plants back by one-half to encourage a flush of new growth. Cut down dead stems in late fall to early spring. Propagate tansy by digging and dividing clumps in spring or fall.

To harvest tansy for drying, cut the flowerheads with 18- to 24-inch stems when the blooms are fully open and developed but before they start to turn dull or brown. Strip the leaves off the stems before drying.

How to Use It

Tansy's colorful blooms are a welcome addition to fresh or dried flower arrangements. You can also add the dried flowers to wreaths, potpourri, and other crafts. Fernleaf tansy makes an attractive container plant. The leaves have a reputation for repelling ants and flies; try it for yourself by growing tansy near doorways.

Did You Know?

Native to Europe and Asia, tansy was thought to promote immortality and was used in ancient times to embalm the dead.

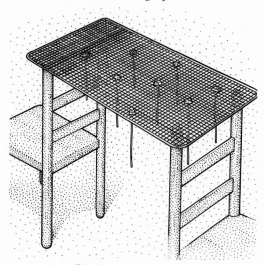

To dry tansy flowers for arrangements, slip the stems through a screen to hold the flowerheads upright.

66

T

Tarragon
Artemisia dracunculus

⬆	3'
☀	full
💧	avg

What It Looks Like

French tarragon, the kind favored for cooking, forms 2-foot-wide, shrubby clumps of branching stems with short, narrow, dark green leaves. The 2- to 3-foot-tall stems tend to be woody at the base. Tiny, yellowish green flowers may appear in summer, but they rarely set seed.

Russian tarragon, a close relative, looks much like French tarragon with paler green leaves. Russian tarragon sets seed much more readily, however. It is also generally considered less desirable for cooking, due to its bitter flavor.

How to Grow It

Tarragon is a perennial herb hardy in Zones 4 to 8. It thrives in full sun and average, well-drained soil; it grows poorly in hot, dry areas. Start with a potted plant to be sure you're getting the right herb. Set plants 2 feet apart in spring or fall. Divide every two or three years in spring to keep plants vigorous and to propagate them.

Snip leaves as needed for fresh use, or cut the leafy stems in summer for drying. Handle the leaves gently; they bruise easily.

How to Use It

Add fresh or dried leaves to roasted chicken and chicken salad, green salad, fish and tomato sauces, and cream soups. Tarragon has a relatively strong licorice flavor, so use it lightly. And for best flavor, wait until the last 15 minutes of cooking to add it. To make tarragon vinegar, loosely fill a large glass jar with sprigs of fresh tarragon. Heat (but don't boil) white vinegar, then pour it into the jar to cover the herbs. Let cool, then cover and store in a cool, dark place. Tarragon vinegar is great in salad dressings and marinades.

Did You Know?

Native to southern Europe, tarragon was once used to heal snake bites. Its name, *dracunculus,* means "little dragon." 🌀

𝒟on't pay a fortune for tarragon vinegar at the supermarket! One plant will give you all the leaves you need to make your own for home or gifts.

Thymes
Thymus spp.

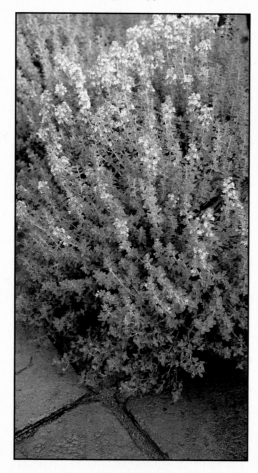

⬆	3"–12"
☀	full
💧	dry

What It Looks Like

Thymes grow as bushy, 6- to 12-inch-tall shrubs or as creeping mats that reach only 3 inches tall. Tiny but pretty flowers bloom in small clusters in early summer. Common thyme (*T. vulgaris*) is a bushy type with aromatic, gray-green leaves and white or pale lavender blooms. It is the kind most commonly used in cooking. Lemon thyme (*T. × citriodorus*) also has a bushy habit, with white flowers and dark green leaves that have a strong lemony scent. Mother-of-thyme (*T. serpyllum*) is a creeper with pink to purple flowers over mats of tiny, dark green, aromatic leaves. These are just a few of the hundreds of species and cultivars that have a wide range of growth habits, colors, and fragrances.

How to Grow It

Thymes are generally hardy in Zones 4 to 9. Grow them in a sunny location, with light, well-drained soil. You can grow thyme from seed sown indoors in early spring or outdoors two or three weeks before the last frost date; do not cover. Seedlings, however, tend to grow slowly, and they will vary in habit and aroma. Buying a selection of already-started plants will give you a wider variety of scents, shapes, and colors. Set plants 6 to 12 inches apart. Propagate thymes by division in spring or by stem cuttings in summer.

For fresh use, pick individual leaves or small sprigs as needed. For drying, harvest just as the flowers begin to bloom in early summer; cut the whole plant to 2 inches above the ground.

How to Use It

Add fresh or dried thyme leaves to soups, stews, poultry stuffing, roasted meats, and vegetable, cheese, or egg dishes. Thyme's delicate flavor is also an important part of French and Cajun cuisine. In the garden, use bushy thymes to edge pathways; grow creeping types between bricks or paving stones. Bushy thymes also make excellent container plants for an indoor, windowsill garden in winter.

Did You Know?

Drinking thyme tea was thought to help one see the fairies in the British Isles. 🌀

T

Wild Strawberry
Fragaria vesca

What It Looks Like

⬆	10"
☀	full
💧	moist

Wild strawberry, also known as woodland strawberry, alpine strawberry, and *fraises des bois*, looks like a smaller version of the regular garden strawberry. Unlike their garden cousins, however, wild strawberry plants rarely spread by runners; they instead form compact, leafy clumps 6 to 10 inches tall and wide. Wild straw-

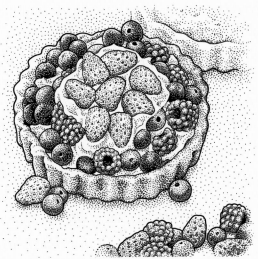

berries also produce their small, white, yellow-centered flowers and bright red fruits all through the summer. 'Improved Ruegen' bears particularly well in late summer to early fall. White-or yellow-fruited wild strawberries are a good choice if your feathered friends tend to steal your harvest; apparently they don't think the fruits are ripe and tend to leave the plants alone!

How to Grow It

This perennial herb is hardy in Zones 5 to 9. It grows best in evenly moist, compost-enriched soil in a sunny to partly shady, sheltered spot. Buy potted plants, or start your own from seed. Sow indoors in late winter or early spring. Do not cover the seed; just press it into the soil surface, and cover pots with clear plastic wrap to keep the seed moist. Set out transplants 8 inches apart in mid- to late spring, around your last frost date. Propagate by division in fall or spring; use a knife to help separate the clumps.

Pick the fruit when it is fully colored; use fresh. Pick leaves in early summer for drying.

How to Use It

The tiny berries of wild strawberry are much sweeter than those of larger strawberry plants. Enjoy them right off the plant, or save a few for decorating desserts. Add the dried leaves to herb tea blends. In the garden, the compact, bushy plants are excellent for edging pathways. They also grow well in containers, so try a few in a deck or patio planter to keep the fruit within easy reach.

Did You Know?

Strawberry fruits are dedicated to the Virgin Mary and the Goddess Venus. 🌀

Wild strawberry's tiny but flavorful fruits make a wonderful garnish for tarts, fruit salads, and other desserts.

W

Wormwood

Artemisia absinthium

How to Grow It

Wormwood and its perennial relatives are usually hardy in Zones 4 to 9. Give them a sunny spot with average, well-drained soil. Their tiny seeds may be slow to grow into garden-size plants, so it's best to start with purchased plants. Set them out in spring at least 2 feet apart. Propagate by taking cuttings from sideshoots, with a bit of old growth at the base, in late summer. Trim back by one-half to two-thirds in spring to shape them.

Gather the top part of the stalks (the upper 12 to 24 inches, depending on the stem length you need) as the flowers open. Hang in bundles in a warm, shady place to dry.

How to Use It

Wormwood looks great in fresh or dried arrangements. You can also add it to potpourri or use it for dried wreaths. Hang or lay bunches or sachets in drawers and closets to keep moths away from clothes.

Did You Know?

The most bitter of all herbs, wormwood has been used in absinthe, vermouth, and other herb-flavored liquors.

🔺	3'
☀	full
💧	avg

What It Looks Like

Wormwood is a large perennial herb, producing shrubby clumps to 3 feet tall and wide. Its sturdy, silvery stems, which tend to be woody at the base, carry many deeply divided, gray-green leaves. Both the leaves and stems have a distinct bitter scent. Wormwood blooms in mid- to late summer, with small, rounded, greenish yellow flowers that are not particularly showy.

W

To create your own herb wreath, use thin floral wire to fasten bundles of dried wormwood to a wire wreath form.

Yarrow
Achillea millefolium

3'

full

avg

What It Looks Like
Common yarrow produces 18- to 24-inch-wide mounds of feathery, green, aromatic leaves. The 1- to 3-foot-tall, leafy flowerstalks are topped with flat clusters of small, white flowers through the summer. 'Cerise Queen' grows 2 feet tall, with bright reddish pink flowers. 'Fire King' reaches the same height, with reddish flowers that fade to pink as they age.

Fernleaf yarrow (*A. filipendulina*) also has deeply cut, green foliage, but its leaves aren't as finely dissected as those of common yarrow. It usually grows to 4 feet tall and 2 feet wide, with broad, flat clusters of small, golden flowers. 'Coronation Gold' is a hybrid with mustard-yellow flowerheads and gray-green leaves on compact, 3-foot stems.

How to Grow It
Yarrows are perennials hardy in Zones 3 to 8. They thrive in full sun and average to sandy, well-drained soil. To raise plants from seed, sow indoors in late winter or outdoors around the last frost date. Scatter the seed thinly over the surface, and press it in lightly; keep moist until seedlings appear (usually a week or less). If you are looking for a particular flower color, it's better to buy named cultivars.

Space plants or thin seedlings to stand 2 feet apart. Common yarrow can spread quickly. Pull out the unwanted runners, or divide established clumps every two or three years in spring or fall to control their spread. Division is also an easy way to propagate yarrow. Plants may need staking if your soil is rich. Cut the dead tops to the ground before spring.

Harvest yarrow when the flower clusters show good color but before they start to turn brown. Hang the flowers in bunches to dry.

How to Use It
Once considered an important medicinal herb, yarrow is now used primarily as an ornamental. The colorful flowerheads look wonderful in the garden and last well in fresh and dried flower arrangements.

Did You Know?
Achillea is named after the Greek warrior Achilles, who used the leaves of yarrow to treat the wounds of his soldiers at the Battle of Troy. 🌐

Y

Harvesting and Preserving Herbs

Chapter 3

Harvesting and Preserving Herbs

I've been harvesting and drying the herbs I grow ever since I began to work in the garden. I know that it's easier to buy dried herbs from a store or mail-order catalog than it is for me to dry my own. But I love the freshness and fragrance of my own dried herbs. I like harvesting them and getting their fragrant oils all over my hands. I enjoy the look and fragrance of my own dried herbs in the kitchen and in floral arrangements. I like the freedom of having a wide variety of dried herbs on hand, so I can add a pinch of this or a scattering of that to get the perfect seasoning for whatever dish I'm preparing for dinner. And naturally, I like knowing that no chemicals have been sprayed on my herbs—they're 100 percent organic!

I know you'll enjoy preserving the flavors and fragrances of your homegrown herbs, too. There are two simple tricks to success: The first secret is harvesting them at the right time, so the herbs are at their flavorful and fragrant peak. The other key is to choose the right preservation technique to keep the best possible flavor. Many herbs dry well, but some are better when frozen or preserved in oil. Read on to find out what to do for every herb.

Harvesting
Your Herbs

One of the greatest rewards of growing herbs is being able to harvest them—full of garden-fresh flavor and fragrance—for cooking and crafts. A flower garden may look pretty for a few months, but an herb garden can bring you pleasure all year long.

When to Harvest

To get the best from any herb, you need to harvest it at the ideal time. The best time of day to harvest herbs, either for preserving or for fresh use, is early in the morning. Gather them after the dew is off the leaves but before the heat of the day begins. The hot sun wilts plants, robs them of moisture, and reduces the flavor of the leaves.

The best time of year to harvest varies widely, depending on how you plan to use the herb. If you just need a fresh sprig or two to liven up a recipe or to garnish a plate, you can harvest any time during the growing season. For preserving, some seasons are better than others, depending on the kind of herb and whether you're harvesting its leaves, flowers, seeds, or roots.

Leafy Herbs: When you plan to dry herb leaves, try to gather them just before the plants start to bloom. At this stage, they are highest in the essential oils that give them their scents and flavors. Most herbs will lose some of these oils in the drying process, so it makes sense to start with as high an oil content as possible. But if you don't have the chance to harvest at the ideal time, it's still worth picking leafy herbs when the plants are blooming rather than lose the whole harvest.

Flowering Herbs: The timing for harvesting herb flowers varies, depending on how you plan to use the herbs. For most herbs, you can harvest when the flowers open fully, or just before they're fully open. It's worth

Try to resist the urge to harvest sage and other perennial herbs during the first year. After that, you can usually harvest twice a year—in spring and summer.

74

Lavender dries best when cut just after the flowers open. Check the individual herb entries in Chapter 2 for recommendations for each herb.

few days until you notice the seeds changing color.

Root Herbs: On herbs such as garlic and horseradish, you usually want the roots rather than the tops. (However, I must put in a plug for fresh garlic greens—they're incredibly delicious in stir-fries and pesto.) Dig garlic bulbs in mid- to late summer after the tops have died back. For other root herbs, wait until fall or early spring, when they are not producing topgrowth. Horseradish spreads vigorously, so the more you harvest, the better!

How to Harvest

Harvest your herbs with sharp scissors or garden shears or with a sharp garden knife. On multistemmed herbs, such as lemon balm and rosemary, snip off shoots from the top of the plant, then strip the leaves you need from those shoots. When you're harvesting fine-leaved plants like thyme, you don't need to strip off the leaves. Just dry (or freeze) and use the shoots, stems and all. On low, clump-forming herbs without distinct stems, such as arugula and parsley, you can take any leaves that are big enough to use. Harvesting the outer leaves first will encourage more new growth, but the young center leaves are usually the most mild and tender.

Picking a leaf here and there for fresh use won't weaken your plants at all. In fact, these tough plants can withstand much heavier harvesting as long as you do it wisely. Most annual and biennial herbs can recover from several harvests a

Harvesting and Preserving

collecting them at different stages, from just-opening buds to fully open flowers, to see which dry best for your purposes.

If you don't need the stems, just the flowerheads, cut them off above the uppermost leaves on the stems. For crafts, harvest the flowerheads with 6 inches or more of stem.

Seed-Producing Herbs: Harvesting herb seeds is really straightforward: You need to collect them when they're ripe but before they fall off the plant. It's usually easy to tell when the seeds are ripe, since they darken from green to tan or brown. Start watching your herbs about a week after the flowers fade, and keep checking every

season as long as you don't take more than half of the topgrowth at each cutting. Exceptions are herbs you are growing for their seed, such as caraway and dill. If you want the biggest harvest of seed, avoid harvesting more than a leaf or two now and then. For coriander, where you may want to harvest both the leaves (better known as cilantro, a key ingredient in Mexican and Chinese food) and the seeds, grow a double crop so you'll have plenty of both. Don't harvest leaves from plants that you want to set seed.

With perennial herbs, it's best to resist the urge to harvest the first year, so the plants have a chance to get established in the garden. (Here again, picking a leaf or two as needed is okay.) After the first

year, you can generally get two harvests: one in late spring and one in mid- to late summer. You can cut off up to two-thirds of the topgrowth during the spring harvest. At the second picking, it's best to take no more than one-third of the topgrowth. Popular perennial herbs include bee balm, chives, lavender, lemon balm, the mints, oregano, rosemary, sage, and thyme. You'll find many more in Chapter 2, "Fifty Herb Biographies," starting on page 20.

Schedule this second harvest 40 to 60 days before your first fall frost, so your herbs will have a chance to produce and store enough food to survive the winter and produce new growth next spring. (If you live in a frost-free area, continue to harvest lightly through late fall.)

76

Harvest leafy herbs for drying just before they flower. They'll be richest in essential oils then and will keep the best and strongest flavor.

Drying Herbs

The goal of drying herbs is to remove as much moisture as possible, as quickly as possible. Fast drying will help to preserve the fragrance, flavor, and color as well as reduce the chance of mold developing.

Store dried herbs in airtight containers away from bright light. Dark glass bottles work well for dried leaves, petals, and seeds. Resealable plastic bags are another good choice if you squeeze out all the air before sealing and storing them in a dark, cool area. For crafts, store long-stemmed herbs in cardboard boxes with tight-fitting lids. Always label any container clearly before storage, with the name of the herb and the packaging date. For the best flavor and fragrance, plan to replace your dried herbs every year.

Drying Leafy Herbs

Herbs with pungently aromatic leaves, such as rosemary, sage, and thyme, tend to hold their flavor and fragrance well when dried. Experiment with air, oven, and microwave drying to see which method produces the best results for you. The end result of any process should be herbs that feel dry and crispy to the touch, like a cornflake.

Air Drying: This is probably the most widely used drying technique with home herb gardeners, and with good reason: It's easy, and you usually get good results. The secret is providing the ideal atmosphere for fast drying. You need a spot that is dry and dark with good air circulation. An attic, barn, or garage loft can be ideal if the site is well ventilated. Some gardeners even have good luck drying herbs in their car! (Lay the herbs on screens, cover them with paper towels, and open the windows a bit.)

Hanging works well for herbs with long stems. Gather them into bundles, with four to six stems of one kind of herb in each bundle. Fasten the stem end of the bundles with rubber bands. The bands will contract as the stems dry, holding them firmly. Label the bunches before hanging them to dry.

Once your herbs are dry, strip the leaves from the stems (if you haven't already). Discard the stems, or save them for use in potpourri.

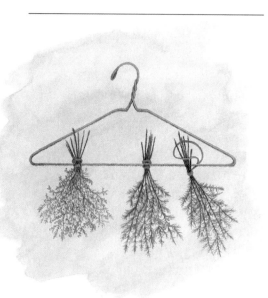

Coathangers make handy drying racks, holding three to six herb bundles each. Label individual bunches or the hanger itself.

Many herbs also dry well when laid on screening (such as old window screens) propped up on bricks or chairs for good air circulation on all sides. This setup is ideal for drying individual leaves, flowerheads, and petals easily. Stir the herbs every day or two to promote even drying.

Oven Drying: If you don't have an ideal spot to hang herbs for air drying or if you live in a humid climate, oven drying may be a better option than air drying. Spread your herbs evenly on cookie sheets and place them in the oven; leave the door open partway to let the moisture escape. Set the oven on its lowest temperature setting. (In a gas oven, the warmth from the pilot light can be enough for drying

Screen trays are ideal for air drying many leafy and flowering herbs. For faster drying, prop up filled screens on bricks or blocks to allow good air circulation on all sides.

herbs.) Stir the herbs every half hour or so to encourage even drying.

The drying time will vary depending on the herbs and the oven, from a few hours to a day or two (if you're just using the pilot light). The herbs are done when they feel dry and crispy.

Microwave Drying: If you have just a few herbs to dry, you could try drying them in a microwave oven. Place a single layer of leaves on a paper towel on a microwave-safe plate. Lay another paper towel on top, and microwave on high for one minute. Watch the herbs continually during the drying process, and stop the oven if you smell the herbs burning. If needed, repeat the heating for 30 seconds at a time until the herbs are fully dry.

While these general instructions work well with most microwaves, you should always read the manufacturer's

To dry leafy herbs in a microwave, sandwich them between two paper towels on a microwave-safe plate.

TOP 10 HERBS FOR DRYING

DRYING IS AN EASY TECHNIQUE THAT'S A TRADITIONAL FAVORITE FOR PRESERVING MANY LEAFY HERBS. SOME HERBS, HOWEVER, HOLD THEIR FLAVOR BETTER THAN OTHERS WHEN DRIED. BEST BETS FOR TASTY DRIED HERBS INCLUDE:

ANISE HYSSOP
(*Agastache foeniculum*)

BEE BALM
(*Monarda didyma*)

CATNIP
(*Nepeta cataria*)

MINTS
(*Mentha* spp.)

OREGANOS
(*Origanum* spp.)

ROMAN CHAMOMILE
(*Chamaemelum nobile*)

ROSEMARY
(*Rosmarinus officinalis*)

SAGE
(*Salvia officinalis*)

SAVORIES
(*Satureja* spp.)

THYMES
(*Thymus* spp.)

instructions for your particular model before using it to dry herbs. You may need to use a lower setting or shorter heating periods to get good results.

Drying Flowering Herbs

Fast drying is as important for flowering herbs as it is for leafy herbs, since you want to keep the colors as bright as possible. If you just need the petals or flowerheads—for example, for cooking or potpourri—you can use any of the techniques discussed above for leaves: air drying on screens (or sheets of paper), oven drying, or microwave drying. Petals are generally much thinner than leaves, so they will dry much more quickly.

To dry long-stemmed herbs for crafts, such as tansy and yarrow, you have two options. You could hang them upside down in bunches, as you would for leafy herbs. Or you could slide their stems down through a horizontal wire-mesh screen, so the flowerheads rest on the screen. Both of these techniques will help the flowerheads to dry in a natural-looking position. Oven and microwave drying usually give disappointing results, since the stems and flowerheads dry unevenly, and the heads will be mis-shapen from lying on one side.

If you enjoy herbal crafts, don't overlook the fun and beauty of pressed flowers. (Pressing is a special kind of drying.) You can use flowering herbs like bee balm, calendula, chives, lavender, and nasturtium to make beautiful pressed flowers. (Don't forget the old roses,

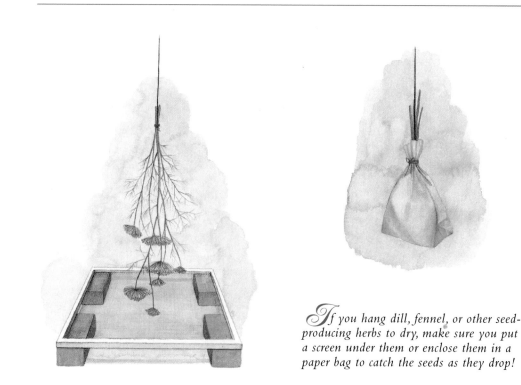

If you hang dill, fennel, or other seed-producing herbs to dry, make sure you put a screen under them or enclose them in a paper bag to catch the seeds as they drop!

To make a garlic braid, keep the leafy tops on at harvest time, then braid them evenly to the size you like. For extra color, add dried herb leaves and flowers.

the flowers out in the phone book, making sure they don't touch each other. Then weight the book down with the dictionaries. Or use layers of newspaper instead of a phone book. Of course, you can also buy or make an attractive wooden flower press.

Drying Herb Seeds

It's easy to dry seeds, since their moisture content is already fairly low by the time they're ripe. One option is to lay harvested seedheads on a screen for two or three days. Then shake off and collect the seeds. If you've harvested the seedheads with long stems, you can hang them to dry instead. Place a screen under the bunches to catch the seeds as they drop. Or put the heads in a paper bag, stem ends up. Gather the top of the bag around the stems, tie it with string, and then hang the bagged herbs in a warm, dry place. As the seeds dry, they will drop into the bottom of the bag—usually in about two weeks.

too—single-flowered types are best for pressing. Violets also make lovely pressed flowers and look delightful with herbs and roses.) Herb foliage—especially ferny rue and feathery dill leaves—look good pressed, and it complements your pressed-flower compositions. Once you've pressed a nice assortment of foliage and flowers, you can make greeting cards, pictures, decorated lampshades and napkin rings—the list is endless! And need I say that they make great gifts?

You can make a simple herb flower press from an old phone book and a couple of dictionary-size books. Spread

Storing and Enjoying Dried Herbs

Once you've harvested and dried your herbs, there are plenty of ways to store and display them. You can put culinary herb leaves and seeds in glass jars—labeled and dated, of course! They'll last longer and stay fresher if the jars are made of colored glass. Or create a *bouquet garni* by combining soup or stew herbs—bay, parsley, and thyme, plus whatever you like—in small cheesecloth bags. Just toss a bag into your soup or stew and remove before serving.

Freezing Herbs

Many leafy herbs also keep their flavor well when frozen, and this technique couldn't be easier! Simply place your herbs in resealable plastic freezer bags. You can freeze whole sprigs or chop the herbs first. Squeeze the air out of each bag, then seal it. Label with the name of the herb and the storage date. For best flavor, use frozen herbs within six months.

Another way to freeze herbs is to puree them with water or oil and pour them into ice-cube trays. When the cubes are frozen, transfer them to labeled resealable plastic bags. Toss individual cubes into soups, stews, and other foods during cooking. When you use herb ice cubes, bear in mind that you're adding water as well as herbs. So either reduce the amount of liquid in the recipe accordingly or be prepared to let it cook a little longer. You can have fun making up mixed-herb cubes for specific recipes, such as basil-oregano-thyme cubes for spaghetti sauce. Here's a final tip for herb ice cubes: If you haven't tried lemon balm or mint ice cubes in iced tea, you're really missing out!

Frozen herbs don't have that fresh-picked look, so don't use them for green salads or garnishes, but they'll still be great in soups, stews, and other cooked dishes. Use the same amount of frozen herbs as you would fresh.

Many herbs look alike when frozen or dried, so always label bags and jars carefully before storing. It's smart to add the date, too, since you'll want to replace unused herbs every 6 to 12 months.

mint

BEST BETS FOR FREEZING

FREEZING IS A FAST AND EASY WAY TO PRESERVE MANY CULINARY HERBS FOR WINTER RECIPES. HERE'S A LIST OF SOME HERBS THAT KEEP THEIR FLAVOR BEST WHEN FROZEN. IT'S ALSO WORTH EXPERIMENTING WITH OTHERS TO SEE WHICH WORK WELL FOR YOU.

CHERVIL
(*Anthriscus cerefolium*)

MINTS
(*Mentha* spp.)

DILL
(*Anethum graveolens*)

PARSLEY
(*Petroselinum crispum*)

FENNEL
(*Foeniculum vulgare*)

SAGE
(*Salvia officinalis*)

GREEK OREGANO
(*Origanum heracleoticum*)

TARRAGON
(*Artemisia dracunculus*)

MARJORAM
(*Origanum majorana*)

THYMES
(*Thymus* spp.)

Herb leaves and flowers look beautiful when frozen in ice. Preserve them in individual ice cubes to chill and garnish your favorite tea or punch, or freeze them into an ice bowl to make an eye-catching centerpiece.

Making Herbal Vinegars and Oils

erbal vinegars and oils are both wonderful ways to preserve a wide variety of culinary herbs. Besides adding fabulous flavor to your own recipes, these beautiful bottled vinegars and oils make great gifts for your favorite cooks!

Herbal Vinegars: If you're looking for a way to reduce your salt and fat consumption, take the salt shaker and butter dish off your dining table and add a bottle of herb-flavored vinegar instead. I've found that a dash of herbal vinegar really brightens up a dish and keeps me from reaching for that extra pat of butter.

You can use practically any edible herb to flavor vinegar, depending on what you want to use it for. I'm fond of tarragon vinegar for salad dressings, garlic vinegar for Asian dishes, and garlic-cilantro vinegar for sprinkling on steamed broccoli. Other herbs that taste especially good in vinegar include basil, chive blossoms, dill, rosemary, and thyme. I heartily encourage you to experiment with different combinations of herbs to find the flavors you like best.

The vinegar you use will also influence the flavor of the finished product, so it's worth trying different kinds to find your favorites. Apple cider and white wine vinegar are probably the best because they take on more of the flavor of whatever herbs you add. (White wine vinegar also takes on a pretty pink color if you add purple basil.)

Balsamic vinegar and sherry vinegar can be infused with herbs, but they are already so flavorful that the flavor of the herbs often gets lost. White vinegar is another possibility, but I find that it doesn't have the inherent good flavor that's needed to bring out the best in the herbs I use.

To make herb vinegar, stuff a large, wide-mouthed jar as full of herbs as possible. Most people put a sprig or two

Herbal vinegars keep their flavors best if you store them in a cool, dark place. Make a few extra bottles if you want to use them to decorate your kitchen.

in and expect it to be flavorful. But vinegar needs a lot of herbs to really taste good! Don't heat the vinegar at all; simply pour it in to cover the herbs and place a lid on the bottle. (If you are using a metal lid, cover the top of the jar with a piece of plastic wrap before you put the lid on to prevent a reaction between the metal and the acid in the vinegar.)

Store the prepared vinegar in a cool, dark place. Let it rest for two to three weeks, and then strain off and reserve the liquid. If you are keeping the vinegar for yourself, repack the same jar with fresh herbs, and pour the reserved vinegar back in. If you are giving the vinegar as a gift, add a few sprigs of fresh herbs to a decorative bottle, pour in the already-flavored vinegar, and seal the bottle.

After the initial two- to three-week period, your herbal vinegar is ready to use. Herbal vinegars will stay fresh for at least three months, but for best flavor, make small batches and use them as quickly as possible.

Herb-Flavored Oils: Herbal oils are popular with gourmet chefs, but you don't have to pay gourmet prices for these flavorful mixtures when you grow your own herbs. Basil, dill, French tarragon, garlic, Greek oregano, rosemary, sage, and thyme are some of the best choices for flavoring herbal oils.

To make an herb-infused oil, loosely fill a wide-mouthed jar or bottle with your favorite herb or combination of herbs. Then fill the bottle with olive oil or your favorite vegetable oil. Some people think that warming the oil brings out the flavor better, but I haven't

Olive oil is my favorite base for herb-flavored oil, but you can use vegetable or safflower oil if you prefer.

noticed any difference, so I usually just use it at room temperature.

The flavor of the herbs will begin to infuse the oil almost immediately, but for best flavor and fragrance, let the mixture sit for a week before you use it or repackage it in a decorative bottle for gift-giving. Keep the oil in your refrigerator or another cool, dark place for maximum freshness. Herbal oils should stay fresh for up to six months, but for best results, try to use them up within a few weeks.

One word of caution: When preparing any garlic-flavored oil, it's smart to soak the garlic in vinegar overnight first to prevent bacterial contamination. Strain out the garlic, place it in a clean container, add the oil, then refrigerate immediately.

Chapter
4

Cooking with Herbs

Cooking
with Herbs

Herbs add a fresh sparkling flavor to foods that other seasonings just can't match. I really love to cook, and herbs are at the heart of my recipes at home and in this book.

This chapter will introduce you to the wonderful world of cooking with herbs. I encourage you to try these 50 easy-to-follow recipes for using herbs in soups, salads, vegetables, meat and poultry, fish, pasta, breads, and desserts.

I entertain outside in warm weather. I can walk over to the herb garden, snip a few leaves, add them to the recipe, and make my dishes the best they can be.

Growing your own herbs gives you the very best freshness and flavor. Plus, if you dry or preserve your own homegrown herbs, you can keep that flavor all year long. As an added bonus, it's healthier to use herbs to add flavor to our foods as a substitute for excess fats and salt.

My suggestions for which herbs to use are based on what I like. Use them as a starting point, but feel free to try others to find out your own favorites. Experiment! Enjoy!

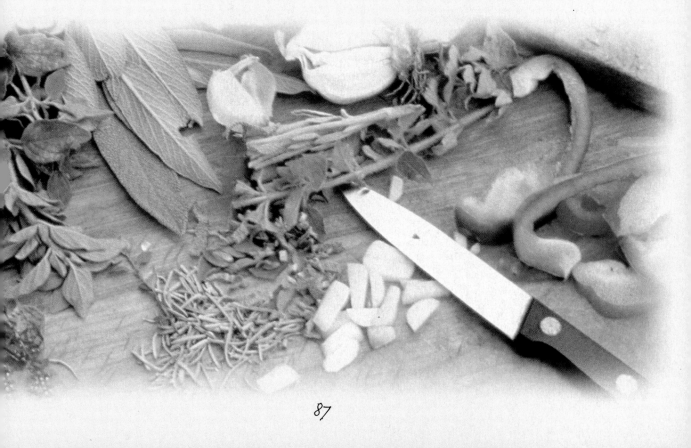

Fennel, Tomato, and White Bean Soup

This bean-and-vegetable soup makes a wonderfully satisfying meal. A simple version of the more familiar minestrone, it highlights the unique licorice-like flavor of Florence fennel. Oregano and sage enhance the flavor of the beans and tomatoes.

1 bulb Florence fennel

1 teaspoon olive oil

1 medium onion, chopped fine

2 cloves garlic, minced

4 cups chicken broth

1 teaspoon each fresh oregano and sage, minced

2 cups fresh tomatoes or drained, seeded, canned tomatoes, chopped

2 cups cooked cannelli or other white beans

Salt and pepper, to taste

1 Trim the stalks and feathery leaves from the Florence fennel bulb. Chop the bulb into small cubes about the same size as the beans. Add the cubes to a soup pot, along with the olive oil, onion, garlic, and chicken broth. Cook over medium heat for 15 minutes, or until the fennel is tender.

2 Add the oregano, sage, and tomatoes, and cook over medium heat for 10 minutes. Add the beans, and cook over medium heat for 5 minutes. Salt and pepper to taste.

Serves 4 to 6

88

Spring Herb and Vegetable Soup

This is a very light and brothy soup. It features annual and perennial herbs, along with first-of-the-season vegetables from the late spring and early summer garden. Wait until the last minute to add the minced herbs so they keep their fresh, bright green color.

4 cups chicken or beef broth

1 cup fresh carrots, diced

2 leek stalks, white parts only, carefully cleaned and sliced thin

1 cup fresh garden peas, shucked

½ cup fresh herbs (including chervil, chives, lovage, parsley, sorrel, and tarragon, in any combination you like), minced

Salt and pepper, to taste

1 Bring the stock to a boil in a medium-size soup pot. Add the carrots, leeks, and peas. Reduce the heat to medium, and cook until the vegetables are tender, about 10 minutes.

2 Add the minced fresh herbs, and salt and pepper to taste. Simmer for 1 minute. Serve immediately.

Serves 4

Leek and Potato Soup

Herbs used:

Chervil, chives,
and parsley

This flavorful creamy soup can be served hot or cool. If you want to dress it up, add a small spoonful of low-fat sour cream to each serving, and sprinkle with fresh herbs.

4 leek stalks, white parts only, washed and thinly sliced

1 tablespoon unsalted margarine or vegetable oil

4 medium white potatoes, peeled and quartered

1 quart chicken stock

1 pint half-and-half

1 tablespoon each fresh chervil, chives, and parsley, minced and mixed

Salt and pepper, to taste

1 In a 4-quart soup pot, sauté the leeks in unsalted margarine or oil over medium heat for 3 minutes. Add the potatoes and chicken stock. Bring to a boil, reduce the heat to medium, cover, and simmer for 20 minutes. Turn off the heat, and let cool for 5 minutes.

2 Pour the leeks, potatoes, and chicken stock into a food processor or blender. Puree, then return to the soup pot. Add the half-and-half and about three-quarters of the minced herbs.

Simmer over low heat for 10 minutes. Do not boil or the milk will curdle. Salt and pepper to taste. Serve the soup in bowls, and sprinkle the remaining herbs on top.

Serves 4

89

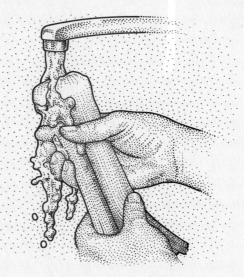

Wash leeks under
running water to remove
clinging soil.

Cape Cod Chowder with Herbs

Herbs used:

Lovage, sage, savory, and/or thyme

It seems there are as many ways to make chowder on Cape Cod as there are people who eat it. Many chowder lovers enjoy the zesty flavor that herbs add to this traditional favorite.

3 strips of lean country bacon

2 medium potatoes, peeled and chopped fine

1 medium onion, chopped fine

¼ cup lovage leaves and stalks, chopped fine

2 cups clam broth, fish stock, water, or a combination

2 tablespoons fresh sage, savory, thyme, or a combination, minced

2 cups milk

1 pint fresh clams, minced

¼ teaspoon salt

⅛ teaspoon freshly ground black pepper

Pilot crackers

Chop the bacon, and place it in a soup pot over medium heat. Cook the bacon until it is almost crisp, and drain off the fat. Add the chopped potatoes, onions, and lovage to the pot, cover with the liquid, and simmer until the potatoes are tender, about 15 minutes.

Cool the mixture slightly, and mash the potatoes lightly, just enough to break them up a bit. Add the fresh herbs to the potato mixture, and stir to blend well. Add the milk and heat through, but do not boil.

Add the clams, salt, and pepper, and cook for 2 or 3 minutes at medium heat until the clams are just cooked. Don't overcook the clams, or they will be tough. Serve with pilot crackers.

Serves 4 to 6

Regional Chowder Variations

The chowder you find served all over Cape Cod is the same creamy white chowder you will also find served in Boston, Portsmouth, Portland, New Bedford, and most of eastern New England. You will also find creamy chowder along the northwest coast of Oregon where a lot of New England fishermen settled.

But in coastal Connecticut, the fishing families often drop the milk or cream from their soup and enjoy their chowder with a seafood broth. Once you get into New York State and closer to Manhattan, the chowder really begins to change. The cream is completely gone, and the chowder turns red with tomatoes and green with celery, parsley, and more and more herbs like basil, oregano, and tarragon.

Despite regional claims to the contrary, all of these chowders are good as long as the clams are not overcooked and the herbs are of the best quality.

Cold Shrimp Bisque with Cucumber

This cool, refreshing soup includes the herb salad burnet, which tastes a lot like cucumber. If you don't have salad burnet on hand, you might try borage, which also tastes like cucumber, or even dill, which is a very good flavoring for shrimp and cucumber.

1 cup salad burnet leaves (whole), washed and dried

1 pound medium shrimp, shells on

2 cups water

2 large cucumbers

2 cups plain yogurt

Salt and freshly ground white pepper, to taste

1 Divide the salad burnet leaves into two bunches. Mince half of them, and place the rest in a plastic bag to save for the garnish.

2 Place the shrimp in a soup pot, and add the water. Bring the contents to a boil, reduce heat to low, and simmer for 2 minutes. Turn off the heat, and allow the shrimp to cool slightly in the liquid.

3 Remove the shrimp, and peel them. Return the peels and tails to the liquid, and simmer over medium heat for 10 minutes. Drain the liquid through a strainer. Reserve the liquid, and discard the peels and tails.

4 Peel the cucumbers. Cut them in half lengthwise. Using a spoon, scrape out the seeds and discard them. Place the cucumber, the minced burnet leaves, and half of the shrimp in a food processor, and pulse until smooth. Add a little shrimp liquid if necessary to get a smooth consistency.

5 Place the ground mixture of shrimp, burnet, and cucumbers in a large bowl, along with three-quarters of the yogurt and enough shrimp liquid to form a creamy soup. Salt and pepper to taste, cover, and refrigerate for 1 hour.

6 Remove the soup from the refrigerator, stir, and add more salt and pepper if necessary. Ladle the soup into bowls, top with a spoonful of yogurt, and arrange the remaining burnet leaves on top of the soup to form an attractive garnish.

Serves 4

Chinese Chicken Noodle Soup

Herbs used:
Arugula, garlic
chives, coriander
leaves (cilantro),
and garlic

This traditional favorite is a great way to use leftover chicken. The peppery-tasting arugula, distinctive coriander leaves (cilantro), and garlic chives really perk up the flavor and add color.

1 cup fresh arugula, chopped

½ cup fresh garlic chives, minced

½ cup coriander leaves (cilantro)

1 quart homemade or canned chicken stock

3 cloves garlic, minced

1 tablespoon fresh ginger, minced

½ pound Chinese wheat noodles or vermicelli

2 cups cooked chicken, chopped

1 teaspoon toasted sesame oil

1 teaspoon soy sauce

92

1 Wash and dry the arugula, chives, and coriander. Coarsely chop the arugula, mince the chives and coriander, and set all the herbs aside.

2 Place the chicken stock, garlic, and ginger in a medium-size soup pot, and bring to a boil. Reduce heat to medium low, and simmer for 5 minutes.

3 Cook the noodles to the al dente stage, according to package instructions. Drain. Add the noodles to the chicken stock along with the cooked chicken, sesame oil, and soy sauce. Simmer over medium heat for 2 or 3 minutes to heat thoroughly.

4 Add the arugula, chives, and coriander, and cook for 1 minute over medium high heat. Serve immediately.

Serves 4

Add herbs to soup just
before serving to avoid
overcooking them.

Summer Soup Provençal

Herbs used:

Garlic, parsley, basil, rosemary, and thyme

In the countries around the Mediterranean Sea, cooks prepare delightful summer soups with the fresh vegetables and herbs available in the marketplace. Basil, rosemary, and thyme grow wild around the "wine dark sea" and are classic flavors in this soup.

1 teaspoon olive oil

1 medium onion, chopped fine

1 clove garlic, minced

½ cup each fresh carrots, green beans, and zucchini, diced

2 large fresh tomatoes, chopped

1 quart chicken, beef, or veal stock

1 cup orzo, elbow, or ditalini pasta

¼ cup fresh flat-leaf (Italian) parsley, minced

2 tablespoons fresh basil (any kind), minced

1 tablespoon each fresh rosemary and thyme leaves, minced

Salt and pepper, to taste

Place the olive oil, onion, garlic, carrots, green beans, and zucchini in a soup pot over medium heat, and cook for 5 minutes, stirring often.

Add the tomatoes, stock, and pasta. Bring the soup to a boil, reduce heat to medium, and cook for about 10 minutes until the pasta is tender. (If you prefer, you can cook the pasta separately and add it after the tomatoes and stock have cooked for 5 minutes.)

Add the herbs, and cook for 3 minutes. Salt and pepper to taste. For an extra added taste treat, sprinkle freshly grated Parmesan or Romano cheese, or drizzle a little herb-infused olive oil over individual servings.

Serves 4 to 6

93

The Best Garlic Bread

Garlic bread is the best bread to serve with *Summer Soup Provençal.* But with the spread of well-made, crusty European-style breads, garlic bread has taken on a new look in recent years. All of the fashionable restaurants are now serving garlic bread with a new earthy appeal. Instead of spreading butter over your soft Italian loaf and sprinkling it with garlic powder, do what the Europeans do: Rub a fresh garlic clove over a 1-inch-thick slice of crusty bread, drizzle that with fruity green olive oil, and broil it in the oven or toast it over your barbecue grill. Top the bread with fresh sliced tomato and fresh herbs to really liven up your new style of garlic bread.

Mesclun Salad with Herb Vinaigrette

Mesclun is a blend of garden-fresh salad greens, usually including red and green lettuce, curly endive, chicory, arugula, and other tender greens and herbs. Many seed companies sell mesclun mixes, but you can also blend your own from your favorite flavors.

2 tablespoons balsamic, raspberry, or sherry vinegar

1 tablespoon Dijon or spicy brown mustard

1 tablespoon fresh chervil, dill, or thyme, minced

¼ teaspoon salt

⅛ teaspoon freshly ground black pepper

½ cup extra-virgin olive oil

4 to 6 cups fresh cut mesclun greens, rinsed and dried

2 cups mixed herb leaves, whole

1 In a medium-size mixing bowl, combine the vinegar, mustard, minced herbs, salt, and pepper. Stir to blend well. Slowly add the oil, whisking continuously to form a creamy dressing.

2 Place the greens and herb leaves in a large bowl or platter. Pour the dressing over the mixed greens, toss to coat all the leaves, and serve on salad plates.

Serves 4 to 6

94

Chicken Salad with Herbed Mayonnaise

Perfectly cooked, moist chicken is the secret to great chicken salad. Go one step further and add fresh minced herbs and mayonnaise to transform this simple dish into something truly elegant.

4 cups roasted or poached chicken, cut into bite-size pieces

1 cup celery, minced

2 tablespoons shallots, finely minced

2 tablespoons fresh dill or tarragon, minced

1 cup mayonnaise

1 tablespoon lemon juice

Four large lettuce leaves

Curly parsley or chervil, for garnish

1 Allow cooked chicken to cool. Combine the chicken, celery, shallots, herbs, mayonnaise, and lemon juice in a large mixing bowl. Stir to blend well.

2 Place lettuce leaves on individual plates, and top them with the chicken salad. Garnish with parsley or chervil.

Serves 4

French Potato Salad with Chervil

Herb used:
Chervil

Want to liven up a plain potato salad? Add minced fresh chervil for its bright green color and terrific taste. A few sprigs of feathery chervil make a great-looking garnish.

12 medium red potatoes

½ cup celery, thinly sliced

½ cup shallots, red onions, or scallions, finely chopped

¾ cup low-fat plain yogurt or sour cream

½ cup low-fat or regular mayonnaise

2 tablespoons Dijon or spicy brown mustard

¼ cup fresh chervil leaves, minced

¼ teaspoon salt

⅛ teaspoon freshly ground black pepper

4 or 5 sprigs of chervil, for garnish

1 Place the potatoes in a large pot of water to cover, and boil until tender, about 20 minutes. Drain and cool.

2 Peel the potatoes, if you like, and cut them into ½-inch-thick wedges. Place them in a medium-size mixing bowl. Add the celery and the shallots, red onions, or scallions. Stir gently to blend well.

3 In another medium-size mixing bowl, combine the yogurt or sour cream, mayonnaise, mustard, chervil, salt, and pepper to make the dressing. Stir to blend well.

4 Add the dressing to the potato mixture, and stir to blend well. Place the salad in an attractive bowl, and garnish with the feathery chervil sprigs.

Serves 4 to 6

95

Best Spuds for Potato Salad

Red potatoes are the ideal spuds to make into potato salad because of their waxy texture. Look for tiny marble-size red potatoes. You don't have to peel them, and you'll enjoy the color the red skins add to your potato salad.

Yellow 'Yukon' potatoes are a good alternative. They have a slightly waxy texture if not overcooked, and they add a delicious buttery flavor to the salad. And, of course, their yellow color gives the potato salad a rich, warm, inviting look.

Purple potatoes also add a different look to your potato salad. And for something completely different, try making a potato salad with red, yellow, and purple potatoes!

Savory Savoy Cole Slaw

Herb used:

Lemon or
common thyme

Savoy cabbage has dark green crinkled leaves, which make this slaw a colorful alternative to what you are used to serving. Basil, chervil, dill, lovage, parsley, and tarragon are just some of the herbs you could use in place of or in combination with the thyme.

1 small to medium Savoy or
  regular green cabbage

1 medium red onion, quartered
  and thinly sliced

2 large bell peppers (1 red
  and 1 green), cored, seeded,
  quartered, and thinly sliced

2/3 cup olive or vegetable oil

1/3 cup white or red wine vinegar

1 teaspoon dry English mustard

1 teaspoon sugar

1/4 teaspoon salt

1/8 teaspoon freshly ground
  black pepper

1 tablespoon fresh lemon or
  common thyme leaves,
  removed from the stems

Quarter and core the cabbage, and finely shred the leaves. Place the cabbage in a large mixing bowl. Add the sliced onions and peppers. Stir to blend well.

In another bowl, combine the olive oil, vinegar, dry mustard, sugar, salt, pepper, and half of the thyme leaves. Stir to make a creamy dressing.

Pour the dressing over the slaw, and stir to blend well. Sprinkle with the remaining thyme leaves.

Serves 6 to 8

Super Tips for Cole Slaw

For a super-flavorful cole slaw, take advantage of the seed mixes many seed companies are offering of Chinese greens, Italian greens, or salad greens. It's easy to grow these mixes and add color, crunch, and flavor to your cole slaw.

If you don't want to wait until your greens are grown, you can find many of these greens in grocery stores and farmers' markets. They will typically have greens such as arugula, bok choy, chicory, kale, mizuna, turnip greens, and other wonderful fixings. I've taken to experimenting more with cole slaw by adding different greens to savoy or white cabbage, and then changing the ingredients I add for the dressing. I've made Mexican cole slaw by adding cilantro, lime, and fresh jalapeño to the salad. I've made Asian slaw by adding lime juice, soy sauce, ground peanuts, and dried shrimp. Break out of your cole slaw rut, and try these new flavors—or mix up your own!

Warm Herbed Cheese on Salad Greens

Coating cheese with herbs helps bring out the flavor of both. A moment under the broiler makes this an extra-special treat. I've suggested chives, mint, parsley, and tarragon for the herb coating, but you could also include or substitute your favorite culinary herbs.

½ pound fresh goat cheese

4 tablespoons mixed fresh herbs, including chives, mint, parsley, and tarragon, minced

2 cloves garlic, minced

½ cup unflavored bread crumbs

2 cups fresh arugula leaves

1 small head red leaf lettuce

3 tablespoons extra-virgin olive oil

1 tablespoon balsamic, raspberry, or red wine vinegar

¼ teaspoon salt

⅛ teaspoon freshly ground black pepper

1. Shape cheese into a "log"; cut into equal slices. Combine the herbs, garlic, and bread crumbs; stir to blend well. Coat slices with the mixture. Place on waxed paper; refrigerate.

2. Rinse the arugula and lettuce. Drain and dry well. Whisk the olive oil, vinegar, salt, and pepper to form a smooth dressing; toss with greens and arrange on four salad plates.

3. Place the cheese slices on a broiler pan; broil for 30 seconds, or until golden brown. Carefully flip them over, and broil the other side for 15 seconds, or until golden brown. Place the warm cheese on top of the greens.

Serves 4

97

Tabouli Salad with Mint and Olives

Mint is a common ingredient in Middle Eastern cooking. This delicious mint-seasoned grain dish makes a perfect summer salad for dinners and picnics.

1 cup bulgur wheat

2 cups boiling water

2 ripe tomatoes

½ cup fresh scallions, minced

½ cup fresh parsley, minced

1 tablespoon fresh or 1 teaspoon dried mint, minced

⅓ cup olive oil

Juice of 1 lemon

Mint sprigs, for garnish

1. Place the bulgur in a medium-size salad bowl. Add the boiling water. Stir and let rest for 30 minutes.

2. Core the tomatoes and chop fine. Combine with the scallions, herbs, oil, and lemon juice, and stir to blend well. Cover and refrigerate for at least 30 minutes. Remove from the refrigerator 15 minutes prior to serving, and garnish with sprigs of mint.

Serves 4 to 6

Colorful Cucumber Salad

This stunning salad creation combines freshly sliced cucumbers with sweet, tender lettuce, peppery nasturtium leaves, colorful nasturtium flowers, and cucumber-flavored borage and salad burnet.

2 large cucumbers

1 teaspoon coarse salt

2 cups each whole nasturtium flowers, nasturtium leaves, and lettuce leaves

1/4 cup fresh borage leaves, minced

1 cup low-fat or fat-free sour cream

1/4 cup white wine vinegar or lemon juice

1/4 teaspoon salt

1/8 teaspoon freshly ground black pepper

2 tablespoons fresh salad burnet leaflets

1 Peel the cucumbers, and slice in half lengthwise. Scoop out the seeds and discard them. Thinly slice the cucumbers across the grain, place in a bowl, and sprinkle with 1 teaspoon of coarse salt. Let sit for 30 minutes. Drain off the liquid, rinse the cucumber slices, and let them dry.

2 Inspect the whole nasturtium flowers to be sure they are clean and pretty; discard any that have insects or damaged spots. Wash the nasturtium and lettuce leaves. Dry thoroughly, and tear into bite-size pieces. Combine with the borage leaves, and toss to blend well.

3 On individual salad plates, spread a layer of the lettuce and nasturtium leaves. Place a mound of cucumber in the center.

4 Put the sour cream, vinegar, salt, and pepper in a bowl. Stir to form a creamy dressing. Drizzle over the cucumbers and greens. Arrange a couple of nasturtium flowers around the plate, and sprinkle salad burnet leaves over the salad.

Serves 4 to 6

Salads

Yellow Tomato Salad with Purple Pesto

Herbs used:

Purple basil and
garlic

Minced green basil and ripe red tomatoes have long been a favorite summer salad combination. Yellow tomatoes topped with dark purple basil pesto will give you the same great flavor but with a refreshing twist.

1 cup fresh purple basil leaves

2 cloves garlic, chopped

¼ cup walnuts or pine nuts

4 tablespoons grated
   Parmesan cheese

½ cup olive oil

1 teaspoon water (if needed)

Salt, to taste

4 large red leaf lettuce leaves

4 large ripe yellow tomatoes

4 to 8 whole purple basil leaves,
   for garnish

1 Wash and dry the purple basil leaves. Coarsely chop and place the basil in a blender or food processor.

2 Add the garlic, walnuts or pine nuts, and cheese. Pulse to combine ingredients. Slowly add the olive oil to form a creamy paste that resembles slightly runny mayonnaise. Add a teaspoon of water to thin, if necessary. Taste, and add salt if desired.

3 Wash and dry the lettuce leaves. Arrange one leaf on each of four salad plates. Core and slice the yellow tomatoes into slabs, wedges, or your favorite shape. Arrange the tomatoes on top of the lettuce leaves. Spoon a little pesto over the tomatoes, and garnish with basil leaves before serving.

Serves 4

Spoon prepared pesto over
quartered tomatoes to serve.

Tomatoes Stuffed with Herbed Cheese

Broil and serve these simple-to-make stuffed tomatoes with croutons and salad, add them to a hero sandwich, or serve them as appetizers in place of deviled eggs.

8 large, ripe Italian plum tomatoes

4 ounces low-fat Neufchâtel cream cheese

2 ounces chèvre or feta cheese

1 clove garlic, minced

1 tablespoon each fresh basil, mint, parsley, and thyme, minced

¼ teaspoon salt

⅛ teaspoon freshly ground black pepper

1 Cut the tomatoes in half lengthwise, and scoop out the seeds. Drain and reserve.

2 Add the cheeses, garlic, herbs, salt, and pepper to a mixing bowl, and stir to blend well. You could also do this in a food processor. Add a little milk, olive oil, or lemon juice if the mixture seems too dry. (It should be loose but moist enough to hold together when pressed.)

3 Spoon some of the cheese mixture into each tomato half. Serve as is, or broil to lightly brown the cheese.

Serves 4

100

Carrots with Dill and Honey

Herb used:
Dill

Carrots, especially those from your garden or local farmer's market, are naturally sweet. But a touch of honey and a sprinkling of dill makes them taste even better.

1 pound tender fresh carrots

2 teaspoons unsalted butter or margarine

1 tablespoon honey

1 tablespoon fresh dill, minced

Salt and pepper, to taste

Fresh dill, for garnish

1 Wash and peel the carrots, and cut them into bite-size chunks. Cook them in a pot of boiling water until they are tender but still crisp, about 5 to 10 minutes.

2 Drain the carrots. Toss with the butter or margarine, honey, and dill. Salt and pepper to taste. Garnish with fresh dill before serving.

Serves 4 to 6

Yogurt Beets with Dill

Beets, especially fresh ones, are one of our most underappreciated vegetables. Try combining them with tangy low-fat yogurt and fresh dill for a delicious side dish or salad.

4 medium to large fresh beets, with tops

1 cup low-fat yogurt

1 tablespoon fresh dill, minced

1/4 teaspoon salt

1/8 teaspoon freshly ground black pepper

Fresh dill sprigs, for garnish

1 Trim off all but 1 inch of the beet tops and most of the thin roots, and wash carefully. Cook the whole beets in boiling water for 15 to 20 minutes until they are fork-tender. Drain. When cool enough to handle, cut off the tops, peel the beets, and cut them into bite-size pieces.

2 In a separate bowl, mix the yogurt, dill, salt, and pepper. Add the beets, toss lightly, and place on individual plates. Garnish with dill sprigs.

Serves 4

101

Filet Beans with Summer Savory

Tender filet beans, also known as French beans, are expensive in gourmet stores but are easy to grow at home. Summer savory, often referred to as the "green bean herb" in Germany, makes an excellent companion for this flavorful summer vegetable.

1 pound fresh tender green beans

2 teaspoons unsalted butter or margarine

1 tablespoon fresh summer savory, minced

Salt and pepper, to taste

Summer savory sprigs, for garnish

1 Wash and trim the green beans. Cut them up or leave them whole. Cook them in a pot of boiling water for 3 to 4 minutes until they are tender but still crisp.

2 Drain the beans; toss with the butter or margarine and summer savory. Salt and pepper to taste. Garnish with summer savory sprigs before serving.

Serves 4 to 6

Roasted Turnips and Parsnips with Herbs

Turnips and parsnips roasted in the oven is one of the glories of the late fall table. Add a little fresh rosemary (or thyme, if you prefer) and some fruity olive oil for one of the best side vegetable dishes you will ever taste.

1 pound each small white turnips and short yellow parsnips

2 tablespoons olive oil

2 tablespoons fresh rosemary or thyme, or a combination

¼ teaspoon salt

⅛ teaspoon freshly ground black pepper

1 Preheat the oven to 350°F. Wash and peel the turnips and parsnips, and cut them into large chunks.

2 Place the vegetables in a large casserole dish. Drizzle with olive oil, and sprinkle with rosemary or thyme, salt, and pepper. Cover with foil, and bake in the oven for 45 to 60 minutes until fork-tender but not mushy.

Serves 4

Vegetables

Sugar Snap Peas with Mint

Fresh tangy mint is a naturally sweet addition to any kind of garden-fresh peas. This recipe calls for the crispy podded sugar snap peas, but you could substitute an equal amount of snow peas or shelled petite or English peas.

1 pound fresh sugar snap peas

2 teaspoons unsalted butter or margarine

1 tablespoon fresh mint leaves, minced

Salt and pepper, to taste

Fresh mint sprigs, for garnish

1 Cook the peas in a pot of boiling water for 2 to 3 minutes until tender but still crisp.

2 Drain the peas, and toss with the butter and mint. Salt and pepper to taste. Garnish with fresh mint before serving.

Serves 4 to 6

Cardoon with White Beans and Parsley

Herbs used:

Cardoon and parsley

Cardoon cooks like celery and tastes like artichoke. Mixed with white beans, flat-leaved parsley, lemon juice, and olive oil, it makes a unique first course or side dish.

2 pounds fresh, young cardoon stalks

One 16-ounce can cooked white cannelli or ceci beans

3 tablespoons fresh flat-leaf (Italian) parsley, finely chopped

2 tablespoons extra-virgin olive oil

2 tablespoons lemon juice, freshly squeezed

Salt and pepper, to taste

1 Trim the jagged edges off the cardoon stalks. Remove the strings just as you would for celery, by snapping off a small piece at the top and pulling the strings off with a downward motion. Cut the cardoon into bite-size pieces, and simmer in a pot of boiling water for 10 to 15 minutes until fork-tender. Drain, and place in a large mixing bowl.

2 Drain the beans, and add to the cardoon. Add the parsley. Pour the olive oil and lemon juice over the vegetables, and toss. Salt and pepper to taste before serving.

Serves 4

103

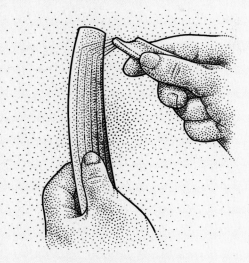

Remove strings from cardoon stems before cutting them into bite-size pieces.

Grilled Lamb with Mediterranean Herbs

Herbs used:

Garlic, oregano, rosemary, and thyme

Lamb is a flavorful meat that tastes even better with the addition of herbs. The meat is simply marinated with herbs and then grilled. If you don't care for lamb, substitute London broil or your favorite beef steak.

1 leg of lamb, about 3 to 5 pounds, boned and butterflied by the butcher

¼ cup extra virgin olive oil

3 cloves garlic, minced

3 tablespoons each fresh or 1 tablespoon each dried oregano, rosemary, and thyme

¼ teaspoon salt

⅛ teaspoon freshly ground black pepper

104

1 Place the leg of lamb in a large roasting pan. Rub it well with the olive oil and garlic. Mix the herbs, salt, and pepper together in a small bowl, and sprinkle them all over the lamb. Cover, and let sit in the refrigerator overnight or at room temperature for 1 hour.

2 Build a fire in a hooded charcoal grill. If you are using a gas grill, turn it on very low. When the coals are ashen gray or the gas grill is evenly heated, place the lamb on the grill about 5 inches from the heat. Cover, and roast for 15 minutes. Turn, and roast for an additional 15 minutes, basting with any additional marinade.

3 A butterflied leg of lamb will have uneven thick and thin parts. When the thickest part is still very rare, pull the meat from the grill. Put the meat on a warm platter, cover it with foil, and let it rest for 15 minutes. The meat will continue to cook during this time, turning very rare into perfectly rare. Now you have rare, medium, and well-done pieces to please your guests' tastes. Pour any juices that collected on the platter over the meat.

Serves 6 to 8

Meat & Poultry

Beef Stew with Lovage

Lovage is a crunchy herb with a taste very similar to celery. This stew is made in a conventional way, but the lovage and the extra herbs give it a unique flavor.

1/3 cup all-purpose flour

1 teaspoon salt

1/4 teaspoon freshly ground black pepper

2 pounds stewing beef or veal, cut into chunks

2 tablespoons vegetable oil

4 cups warm water

1 large onion, chopped

2 bay leaves

3 sage leaves

1 tablespoon fresh or 1 teaspoon dried thyme leaves

2 cups lovage stalks, chopped

2 cups each carrots and potatoes, peeled and chopped

Salt and pepper, to taste

1 Combine the flour with 1 teaspoon salt and 1/4 teaspoon black pepper. Dredge the beef or veal chunks in the flour mixture. In a large stewing pot, brown the meat in the oil in four equal batches.

2 Return all the meat to the pot, and add the water, onion, bay leaves, sage leaves, and thyme. Cover and simmer over medium low heat for 1 1/2 to 2 hours, until the meat is tender.

3 Add the lovage, carrots, potatoes, and additional salt and pepper, if desired. Cover and simmer another 20 to 25 minutes, or until the vegetables are tender. Remove the bay leaves before serving.

Serves 6 to 8

105

Cast Iron for Savory Stews

Call me old-fashioned if you will, but I think beef stew has a better flavor when it's cooked in a large cast-iron pot or Dutch oven. That's because cast iron is thicker than the usual pots. That means you can cook the meat chunks at a slightly higher temperature without burning them. This method helps brown the meat better and leaves a lot of good "browned bits" behind that add flavor to the stew.

I also think cast iron helps distribute the heat better throughout all the food in the pot, so all the food is cooking at the same temperature and will be at the correct stage of tenderness at the same time. Finally, a cast-iron pot can be placed in the oven so the stew can bake slowly over a long period of time. This helps bring out the best flavors of all the ingredients, especially the herbs.

Chicken Breasts with Lemon and Herbs

Quick and easy, chicken breast cutlets are a favorite dinner staple. Adding fresh minced herbs brightens the taste of this classic dish.

4 boneless and skinless chicken breast halves (or 8 medium chicken cutlets)

1 cup all-purpose flour

¼ cup vegetable oil

2 tablespoons unsalted butter

2 tablespoons fresh parsley, minced

2 tablespoons tiny nonpareil capers

2 tablespoons fresh basil, minced

Juice of 1 lemon

½ cup chicken stock

¼ teaspoon salt

⅛ teaspoon freshly ground black pepper

106

1 Place a single chicken breast half flat on the cutting board. Place one hand flat on top of the breast. Using a sharp knife with the blade held parallel with the cutting board, slice the breast in half, making two thin cutlets.

2 Place the flour in a large flat bowl. Dredge the cutlets in the flour. Heat the vegetable oil in large, heavy skillet. Fry the cutlets over medium-high heat, 2 minutes on each side. Remove from the pan, cover, and keep warm.

3 Pour the frying oil out of the pan, and add the butter to the same pan. Add the parsley, capers, and basil, and cook over medium heat for 1 minute, stirring often.

4 Add the lemon juice, chicken stock, salt, and pepper. Bring the sauce to a boil, and cook over high heat for 2 minutes, scraping up any browned bits and making a smooth, creamy sauce. Pour over the chicken cutlets.

Serves 4

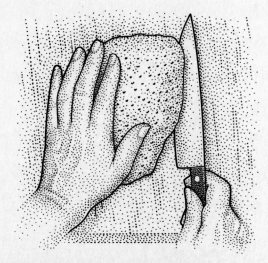

Make your own chicken cutlets by slicing breast pieces horizontally.

Herb-Roasted Cornish Hens

Herbs used:
Tarragon
and garlic

Cornish game hens are a festive and delicious way to serve poultry. For this dish, you rub the hens with a tarragon-butter mixture that infuses the meat with flavor as it roasts.

4 Cornish game hens

3 tablespoons fresh
  or 1 tablespoon dried tarragon

2 cloves garlic, minced

2 tablespoons unsalted butter
  or margarine

½ teaspoon salt

¼ teaspoon freshly ground
  black pepper

½ cup white wine

4 to 6 sprigs of fresh tarragon,
  for garnish

1. Preheat the oven to 350°F. Wash and dry the hens, and place them in a large, low-sided roasting pan. Mash the tarragon with the garlic, butter or margarine, salt, and pepper. Rub the hens inside and out with the tarragon mixture.

2. Place the hens breast side down on the roasting pan, and place them in the oven. Cook for 30 minutes and turn. Baste with any pan drippings. Cook for another 30 minutes, or until the juices run clear.

3. Remove the hens from the pan, cover, and keep warm. Place the pan over medium heat, and add the white wine to the drippings. Stir to form a simple, light sauce.

4. Place whole or halved hens on serving plates. Pour the light sauce over the hens, and garnish each with a sprig of tarragon.

Serves 4 to 6

107

More Herbs for Cornish Hens

Tarragon is the classic French herb to use with roasted game hens, but it is only one option. Southern cooks might use thyme with their hens and then thicken the sauce with a little cream. I am particularly fond of roasting chicken and pork with fresh rosemary, then adding lemon juice and a couple of capers to the sauce for a Mediterranean flavor.

Let your imagination give you ideas, but be sure not to cook these tiny birds too much. They will easily become dry and tough with too much cooking. And don't worry about not cooking them long enough for your taste: If you find you've undercooked them, you can always pop them back in the oven for 15 minutes to finish them off.

Paella with Saffron

Herbs used:

Garlic, saffron, and parsley

Paella is a traditional Spanish rice dish made with chicken, seafood, fish, sausage, vegetables, or whatever looks best in the market that day. I like mine with chicken. Pungent, reddish yellow saffron adds color and flavor to this all-in-one casserole dish.

1½ pounds boneless chicken thighs, cut into small bite-size pieces

1 teaspoon olive oil

1 cup red bell pepper, seeded and chopped

½ cup onion, chopped

2 cloves garlic, minced

2 ripe tomatoes, peeled and chopped

¼ teaspoon saffron threads

2 cups short grain white rice (uncooked)

4 cups chicken stock, warmed

1 cup fresh or frozen peas

¼ cup fresh parsley, minced

1 Brown the chicken in the olive oil over medium heat until golden. Remove from the pan, and set aside.

2 Drain off all but 1 teaspoon of oil from the pan. Add the peppers, onions, and garlic, and cook for 2 minutes. Add the tomatoes and saffron. Cook 1 minute. Add the rice, and stir to blend well.

3 Preheat the oven to 350°F. Arrange the chicken pieces in a large casserole pan. Spoon the vegetable-rice mixture over the chicken, and pour the chicken stock over all. Scatter the peas over the mixture. Cover, and place in the oven.

4 Bake in the oven for 15 to 20 minutes, or until the rice is cooked. Add more stock if the rice begins to dry out, or cook a little longer if the dish is still soupy. Remove from the oven, sprinkle with parsley, and serve.

Serves 4 to 6

108

Try Sardines with Paella

The first paella I ever ate was cooked over an open wood fire in Spain. It tasted wonderful. The appetizers we ate before we cooked the paella were fresh-caught sardines. Most of us know sardines only as an oily fish found in a can. But fresh sardines are much sweeter and a real delight to eat.

If you can get your hands on fresh sardines or frozen ones that have been thawed, clean them and scrape off any scales, leaving the head intact. Rub them with olive oil, minced garlic, salt, pepper, and minced parsley. Place them on a fish rack over your prepared barbecue grill, and grill for 5 to 10 minutes, turning only once.

Fennel Shish Kebab
with Pork Tenderloin and Rosemary

Herbs used:

Rosemary and
Florence fennel

Florence fennel, also known as finocchio, is a licorice-flavored, celery-like vegetable that cooks perfectly over a grill. Paired with tender, marinated pork, it is a sure crowd-pleaser.

3 pounds boneless pork tenderloin

½ cup orange juice

½ cup soy sauce

¼ cup fresh or 2 tablespoons dried rosemary leaves

¼ teaspoon salt

⅛ teaspoon freshly ground black pepper

4 medium Florence fennel bulbs, separated into "scales" and cut into bite-size pieces

1 Cut the pork into 1-inch cubes, and place them in a large bowl. Pour the orange juice and soy sauce over the meat. Add the rosemary leaves, salt, and pepper. Toss all to combine the ingredients and coat the pork. Marinate for 1 hour.

2 Prepare a charcoal or gas grill, or preheat the broiler in your oven. Arrange alternating pieces of fennel and pork on skewers. Cook for 10 to 15 minutes, turning often, until the meat is no longer pink in the center.

Serves 4 to 6

Anise Hyssop Herb Jelly

Herb used:

Anise hyssop
or mint

Anise hyssop is a naturally sweet herb. It makes a unique jelly that is great with roast lamb or beef curry. Mint makes a pleasant alternative to use in this recipe, if you don't have any anise hyssop.

1 cup fresh anise hyssop or mint leaves, washed and dried

4 cups apple juice or cider

1¾ ounce powdered fruit pectin

4½ cups granulated sugar

1 Combine anise hyssop leaves, apple juice or cider, pectin, and sugar in large pot. Bring to a boil.

2 Boil for 1 minute, stirring constantly. Remove from heat. Strain out the leaves, pour into six scalded, half-pint jars, and seal.

Makes approximately 3 pints

Poached Cod with Green Herb Sauce

The secret of this moist, flavorful fish dish is the herb-infused poaching liquid. Instead of cod, you could substitute trout, small whole salmon, monkfish, shark, or another firm-fleshed fish of your choice. The herb sauce adds a great finishing touch.

For the fish:

1 quart water

1 cup dry white wine

1 small carrot, peeled and chopped

1 small onion or shallot, chopped

1 tablespoon fresh parsley, minced

1 bay leaf

1/4 teaspoon freshly ground black pepper

4 cod steaks, 1½ to 2 pounds total

For the herb sauce:

½ cup olive oil

3 tablespoons white wine vinegar

1 tablespoon Dijon or spicy brown mustard

½ cup fresh flat-leafed (Italian) parsley, minced

1 large or 2 small shallots, chopped

1 tablespoon each fresh chives and tarragon, minced

1 clove garlic, minced

1 Combine the water, wine, carrots, onions or shallots, parsley, bay leaf, and pepper in a fish poacher or a pot large enough to hold the fish. Bring the mixture to the boil, reduce heat to medium high, and simmer for 10 minutes.

2 Gently place the fish in the poaching liquid. Cover with a tight-fitting lid, and continue cooking at medium-high heat, but do not boil. After 10 minutes, turn off the heat. Let the fish rest in the poaching liquid while you make the herb sauce.

3 Place all of the sauce ingredients in a food processor, and blend to form a smooth dressing. Place the poached fish on individual plates, and serve with the sauce.

Serves 4

Seviche with Cilantro and Lime

Herbs used:
Garlic, coriander (cilantro), and/or parsley

Seviche is sort of like Mexican sushi. But in this case, the fish is marinated by lime juice, which retains all of the wonderful flavor. Instead of tuna and scallops, you could use grouper, shrimp, calamari, salmon, or your favorite fish.

3/4 pound small bay scallops

1/4 pound fresh tuna, thinly sliced

Juice of 2 limes

1/4 cup olive oil

1 medium ripe tomato, cored and chopped fine

2 fresh serrano or jalapeño peppers, seeded and thinly sliced

1/2 cup red or green bell peppers, seeded and chopped fine

1/2 medium red onion, sliced very thin

2 cloves garlic, minced

1/4 cup fresh coriander leaves (cilantro), parsley, or a mix, minced

Salt and pepper, to taste

2 cups thinly sliced lettuce leaves

1 Place the scallops and tuna in a bowl, and cover with the lime juice. Cover and refrigerate for 2 to 3 hours. The acid in the lime juice marinates the fish and makes it seem like it's no longer raw.

2 To make the dressing, drain the lime juice from the fish, and whisk it with the olive oil. Stir in the tomatoes, peppers, onions, garlic, and coriander. Salt and pepper to taste.

3 Add the marinated fish and stir, making sure the fish and vegetables are all coated with the dressing. Make a bed of chopped lettuce on four individual salad plates. Spoon the seviche on the lettuce.

Serves 4

For That Festive Feeling...

Another way people along the magnificent coastal regions of Mexico enjoy raw seafood is in a "coktel de mariscos," or seafood cocktail.

Place fresh shucked oysters, raw scallops, and lightly poached shrimp in a large bowl. Sprinkle with fresh lime juice, and let rest for 30 minutes. Add bottled chili sauce or ketchup, toss, and serve.

Serve this with cold beer under an open-sided bamboo shack with a marimba band, and you will have recreated a nightclub on the southern coast of Oaxaca.

Sole Cutlets with Homemade Tartar Sauce

You don't need to drop fish fillets into deep fat to get them crispy; simply bread and sauté them in a nonstick skillet with a small amount of oil. With homemade tartar sauce spiked with fresh herbs, you've put a low-fat twist on fried fish.

For the tartar sauce:

1 cup homemade or top-quality bottled mayonnaise

2 tablespoons cornichons or sweet pickles, finely minced

1 tablespoon shallot, finely minced

1 tablespoon tiny nonpareil capers, rinsed and drained

½ tablespoon each fresh parsley and tarragon, minced

1 teaspoon lemon juice

1 teaspoon Dijon mustard

2 dashes Tabasco or other hot sauce

For the fish cutlets:

2 large eggs

2 tablespoons water

½ cup all-purpose flour

2 cups flavored or unflavored bread crumbs

8 fillets of sole, flounder, halibut, or other flat fish

1 to 2 tablespoons olive or vegetable oil

Fresh parsley and lemon wedges, for garnish

1 To prepare the tartar sauce, mix all the sauce ingredients in a small bowl, and stir to blend well. Cover and keep refrigerated until serving time.

2 Place the eggs and water in a bowl, and stir to blend well. Place the flour in another bowl and the bread crumbs in a third bowl.

3 Dredge the fish fillets in the flour, and shake off any excess. Dip the floured fillets in the egg mix, and let any extra drip off. Then roll the fillets in the bread crumbs.

4 Put the oil in a skillet, and fry the breaded fillets for 1 to 2 minutes per side over medium heat until they are crispy and brown. Serve with the tartar sauce, and garnish with parsley and lemon wedges.

Serves 4

Broiled Tuna with Fresh Herbs

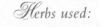
Fish marinated with a mixture of aromatic herbs and broiled over a charcoal or gas grill is packed with incredible flavor. Tuna is one of the best fish to grill because it holds its shape well. Cook it medium to rare for the best flavor.

1½ to 2 pounds fresh tuna steaks

½ cup olive or vegetable oil

1 tablespoon each soy sauce and white wine vinegar

1 tablespoon fresh or 1 teaspoon dried chives

1 tablespoon fresh or 1 teaspoon dried rosemary leaves

1 tablespoon fresh or 1 teaspoon dried thyme leaves

¼ teaspoon salt

⅛ teaspoon freshly ground black pepper

A few sprigs of rosemary

1 Place the tuna steaks in a glass baking pan or casserole dish. Pour the oil, soy sauce, and vinegar over the fish. Sprinkle the fish with the herbs, and let marinate for 1 hour.

2 Prepare the charcoal or gas grill. Place the steaks on the grill, sprinkle them with salt and pepper, and cook over glowing coals for 4 to 5 minutes per side. Use a few sprigs of rosemary as a brush to baste the fish with any remaining herb marinade.

Serves 4 to 6

113

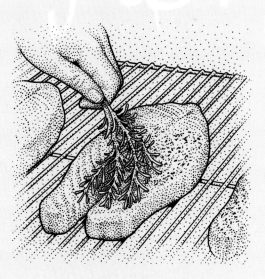

For extra flavor, use a rosemary brush to marinate steaks.

Shrimp with Herbs and Feta

Herbs used:
Garlic, Greek oregano, and anise hyssop or anise

Oregano and anise are two flavors long associated with Greek food. If you really want a Hellenic feast, serve this easy-to-make dish with a plate of cucumbers, some crusty bread, and a cold bottle of Retsina.

1 tablespoon extra-virgin olive oil

1 large leek or 1 medium onion, chopped

2 cloves garlic, minced

4 medium ripe tomatoes, peeled, seeded, and chopped

1 tablespoon fresh or 1 teaspoon dried Greek oregano

¼ teaspoon salt

⅛ teaspoon freshly ground black pepper

1½ pounds medium shrimp, peeled and cleaned

¼ pound feta cheese, crumbled

1 cup black or green Greek olives

2 tablespoons fresh anise hyssop or anise leaves, minced

114

1. Heat the olive oil in a large skillet over medium heat, and sauté the leeks or onions and garlic for 5 minutes. Add the tomatoes, and cook for 5 minutes. Add the Greek oregano, salt, and pepper, and cook for 1 minute.

2. Preheat the oven to 450°F. Place the shrimp in a large glass or metal casserole dish. Spoon the tomato mixture over the shrimp. Sprinkle with the feta cheese, olives, and anise hyssop or anise leaves. Place the dish in the oven, and bake for 10 minutes until the shrimp is pink and the cheese has melted. Serve with rice.

Serves 4 to 6

Fun with Feta

Feta cheese is traditionally a sheep or goat milk cheese. (Think about it—do you usually see cows grazing in pictures of the Greek countryside?) But now, a lot of feta is made from cow's milk, and a lot of it is made in America. And there are several types of feta. Some is firm, some soft, some sharp, and some a little drier than others.

If you are lucky enough to have a Greek or Middle Eastern neighborhood in your city, find a food store there and try the various types of feta you can buy. They really are different. You'll enjoy exploring.

While you are there, try the different types of olives the store may have. Some might even be packaged in barrels, so you can choose the ones that look most intriguing. Many will have herbs like bay leaf or oregano in the barrel to give them flavor.

Fish Fillets in Tomato Herb Sauce Marseilles

115

Herbs used:
Florence fennel, garlic, bay, tarragon, saffron, and parsley

Fennel, bay, tarragon, and saffron mixed with tomatoes and fish are the true flavors of the food around the ancient Mediterranean port city of Marseilles. In place of the monkfish, you could use cod, shark, red snapper, or another firm-fleshed white fish. Serve with white rice.

1 medium onion, chopped fine

1 tablespoon olive oil

1 medium Florence fennel bulb

3 cloves garlic, minced

One 28-ounce can plum tomatoes

1 bay leaf

1 tablespoon fresh or 1 teaspoon dried tarragon, minced

6 to 8 saffron threads

½ cup minced fresh parsley

¼ teaspoon salt

⅛ teaspoon freshly ground black pepper

Four 4-ounce fillets of monkfish

1 In a large saucepan, sauté the onion in the olive oil over medium-high heat for 3 minutes, stirring often. Trim the fennel bulb and chop fine. Add the fennel and garlic, and lower the heat to medium. Sauté for 5 minutes. Add the tomatoes, bay leaf, tarragon, saffron, parsley, salt, and pepper. Stir to mix, breaking up the tomatoes into smaller pieces. Bring to a boil, and reduce heat to medium-low. Cover; simmer for 20 minutes.

2 Preheat the oven to 425°F. Wash and dry fish fillets; place in an ovenproof casserole dish. Pour the sauce over the fillets; bake for 10 minutes. Remove and discard bay leaf.

Serves 4

Salmon with Dill Sauce

Herb used:
Dill

The flavor of fresh dill and salmon is a marriage made in heaven. Perfectly broiled fresh salmon steaks topped with a spoonful of mustardy dill sauce will make a truly unforgettable dish.

½ cup Dijon mustard

Juice of 1 lemon

2 tablespoons fresh dill, minced

¼ teaspoon salt

⅛ teaspoon freshly ground black pepper

4 boneless salmon steaks, about ½ pound each

Fresh dill sprigs and lemon wedges, for garnish

1 Make the sauce by mixing the mustard, lemon juice, dill, salt, and pepper in a bowl.

2 Broil the salmon steaks for 4 to 5 minutes on each side. Do not overcook.

3 Spoon a dollop of mustard-dill sauce on top of each salmon steak. Garnish with dill sprigs and lemon wedges, and pass extra sauce in a bowl on the side.

Serves 4

Pasta Primavera with Fresh Herbs

The original pasta primavera is not made with a creamy white sauce. In this authentic version, fresh herbs and vegetables are gently sautéed and tossed with perfectly cooked pasta. A little sprinkle of grated cheese on top rounds out the flavor.

- 1 tablespoon olive oil
- 1 cup cardoon, cut in bite-size pieces
- 1 cup Florence fennel, cut in bite-size pieces
- 1 cup lovage, cut in bite-size pieces
- 1 medium onion, diced
- 1 cup fresh arugula, chopped
- 1 large ripe tomato, peeled, seeded, and chopped
- 1 tablespoon each fresh basil, oregano, and flat-leaf parsley, minced
- ½ cup chicken stock, white wine, or water
- ¼ teaspoon salt
- ⅛ teaspoon freshly ground black pepper
- 1 pound bow-tie, wagon-wheel, corkscrew, or other macaroni pasta

116

1 Place a large skillet over medium heat, and add the olive oil. Sauté the cardoon, fennel, lovage, and onions for 3 to 5 minutes, or until they are tender but still crunchy.

2 Add the arugula, and cook for 1 minute. Add the tomatoes, herbs, stock, salt, and pepper, and cook for 2 minutes. Cover, and keep warm until the pasta is cooked.

3 Cook the pasta in boiling water until al dente, according to package instructions. Drain, and toss with the herbs and vegetables. If you are not on a fat-restricted diet, add a little more olive oil for flavor.

Serves 4 to 6

Test the firmness of the pasta by cutting it with the side of a fork.

Sesame Noodles with Garden Herbs

This dish is based on the popular sesame noodle dish often served in Chinese restaurants. The garlic chives give it a different look and special flavor.

⅓ cup smooth or chunky peanut butter

⅓ cup sesame paste

½ cup water

2 tablespoons each dry sherry, white vinegar, and soy sauce

1 tablespoon oriental sesame oil

1 teaspoon fresh ginger, minced

1 cup garlic chives, cut into ½-inch-long pieces

1 pound Chinese wheat noodles or vermicelli

3 scallions, green parts only, sliced fine

⅓ cup coriander leaves (cilantro), chopped

1 In a medium-size bowl, combine the peanut butter, sesame paste, water, sherry, vinegar, soy sauce, sesame oil, and ginger. Stir to blend well.

2 Drop the garlic chives into a pan of boiling water, and cook for 1 minute. Drain. Cook the noodles until al dente, according to package instructions. Drain.

3 Place the noodles in a serving dish. Add the peanut-sesame mixture and the garlic chives; toss to mix. Sprinkle the scallions and coriander leaves on top.

Serves 4 to 6

117

Low-Fat Sesame Noodles

If you like sesame noodles but you don't want all the extra fat and calories of sesame and peanut butter, you can simply leave them out. You will still get plenty of sesame flavor by using a little sesame oil, and you can enhance that flavor by sprinkling a few toasted sesame seeds over the dish.

Another variation on this dish is to add a few tiny shrimp and a couple of tablespoons of oyster sauce, grated carrots, tiny bits of surimi, a dash of curry powder, lemon grass, turnip greens, or many other ingredients.

I've found that Chinese noodles make wonderful low-fat dishes if you simply let your imagination and your tastebuds roam.

Linguine with Many-Basils Pesto

This easy-to-prepare pesto is a good way to show off the many different types of basil you are growing or simply to showcase one that is your favorite. You will find that your own homemade pesto is far superior to what you can buy in the store.

2 cups packed fresh basil leaves

⅓ cup walnuts or pine nuts

1 large clove garlic, chopped

½ cup olive oil

⅓ cup Parmesan or Romano cheese, grated

1 pound linguine or thin spaghetti pasta

1 Place the basil, nuts, and garlic in a food processor, and grind to a paste. With the motor running, slowly add the olive oil to form a creamy mixture. Add the cheese, and pulse briefly to combine.

2 Cook the pasta in boiling water until al dente, according to package instructions. Scoop out ½ cup of the cooking water and reserve. Drain the pasta. Mix the pesto with the hot water. Pour over the pasta, and toss.

Serve 4 to 6

Other Great Pasta Dishes

Think of linguine with pesto as a jumping-off place for you to discover an infinite variety of healthy and delicious Italian-inspired pasta dishes using fresh herbs. Instead of making pesto, you can simply add the pesto ingredients to the dish whole, chopped, or minced. The flavor will be the same, but the texture will be deliciously different.

Another Italian pasta dish that I like features fresh oregano, sun-dried tomatoes, and ricotta salta, a firm cheese that has a tart flavor like feta.

The classic version of linguine with clam sauce is properly made by cooking several cloves of fresh-chopped garlic (the more the better!) and a handful of minced Italian flat-leaf parlsey in good olive oil. Shuck the clams at the last minute, toss them in with the garlic sauce for 2 minutes, and blend them in with fresh hot linguine. And never, never add cheese to linguine with clam sauce!

Pad Thai Noodles with Basil

Unlike Chinese cooking, Thai cooking uses a lot of fragrant herbs, including basil. Pad thai noodles is one of the most popular dishes served in the growing number of Thai restaurants.

¾ pound Chinese rice noodles or vermicelli noodles

½ cup garlic chives or scallions, chopped

2 cloves garlic, minced

1 cup carrots, thinly sliced

½ pound medium shrimp, shells on

1 cup mung bean sprouts

1 tablespoon vegetable oil

½ cup fresh Thai basil or other basil leaves, minced

3 tablespoons lime juice

1 tablespoon nam pla fish sauce or soy sauce

Lettuce leaves, lemon wedges, bean sprouts, and sprigs of basil, for garnish

2 tablespoons roasted peanuts, crushed

1 Soak the rice noodles in a bowl of warm water until they are soft and tender, about 20 minutes. Drain. Set the noodles aside.

2 In a wok or deep-sided skillet, sauté the garlic chives or scallions, garlic, carrots, shrimp, and bean sprouts in the vegetable oil over medium-high heat for 3 minutes. Lower the heat to medium, and sauté for another 3 minutes, or until the shrimp is cooked and the carrots are tender.

3 Add the basil, lime juice, and fish or soy sauce to the skillet, and stir to blend well. Add the noodles, and stir to blend well. Cook for 2 to 3 minutes until the ingredients are evenly warm.

4 Spoon the pad thai onto a large warmed platter, and garnish with lettuce, lemon wedges, more bean sprouts, and sprigs of fresh basil. Sprinkle the crushed peanuts over the top.

Serves 4

119

Satay: A Thai Treat

One of the most common dishes in Thai cooking is satay, skewered thin slices of pork, beef, or chicken cooked over a charcoal fire. To make your own, simply thread thin slices or spear small chunks of your favorite meat on bamboo or wooden skewers. You could use metal skewers, but I don't because they do get hot! Marinate the satay in a blend of soy sauce or fish sauce, lime juice, garlic, and a little sprinkling of curry powder. Broil until the meat is cooked to your liking—5 minutes for medium rare to 10 minutes for well done—and serve. Satay is perfect company for pad thai noodles.

Pissaladière

This pizza has neither cheese nor tomatoes. Instead, it features the wonderful fragrances and flavors of rosemary or sage and slowly cooked onions. It is popular in parts of Italy and the south of France and may quickly become a favorite with you.

1 ball premade pizza dough, about 1 pound

3 medium or 2 large red onions, thinly sliced

2 tablespoons olive oil

2 tablespoons fresh rosemary or sage leaves, chopped

2 tablespoons small black olives

1 small tin or jar anchovy fillets (optional)

1 Spread the dough on a pizza pan or cookie sheet. Preheat the oven to 450°F. Sauté the onions in olive oil over medium-high heat for 5 to 7 minutes, or until onions are soft and slightly brown. Add the herbs, and stir to blend well.

2 Spread the onions and herbs over the pizza, and arrange the olives and anchovies on top. Bake in the preheated oven for 10 to 15 minutes, or until the crust is a golden brown. Remove from the oven, and cut into wedges.

Serves 2 to 4

120

Calendula-Cheddar Drop Biscuits

Beautiful calendula flowers give a nice yellow color to baked goods. This is an extremely easy recipe that has proven very popular for both formal buffets and casual family dinners.

1 tablespoon fresh or 1 teaspoon dried calendula petals

2 cups all-purpose flour, sifted

3 teaspoons baking powder

½ teaspoon salt

⅓ cup shortening, unsalted margarine, or butter

1 cup milk

1 cup shredded cheddar cheese

1 Preheat the oven to 450°F. Mix the calendula petals, flour, baking powder, and salt. Stir to blend well. Add the shortening, and mix to form a grainy texture. Add the milk, and stir to blend well. Add the cheese, and stir well.

2 Drop tablespoons of the mixture onto a greased baking sheet, and bake in the preheated oven for 10 to 12 minutes, or until golden brown.

Makes approximately 1 dozen biscuits

Anise Seed Anadama Bread

Anadama bread, with molasses and cornmeal, is an American classic. The simple addition of anise seeds gives this chewy bread a special flavor.

½ cup yellow cornmeal
2 cups water
1 package dry yeast
½ cup warm water
½ cup molasses
2 teaspoons salt
1 tablespoon anise seed
1 tablespoon butter
4½ cups unbleached white flour
Butter, for greasing pans

1 Place the cornmeal in a large mixing bowl. Bring the 2 cups of water to a boil, and pour it over the cornmeal, stirring to blend well. Let rest for 30 minutes.

2 Stir the yeast and ½ cup warm water together in small bowl. Let stand for 5 minutes.

3 Add the yeast mixture, molasses, salt, anise seed, and butter to the cornmeal; stir. Add the flour, and stir to blend thoroughly. Grease two loaf pans, and spoon the batter evenly into the pans. Let rise in a warm place for 1 hour, or until doubled in bulk. Bake the bread in a preheated 350°F oven for 45 minutes. Remove the loaves from the pans, and let cool.

Makes 2 loaves

121

Professional Bread Tip

I know a thing or two about breadmaking—I've been baking homemade bread since my college days in the late 1960s and early 1970s. I once worked as a baker at the Paquin Street Cafe, an alternative health food restaurant in Columbia, Missouri.

I think the secret to making bread that has good flavor is to use the very best flour you can find—whether it's organically grown whole wheat or sifted white flour. Wheat is like any other food you grow: The more it's processed, the more of its flavor you lose. Furthermore, at the Paquin Street Cafe, we always kept our wheat in a refrigerated room to preserve the wheat germ, which can spoil.

So when you're planning to make bread, remember my #1 rule: Make bread any way you like, but always find the freshest flour you can.

Italian Country Herb Bread

Herbs used:
Garlic, basil,
oregano, and
parsley

This is a wonderful bread to serve with Italian pasta dishes or to slice and toast into croutons. Top it with salami and you have a perfect Italian sandwich, or spread butter on it and sprinkle with garlic salt for garlic bread.

2 tablespoons vegetable oil

2 tablespoons sugar

2 teaspoons salt

1 cup hot milk

1 cup hot water

1 package dry yeast

1/4 cup warm water

3 cups white flour

3 cups whole wheat flour

1 clove garlic, minced

1/2 cup mixed fresh basil, oregano, and parsley, minced

1 In a large bowl, mix the vegetable oil, sugar, and salt. Stir in the hot milk and hot water. Let cool.

2 Mix the yeast and warm water in a small bowl, and let stand 5 minutes so the yeast can dissolve.

3 Mix the white and whole wheat flour. Add the yeast mixture and half the flour to the liquid mixture in the large bowl. Stir to blend well. Add the garlic and herbs, and stir to blend well. Add the remaining flour, and stir to form a ball.

4 Knead the dough for 10 minutes. Place in a warm, lightly oiled bowl. Cover with a towel, and place in a warm place for 1 hour.

5 Punch the dough down, and form it into two round loaves. Place on baking sheets, and let rise for 1 hour.

6 Bake the loaves in a preheated 425°F oven for 15 minutes. Reduce heat to 375°F, and bake for an additional 30 minutes, or until the crust is golden brown. Let cool.

Makes 2 loaves

Breads

Neapolitan Pizza with Fresh Basil

Herbs used:
Basil
and garlic

My favorite way to make pizza is with fresh tomato slices, fresh minced herbs, and mozzarella cheese. Starting with premade pizza dough (available in the refrigerated section of your supermarket) makes this pizza as easy to make as it is good to eat.

2 balls premade pizza dough, about 1 pound each

2 large red or yellow tomatoes, peeled, seeded, and sliced thin

1 cup fresh whole basil leaves, washed and dried

4 cloves garlic, minced

½ pound mozzarella cheese, sliced thin or grated

2 tablespoons fruity green olive oil

Freshly ground black pepper

1 Preheat the oven to 450°F. Spread the premade pizza dough over pizza pans or cookie sheets.

2 Arrange the tomato slices and basil over the dough. Sprinkle with minced garlic. Spread with the mozzarella cheese, and drizzle with olive oil. Top with a few gratings of black pepper.

3 Place the pizzas in the oven, and bake for 15 to 20 minutes until the cheese is melted and the bottom crust is golden brown. Remove from the oven, let rest for 2 to 3 minutes, and slice into wedges.

Serves 4 to 6

Pondering Pizza

Less is better with pizza as far as I'm concerned. The more goopy or greasy stuff you put on top, the farther away from true pizza enjoyment you are.

Basil, not oregano, is the key herb in making great pizza. If all of those pizzerias would only put a shaker of dried basil on the table instead of a shaker of dried oregano, their pizza would be a whole lot better.

But the very best pizza is made in a coal- or wood-fired oven. The dry heat and smoke adds a dimension to pizza that cannot be explained, only appreciated. Patsy's under the Brooklyn Bridge and Totonno's on Coney Island still make simple Neapolitan pizza in coal-fired ovens—they make the trip to Brooklyn worth the effort! You can now find wood-burning pizza parlors all over the country—try one and see what I mean!

Apple-Mint Pudding

Herb used:
Apple or
pineapple mint

No doubt about it—homemade pudding does taste better than the kind you make from a package. But if you are in a hurry, you can simply add apple mint to your favorite brand of boxed vanilla pudding and enjoy.

2 cups milk

¾ cup sugar

2 tablespoons cornstarch

¼ teaspoon salt

2 egg yolks, beaten

2 tablespoons butter or margarine

1 teaspoon pure vanilla extract

1 teaspoon apple or pineapple mint, finely minced

Sprigs of fresh mint, for garnish

1 Combine the milk, sugar, cornstarch, and salt in a medium saucepan. Stir to blend well. Cook the mixture over medium-low heat, stirring all the time, until it is thick. Remove from the heat, and cool slightly.

2 Spoon a small amount of the hot pudding mixture into the beaten egg yolks, and stir. Pour the egg mixture into the pudding mixture, and cook for 2 minutes.

3 Remove from the heat. Add the butter, vanilla, and mint; stir. Pour into individual dessert dishes. Cool, and serve with a sprig of mint.

Serves 4 to 6

124

Anise Ice Cream

Herb used:
Anise seed

Let's face it, ice cream is not a low-fat food. But if you take just a small portion, you can still enjoy this flavorful, herb-infused delight without too much guilt!

4 eggs

2½ cups sugar

7 cups milk

3 cups whipping cream

2½ tablespoons pure vanilla extract

1 tablespoon anise seed, whole

1 Beat the eggs until light and fluffy. Add the sugar gradually, beating until thick. Add the milk, cream, vanilla, and anise seed. Stir to blend well.

2 Pour into a 5-quart ice-cream maker. Follow manufacturer's instructions for making the ice cream. Scoop into dishes to serve. Freeze the rest.

Makes 1 gallon

Chocolate Mint Angel Food Cake

Herb used:
Chocolate mint

Chocolate mint is one of the prettiest of the mints to grow, and it really does have a strong flavor of chocolate. This is a very light cake that is perfect with afternoon coffee.

1 cup sifted cake flour

1½ cups granulated sugar

12 egg whites

1½ teaspoons cream of tartar

1 teaspoon pure vanilla extract

¼ teaspoon salt

1 tablespoon chocolate mint, finely minced

Confectioners' sugar

Sprigs of chocolate mint, for garnish

1 Preheat the oven to 375°F. Sift the flour with half of the sugar.

2 In a separate bowl, whip the egg whites until almost firm. Add the cream of tartar, vanilla, and salt, and continue whipping lightly. Whip in the remaining sugar a tablespoon at a time until stiff peaks form.

3 Add the chocolate mint. Gently fold the flour and sugar mixture, a little at a time into the egg whites. Spoon the mixture into an ungreased angel food cake pan, and bake for 35 to 40 minutes.

4 Invert the cake pan on a soda bottle, and cool completely. Unmold, and dust with confectioners' sugar. Garnish with chocolate mint sprigs.

Serves 8 to 10

Whip egg whites to stiff peak stage before adding the mint.

Chapter 5

Ten Great Herb Garden Designs

When you think of herbs, their flavor and fragrance are the first things that come to mind. But many herbs are attractive enough to hold their own against any garden flower.

These ten herb gardens showcase some of the most useful and beautiful herbs you can grow. Plant the designs as is, or use them to get ideas and inspiration for creating your own beautiful easy herb gardens.

Ten Great Herb Garden Designs

An Early American Herb Garden

When you consider that herbs have been an important part of our lives for thousands of years, it's not surprising that these practical plants also offer a fascinating history of lore and legend.

A typical early herb garden was fenced or walled to keep the livestock out, and it was usually close to the house for easy access. However, the actual layout of the garden varied widely, depending on what the family found convenient or attractive. The simple but beautiful garden featured here is a good place to start in your travels back into the history of herbs.

An Early American Herb Garden

Take a trip back in time by recreating a colonial-style herb garden in your own backyard. You'll enjoy the look and fragrance of these old-time herbs and roses.

Seeds to Buy

It's simple to raise these herbs from seed. Sow the seed directly into the garden, right where you want the plants to grow.

- ❧ BORAGE (1 PACKET)
- ❧ CALENDULA (1 PACKET)
- ❧ CARAWAY (1 PACKET)
- ❧ DILL (1 PACKET)

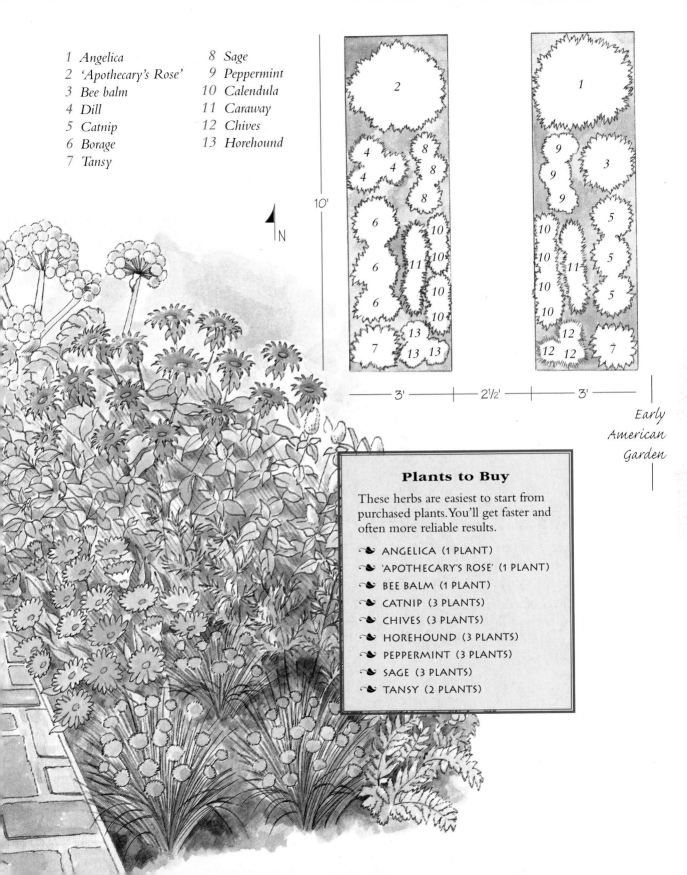

1 Angelica
2 'Apothecary's Rose'
3 Bee balm
4 Dill
5 Catnip
6 Borage
7 Tansy
8 Sage
9 Peppermint
10 Calendula
11 Caraway
12 Chives
13 Horehound

10'

N

3' — 2½' — 3'

Early
American
Garden

Plants to Buy

These herbs are easiest to start from
purchased plants. You'll get faster and
often more reliable results.

- ANGELICA (1 PLANT)
- 'APOTHECARY'S ROSE' (1 PLANT)
- BEE BALM (1 PLANT)
- CATNIP (3 PLANTS)
- CHIVES (3 PLANTS)
- HOREHOUND (3 PLANTS)
- PEPPERMINT (3 PLANTS)
- SAGE (3 PLANTS)
- TANSY (2 PLANTS)

The Plant Guide

An Early American Herb Garden

Herbs in colonial and pre–Civil War America were important sources of food, flavorings, medicine, dyes, repellents, flowers, and fragrance. In those days, the herb garden was the grocery store, the pharmacy, and the flower shop all in one!

This garden contains over a dozen different herbs in a pair of long, rectangular beds, each 10 feet long and 3 feet wide. It includes a sampling of some of the most attractive and useful herbs grown in early America. Besides enjoying the beauty and history of your herbs, you can also use them to flavor your food, make soothing teas, and create pretty and fragrant bouquets. Your herb garden may not replace a trip to the mall or the grocery store, but it will bring you years of fragrance, color, and flavor with a minimum of care.

Seeds

Sow these fast-growing annuals and biennials directly in the garden in spring. After the first year, you may not have to plant again because these herbs will often self-sow.

BORAGE
Borago officinalis

This easy-to-grow annual produces cucumber-flavored leaves that were added to salad and steeped to make tea. Bees are attracted to the pretty blue flowers and make a pleasant-tasting honey from them. Borage self-sows freely, so you'll probably only have to plant it once. If the self-sown seedlings aren't where you want them, you can move them to the desired location when they are still small (with one or two pairs of leaves). Borage grows 2 to 3 feet tall and tends to sprawl a bit as it matures. In this garden, you'll only need three plants, spaced about 1 foot apart. Buy one packet.

CALENDULA
Calendula officinalis

Calendulas, also commonly called pot marigolds, were brought to the Americas by early settlers, who used the leaves, stems, and flowers to dress wounds and heal bee and wasp stings. The fresh flower petals make a cheerful garnish for salads, and they give a wonderful orange-yellow color to breads. Sow in early spring as soon as you can work the soil. You'll want about four plants on each side of the main path, spaced about 1 foot apart. Pinch off spent flowers to prolong the bloom, or allow them to self-sow. Calendulas usually grow 1 to 2 feet tall. Buy one packet.

CARAWAY
Carum carvi

Caraway generally grows as a biennial, producing feathery leaves during

132

Key

TEA

CRAFT

COOKING

the first year and seed-bearing flowers the second spring. You can use the leaves in salads, but the tangy brown seeds are the real reason to grow caraway. They are a favorite for breads, stews, and cabbage dishes. Sow in early spring or in fall for an earlier harvest the next year. Thin seedlings to stand 6 to 8 inches apart. Leave a few seedheads unharvested to get self-sown seedlings. Plants reach 1 to 2 feet tall in bloom. Buy one packet.

DILL
Anethum graveolens

Early Americans used refreshing dill leaves the same way we use them today: minced and added to fish, sauces, and vegetable dishes. Dill leaves, stalks, and seeds are also an important flavoring in making pickled cucumbers and tomatoes. Sow seed in early to midspring. You'll want a clump of three plants, spaced about 1 foot apart. This annual herb self-sows freely if you don't harvest all of the seed. Plants reach 2 to 3 feet tall in bloom. Buy one packet.

Plants

Buy plants of the following herbs, or grow your own from divisions, cuttings, or seed sown indoors in pots.

ANGELICA
Angelica archangelica

This biennial herb forms bushy clumps the first year and tall, leafy flowering stems the following spring and early summer. Early Americans

ate the young second-year shoots as a vegetable, and they boiled the stalks and rolled them in sugar as a confection. The leaves were also used as a medicinal tea. If you cut down the flower stems right after bloom, the plant may live for a few more years. Or let the seeds develop and drop to get self-sown seedlings. Angelica can reach up to 8 feet tall in full bloom. Zones 4 to 9. Buy one plant.

'APOTHECARY'S ROSE'
Rosa gallica 'Apothecary's Rose', also called *R. gallica* var. *officinalis*

This cold-hardy shrub rose produces fragrant pink to red flowers in June. It's been grown for medicinal purposes for hundreds of years—hence its name. The Shakers steeped the petals in water to produce rose water, which they used as an alternative to vanilla as a flavoring. The petals are also wonderful in potpourri. The flowers are followed by round red fruits, called hips, that are high in vitamin C; they make a tangy tea. 'Apothecary's Rose' usually doesn't need much pruning—just a little light trimming after bloom to shape the plant. A mature plant will reach 3 to 4 feet tall. Zones 3 to 8. Buy one plant.

BEE BALM
Monarda didyma

A native American plant, bee balm is a spreading perennial herb that's both beautiful and useful. The aromatic leaves have long been popular for making

Early American Garden

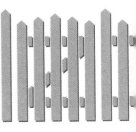

THE LANGUAGE OF HERBS

In the past, people often used bouquets of flowers and herbs to convey special sentiments to a lucky recipient. These small, sentiment-packed bundles were commonly known as "tussie-mussies." You can use flowers and herbs from your own garden to send a message to a special friend; just follow the simple interpretations below to convey your sentiments. Make sure to include a copy of the meanings, so the person you give it to will understand your message!

ANGELICA: inspiration

BASIL: love, good wishes (or hate!)

BEE BALM: virtue

BORAGE: bravery

CALENDULA: sadness

CHAMOMILE: wisdom

CHERVIL: sincerity

DILL: good cheer

LAVENDER: devotion

LEMON BALM: sympathy

MARJORAM: joy

MINT: refreshment

PARSLEY: merriment

ROSE: love, success

RUE: grief

SAGE: long life, wisdom

SCENTED GERANIUM: happiness

SOUTHERNWOOD: constancy

THYME: daring

YARROW: health

Key

TEA

CRAFT

COOKING

a pleasant citrus-flavored tea. In fact, bee balm was once used by colonists as a substitute for the British-taxed black tea. It commonly has red flowers, but cultivars with pink, purple, or white flowers are also available. In mid- to late spring, pinch out up to a half of the stems at ground level to thin out crowded clumps and encourage good air circulation around the remaining stems. Plants grow to 3 feet tall. Zones 4 to 9. Buy one plant.

CATNIP
Nepeta cataria

Catnip forms fast-spreading clumps of fuzzy, green foliage and brushy spikes of small white to pinkish flowers. Its minty leaves make a soothing tea that can be useful for relieving coughs, especially when sweetened with a bit of honey. Cats enjoy catnip leaves, too! Plants will spread quickly, so divide them each spring and replant just a few sections, or grow them in bottomless pots sunk into the soil. Plants grow to 3 feet tall. Zones 3 to 8. Buy three plants; space them about 1 foot apart.

CHIVES
Allium schoenoprasum

Chives has long been grown for its mild onion-flavored foliage. It is a great addition to almost any savory dish. In June, this perennial herb produces pretty pink or lavender flowers that you can add to salads for both flavor and color. Chives will self-sow prolifically if you don't pinch or cut

off the spent flowers. Clumps reach 12 to 14 inches tall in bloom. Zones 3 to 9. Buy three plants, and space them 1 foot apart.

HOREHOUND
Marrubium vulgare

Horehound drops, the old-fashioned candy used to soothe sore throats, are made from the soft, gray leaves of this perennial herb. Horehound grows quickly from transplants, but it's also easy to raise from seed sown either indoors or directly in the garden in early spring. In fact, plants will often self-sow if you don't harvest the tops before they flower. Horehound grows 2 to 3 feet tall. Zones 4 to 9. Buy or grow three plants, and set them about 1 foot apart.

PEPPERMINT
Mentha × piperita

Early settlers in Virginia, Kentucky, and Missouri usually grew a mint bed close to their house. Visitors were offered whiskey with a leaf or two of mint, and the mint julep was born. Mint was also used to make a soothing tea. This garden plan calls for peppermint, but you could easily substitute spearmint or another favorite kind of mint. All mints can spread vigorously, especially in moist soil, so plant them in pots or bottomless buckets sunk into the soil. Different mints vary in height but usually reach about 2 feet tall. Zones 5 to 9. Buy three plants, and space them about 1 foot apart.

Fences are a traditional feature of Early American herb gardens. Choose a rail fence for a rustic look or a picket fence for a more formal appearance.

SAGE
Salvia officinalis

The Shakers grew sage extensively and used it as a digestive aid. While its medicinal use has declined, it is still very popular as a seasoning for stuffing and meat dishes. Common culinary sage has gray-green leaves, but if you'd like extra color, try planting 'Purpurea', with purple-green leaves, 'Icterina', with gold-banded green leaves, or 'Tricolor', with green leaves that are splashed with cream, pink, and purple. You can also find cultivars of the common sage with white or pink flowers, instead of the normal purple-blue blooms. Plants grow 1 to 2 feet tall. Zones 4 to 9. Buy three plants, and space them about 1 foot apart.

TANSY
Tanacetum vulgare

For centuries, gardeners have planted tansy by their doors to keep pests such as ants, flies, and mosquitoes at bay. Indoors, dried tansy was bundled with stored clothing and hung in closets and cabinets to repel troublesome insects. Today, you can still experiment with tansy's insect-repellent properties, and you can enjoy the buttonlike yellow flowers in both fresh and dried bouquets. Tansy roots spread quickly, so it's smart to plant the clumps in a large, bottomless bucket sunk into the soil. You can also divide the clumps every year or two, as needed, to control their spread. Tansy grows to 3 feet tall in bloom. Zones 4 to 9. Buy two plants.

Key

TEA

CRAFT

COOKING

The Seasonal Guide

An Early American Herb Garden

season 1

January and February _____

| J | F | M | A | M | J | J | A | S | O | N | D |

Select a Site

Winter is a good time to start planning your Early American herb garden, beginning with choosing the right site. The key is finding an open spot in full sun (at least six hours of sun a day). Average, well-drained soil will suit all of these herbs. A flat site is ideal, but you could also site this garden on a slight slope. Traditionally, herb gardens were sited close to the house, so it was easy to tend and harvest them. Select an area near the back or front door if you have a choice of suitable spots.

Consider a Garden Fence

A fence or other enclosure—especially a rustic rail or white picket fence— will give your garden a true Early American feel. If you like the look of a wooden picket fence but not the idea of painting it every year, consider installing the vinyl equivalent. Vinyl fences look good for many years with minimal maintenance.

Whatever fence style you choose, it's smart to install it before you plant your garden so you won't have to worry about damaging your established herbs.

To figure out how much space you'll need for the garden plus the fence, first mark out the beds with stakes and string. Be sure to leave a path at least 30 inches wide between the two beds. Then measure 12 to 18 inches out from the outer three sides of each bed to mark the fence lines. This gap will give you a little path between the fences and the beds, so you can reach all parts of the garden without having to step on the loosened soil.

A truly traditional herb garden would be enclosed on all sides, so you may also want to add a gate at either end of the central path.

Buy Seeds and Plants

Although most of these herb plants and seeds will be available from your local garden center or nursery in the spring, it's fun to spend a dreary winter day paging through plant and seed catalogs. General vegetable and flower garden suppliers usually sell a good selection of these basic herbs. Check herb catalog descriptions if you are looking for a particular color of bee balm or sage, or if you're interested in trying some of the more uncommon mints. 'Apothecary's Rose' is a bit unusual, so don't count on finding it at a local nursery or garden center; purchase it from a mail-order supplier. You'll find addresses for some of my favorite mail-order catalogs in "Plants and Supplies" on page 262.

season 2

March,
April, and May _____

| J | F | **M** | **A** | **M** | J | J | A | S | O | N | D |

Prepare the Site

Wait until your soil is completely thawed and dry enough to dig without turning into muddy clumps. If you want to get an extra-early start with your planting, you can also prepare the site in fall, so everything will be ready when spring arrives.

You will be planting two beds, each 10 feet long and 3 feet wide. Mark off the beds with stakes and string (if you haven't already), and remove any rocks, debris, or existing vegetation. Test the soil to check its pH. Add lime or sulfur,

if needed, to raise or lower the pH so it is around neutral (7.0).

Loosen the soil to a depth of 8 inches, either with a spading fork or a rotary tiller. Then spread a 1- to 2-inch layer of compost, composted manure, or other organic material over the beds, and dig that into the top 6 inches of soil. Rake to smooth the soil surface.

If you have created your new herb garden out of an existing lawn area, you could leave the central walkway as a grass path. In that case, you'll want to install plastic, brick, or metal edging strips on each side of the path to keep the grass from creeping into the beds. Another easy-maintenance option is to replace all the grass with a gravel or brick path. Install edging strips or gravel or brick paths after you dig the beds, but before planting.

Plant Your Herbs

Following the planting diagram on page 131, start planting in early spring as soon as the beds are ready. Sow the borage, calendula, caraway, and dill seeds where you want the plants to grow. It's important to keep seeded areas moist. Water lightly every day (unless it rains) until the seedlings appear. When seedlings are a few inches tall, thin them to their recommended spacing. Snip off unwanted seedlings at ground level with scissors; pulling them out may disturb the roots of the remaining seedlings.

Set out the angelica, bee balm, catnip, chives, horehound, mint, sage, and tansy plants as you get them. If the plants were

Try pink-flowered bee balm for a change from the usual red.

growing in a greenhouse when you bought them, make sure you harden them off before planting. (See "Handling Hardening Off" on page 10.) If you don't plan to divide your catnip, mint, and tansy plants every year or two, control their spread by planting them in bottomless pots or buckets sunk into the soil. Leave the top inch of the containers above the soil level to discourage roots from sneaking out over the top.

Set out the rose as soon as it arrives. It will probably be bareroot (with only packing material around the roots). Remove the packing material, snip off any damaged roots, and soak the roots in a bucket of water overnight. The next day, dig a hole big enough to hold all the roots without bending them. Replace some soil in the middle of the hole to form a cone. Set the rose on top of the cone, with the roots spread out evenly over the sides of the cone. If needed, adjust the height of the cone so the crown (where the roots join the stem) will be even with the soil surface. Replace the soil around the roots and water thoroughly.

If you purchase a rose growing in a container, carefully tip the plant on its side and slide it out of the container. "Comb" the outside of the root ball with your fingers to loosen the outer roots and remove excess soil. Then plant the rose at the same depth it was growing in its container.

season 3
June, July, and August

| J | F | M | A | M | **J** | **J** | **A** | S | O | N | D |

Minimize Garden Chores

Once the soil has warmed up, by late spring or early summer, it's time to mulch the garden. Weed thoroughly, then spread 1 inch of compost between the plants, and top that with another inch of shredded bark or chopped leaves. This will discourage more weeds from sprouting and helps to keep the soil moist. If you don't get at least $1/2$ inch of rain each week, pull away a bit of mulch and use a trowel to check the soil underneath every few days. When the top 2 to 3 inches are dry, water thoroughly to soak the soil.

Enjoy Your Herbs

You can start harvesting most of your beautiful easy herbs the first summer. Gather the leaves of bee balm, borage, catnip, chives, dill, horehound, mint, and sage as needed. For drying, pick bee balm and calendula flowers as soon as they open, then hang them upside down to dry. Collect rose petals before the flowers are fully open. Harvest tansy flowers when they are fully open but before they turn brown.

season 4

*September
and October*

J F M A M J J A **S O** N D

Prepare Your Garden
for Winter

If you let your borage, calendula, caraway, and dill plants flower and you don't harvest the seed, they will drop their seed in fall, and you'll probably have a new crop of seedlings in the spring without having to replant. After these annual herbs have dropped their seed, pull them out and toss their remains on the compost pile. Or, if you would prefer not to have the self-sown seedlings, cut off the flowerheads as soon as the flowers fade. Then wait until fall to cut down the remaining stems.

In early winter, when the ground is frozen, cut the tops of the remaining herbs—except for the sage and the rose—to the ground. Add the dead tops to your compost pile.

If you live in Zone 5 or farther north, it's a good idea to give your garden some winter protection. After the ground has frozen, mulch with several inches of loose straw, or use boughs from a Christmas tree after the holidays. This will protect your perennial herbs from damage caused by thawing and freezing during spells of mild winter weather. ✿

Dill and caraway produce lots of seed. Allow some to self-sow for next year.

Keeping your garden going

After the first season, your Early American herb garden will need minimal care to look good for years to come. In late winter, prune the rose to remove any dead wood. Each spring, after the soil thaws and your perennials begin to nudge their way up out of the ground, remove any winter protection.

Once warmer weather arrives, self-sown seedlings of the annual herbs should emerge. If you don't see any seedlings by midspring, replant with new seed. If you allowed the angelica to flower and set seed, you will probably find seedlings where the parent plant was growing; if not, set out a new plant.

Wait until mid- to late spring to prune the sage; cut off winter-damaged tips, and trim lightly to shape the plant. Each year, renew the compost-and-bark or compost-and-leaf mulch layers in late spring to early summer. Trim the rose lightly after flowering to shape the shrub. If the perennial clumps look crowded or begin to flower poorly, divide them in spring or fall. Replant a few of the vigorous outer sections and compost the rest.

Over time, sage can develop tough stems, leaving the base of the plant looking woody and bare. If this happens, mound 3 to 5 inches of sandy soil over the base of the stems in spring. During the summer, water as needed to keep the mound moist. When the stem bases have rooted into the mound (usually by fall or the following spring), cut them off, dig out the old plant, and replant with the rooted stems.

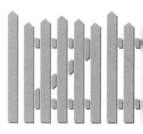

A Beautiful Easy Potpourri Garden

Herbs don't just have pretty flowers—they offer a wealth of fabulous fragrances as well. Growing and drying aromatic herbs for potpourri is a great way to enjoy their scents all through the year. As a plus, home-blended potpourri freshens the air in your house naturally, without your having to buy artificial fragrance sprays.

This simple but elegant garden contains a variety of herbs that retain their fragrance and color well when dried. Even if you never plan to make potpourri, you'll still enjoy the fresh scents and beautiful colors of this easy-care herb garden.

A Beautiful Easy Potpourri Garden

With this scent-sational garden, you'll have the makings for plenty of home-blended potpourri! You'll enjoy the colorful mix of purple, red, gold, and orange flowers.

Plants to Buy

These herbs are easiest to start from purchased plants. You'll get faster and often more reliable results.

- ANISE HYSSOP (1 PLANT)
- 'APOTHECARY'S ROSE' (1 PLANT)
- HYSSOP (1 PLANT)
- LAVENDER (3 PLANTS)
- MINT (1 PLANT)
- ROSEMARY (1 PLANT)
- SAGE (1 PLANT)
- SCENTED GERANIUM (2 PLANTS)
- SOUTHERNWOOD (1 PLANT)
- SWEET WOODRUFF (2 PLANTS)
- THYME (1 PLANT)
- YARROW (1 PLANT)

Seeds to Buy

It's simple to raise this herb from seed. Sow the seed directly into the garden, right where you want the plants to grow.

- CALENDULA (1 PACKET)

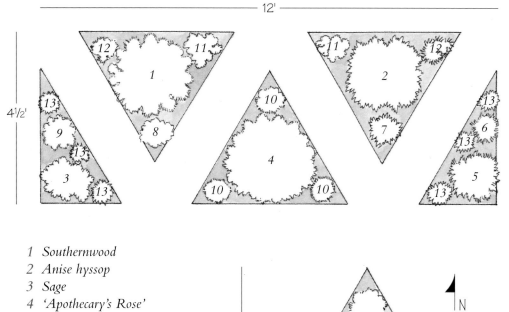

12'

4½'

1 Southernwood
2 Anise hyssop
3 Sage
4 'Apothecary's Rose'
5 Yarrow
6 Hyssop
7 Mint
8 Thyme
9 Rosemary
10 Lavender
11 Scented geranium
12 Sweet woodruff
13 Calendula

3½'

**Section
Dimensions**

N

4'

*Potpourri
Garden*

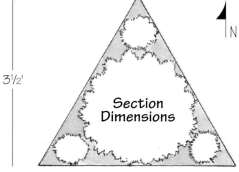

The Plant Guide

A Beautiful Easy Potpourri Garden

People have been growing fragrant herbs for thousands of years, and you can join in the fun with this selection of perfect potpourri herbs. This garden includes a variety of flowering and leafy herbs that hold their fragrance well when dried. It also includes some flowers that keep their colors when dried, so your potpourri will be pretty to look at as well as a pleasure to sniff.

This garden is designed in a rectangle, with a zigzag path that divides the space into five smaller, triangular planting beds. The path and the shape of the beds makes it easy to reach all sides of each section, so planting, maintenance, and harvesting will be a snap. Almost all of these herbs are perennials, so you can just plant them once and enjoy them for years to come.

Seeds

Sow this fast-growing annual directly in the garden in spring. After the first year, you may not have to plant again; this herb will often self-sow.

CALENDULA
Calendula officinalis

Calendulas, also commonly called pot marigolds, produce cheerful bright yellow or orange daisylike flowers. Double-flowered calendulas, such as 'Apricot Bon Bon', bear many more petals on each bloom than single-flowered types do. The flower petals hold their color well when dried, so sprinkle them into potpourri blends to liven up the green tones. Gathering the flowers regularly will extend the bloom season, but leave a few flowers toward the end of the season so they can ripen their seed and self-sow. Calendulas usually grow 1 to 2 feet tall. Thin plants to stand about 1 foot apart. Buy one packet.

Plants

Buy plants of the following herbs, or grow your own from divisions, cuttings, or seed sown indoors in pots.

ANISE HYSSOP
Agastache foeniculum

This pretty perennial herb grows in bushy clumps, with upright, branching stems topped with spikes of lavender-blue flowers in mid- to late summer. Both the leaves and flowers are fragrant when fresh or dried, so they are a great addition to potpourri. (The leaves also make a pleasant tea.) Anise hyssop is usually described as having a licorice-like aroma, although some gardeners liken it to the scent of root beer. It will self-sow prolifically, so pinch off most of the flowerheads before the small, black seeds mature. Plants grow to 3 feet tall. Zones 4 to 9. Buy one plant.

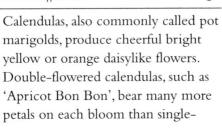

Key

TEA

CRAFT

COOKING

Don't forget to harvest and dry herb flowers for your potpourri. Calendulas, lavender, roses, and other flowers will add splashes of color to your mix.

'APOTHECARY'S ROSE'

Rosa gallica 'Apothecary's Rose', also called *R. gallica* var. *officinalis*

This cold-hardy shrub rose produces fragrant pink to red flowers in June. The dried petals are wonderful in potpourri. 'Apothecary's Rose' usually doesn't need much pruning—just a little light trimming after bloom to shape the plant. A mature plant will reach 3 to 4 feet tall. Zones 3 to 8. If you can't find 'Apothecary's Rose', you could substitute rugosa rose *(R. rugosa)*, eglantine rose *(R. eglanteria)*, or some other sweet-scented rose; their dried petals will be colorful, although not as fragrant. Buy one plant.

HYSSOP

Hyssopus officinalis

Hyssop forms shrubby clumps of narrow, dark green, aromatic leaves. The leafy stems are topped with whorls of blue flowers from summer to early fall. Pink- and white-flowered cultivars are also available. Blend the dried leaves and flowers with more strongly scented herbs to add color and fragrance. Regularly clipping off the flowering tips will encourage plants to produce bushier growth. Plants normally reach 2½ to 3 feet tall. Zones 3 to 9. Buy one plant.

LAVENDER

Lavandula angustifolia

No potpourri garden would be complete without lavender. The bluish purple flowers of this rugged little plant make the most heavenly sachets and potpourri. The stems and leaves are fragrant, too. 'Hidcote' grows 12 to 18 inches tall with dark purple-blue flowers. 'Lady' produces light purple flowers on compact 8- to 10-inch plants that bloom the first year from seed. 'Munstead' reaches 18 inches tall with purple flowers. English lavender is highly prized for its fragrance, but there are many other species and cultivars that vary in scent and flower color. You might enjoy trying a few different kinds to see which you find most appealing. French lavender (*L. dentata*), for instance, has finely toothed, gray-green leaves and pale purple flowers. Spanish lavender (*L. stoechas*) has narrow, silvery foliage and plump, dark purple flower spikes topped with elongated petals. Plants vary in height but can reach up to 3 feet tall. English lavender is hardy in Zones 5 to 8. French and Spanish lavenders are not cold-hardy in most parts of North America, so plan to bring them indoors for the winter, or purchase new plants each spring. Buy three plants.

MINTS
Mentha spp.

Mints come in dozens of different scents and flavors, from apple and grapefruit to the more familiar peppermint and spearmint. Most mints keep at least some fragrance when dried, but peppermint is especially aromatic and long-lasting. All mints can spread vigorously, especially in moist soil, so plant them in a bottomless pot or bucket sunk into the soil. Different mints vary in height but usually reach about 2 feet tall. Zones 5 to 9. Buy one plant.

ROSEMARY
Rosmarinus officinalis

Most gardeners think of rosemary as a cooking herb, but its leaves, stems, and flowers also bring a pungent fragrance to potpourri. In Zones 8 to 10, rosemary can live outdoors through the winter, and it grows as a shrub to 6 feet tall. North of Zone 8, treat it as an annual and buy a new plant each year, or bring your clump indoors for the winter; it will seldom reach more than 3 feet tall. Buy one plant.

SAGE
Salvia officinalis

Sage adds a wonderful aroma and flavor to stuffing, and its leaves, stems, and flowers bring that same warm fragrance to potpourri. Common culinary sage has gray-green leaves, but if you'd like extra color, try planting 'Purpurea', with purple-green leaves, 'Icterina', with gold-banded green leaves, or 'Tricolor', with green leaves that are splashed with cream, pink, and purple. 'Berg-garten' is a handsome selection with especially broad, silvery green foliage. You can also find cultivars of the common sage with white or pink flowers, instead of the normal purple-blue blooms. Plants grow 1 to 2 feet tall. Zones 4 to 9. Buy one plant.

SCENTED GERANIUMS
Pelargonium spp.

Scented geraniums come in dozens of leaf forms and fragrances, including apple, coconut, ginger, lemon, peppermint, and rose—just to name a few! All dry well and are delightful in potpourri. Scented geraniums are only hardy outdoors in frost-free

Key

TEA

CRAFT

COOKING

regions, but you can grow them anywhere as annuals. They also make wonderful houseplants, so you can bring your favorites indoors to grow on a sunny windowsill through the winter. Heights vary, depending on the species and cultivar. Buy two plants.

SOUTHERNWOOD
Artemisia abrotanum

Southernwood's feathery, gray-green leaves add color and fragrance to potpourri. They are also wonderful in dried wreaths and arrangements. The silvery green leaves of its close cousin, wormwood (*Artemisia absinthium*), also dry well, although they have a somewhat bitter scent. Hang the harvested leafy stems in bunches to dry. Strip the dried foliage off the stems before adding it to potpourri. Plants grow to 3 feet tall and wide. Zones 4 to 9. Buy one plant.

SWEET WOODRUFF
Galium odoratum

Sweet woodruff is an attractive garden plant, but you'd never guess that it would be wonderful potpourri ingredient by smelling the fresh leaves; its sweet, vanilla-like scent isn't noticeable until the foliage starts to dry. The dried, leafy stems are also great as a backing for dried wreaths. Sweet woodruff thrives in shady spots, but it can tolerate some sun, as long as the soil is moist. If possible, site it where taller herbs will give it some shade. If the sweet woodruff doesn't thrive there, move it to a shadier spot. Plants grow in spreading

carpets to about 8 inches tall. Zones 4 to 8. Buy two plants.

THYMES
Thymus spp.

Thymes are a traditional favorite in any herb garden because of their compact, shrubby or creeping forms and their aromatic leaves. Although they're most commonly used for cooking, the dried leaves and flowering tops also bring fragrance to potpourri blends. Common or English thyme (*Thymus vulgaris*) adds a piny, woodsy fragrance, while lemon thyme (*T. × citriodorus*) has a citrus scent. Choose either of these, or another kind—whatever scent you find most pleasing. Plants usually grow 6 to 12 inches tall. Zones 4 to 9. Buy one plant.

YARROWS
Achillea spp.

Yarrow's leaves are lightly scented, but it's the flowers you want for potpourri. The dried flowerheads retain much of their fresh colors, and the creams, whites, pinks, rusts, salmon, reds, and yellows add welcome color to the greens of the other herbs. Several species and hybrids are available, in different heights and flower colors; choose the one you like best. 'Cerise Queen', for instance, bears bright reddish pink flowers, while 'Coronation Gold' produces broad, flat, mustard-yellow flowerheads. Height varies, from 1 to 4 feet tall. Zones 3 to 8. Buy one plant.

The Seasonal Guide

A Beautiful Easy Potpourri Garden

season 1

January and February _____

| J | **F** | M | A | M | J | J | A | S | O | N | D |

Select a Site

The dull days of winter are a great time to start thinking about your new potpourri garden. It's critical to choose a spot with at least six hours of direct sun a day. Good drainage is also important. The rectangular shape of this garden makes it fit easily in a corner, against a fence, or along a wall. This garden is pretty enough to site in a highly visible spot, but you might want to choose a more out-of-the-way site if you plan to harvest your herbs heavily for serious potpourri making!

Buy Seeds and Plants

Most of these herb plants and seeds will be available from your local garden center or nursery in the spring. But if you like to plan ahead, this is a good time to look for the herbs you'll need in plant and seed catalogs. General vegetable and flower garden suppliers usually sell a good selection of these basic herbs. Check herb and perennial catalog descriptions if you are looking for a particular color of yarrow, or if you're interested in trying some of the more uncommon mints and scented geraniums. 'Apothecary's Rose' is a bit unusual, so don't count on finding it at a local nursery or garden center; purchase it from a mail-order supplier. You'll find addresses for some of my favorite mail-order catalogs in "Plants and Supplies" on page 262.

season 2

March, April, and May _____

| J | F | **M** | **A** | **M** | J | J | A | S | O | N | D |

Prepare the Site

Before you dig, make sure that the soil is no longer frozen, and that it's dry enough to dig without making muddy clumps. (If you prefer, you could prepare the site for this garden in fall and plant the following spring.)

When you are ready to dig, mark off the outline of the whole garden and the smaller interior beds with stakes and string or with a sprinkling of lime or flour. If you are siting the garden in a corner or along a fence or wall, leave a

12- to 18-inch path around the outside of the garden, so you can easily reach all sides of the beds for planting, maintenance, and harvesting.

If you are creating this garden out of an existing lawn area, you could leave the central walkway as a grass path. Or, for lower maintenance, replace all the grass with a wood-chip, gravel, or brick path. If you choose one of the latter options, remove all existing vegetation from the whole garden site; otherwise, just strip the grass off the individual planting areas. Test the soil to check its pH. Add lime or sulfur, if needed, to raise or lower the pH so it is around neutral (7.0).

Loosen the soil in each of the five triangular beds to a depth of 8 inches. It will probably be easiest to do this with a spading fork, since a tiller could be hard to manage in the odd-shaped beds. Then spread a 1- to 2-inch layer of compost, composted manure, or other organic material over the beds, and dig that into the top 6 inches of soil. Rake to smooth the soil surface.

Install plastic, brick, or metal edging strips around the outside of the entire garden to keep grass from creeping into the beds. If you'll have a grass path through the garden, put in edging strips along the inner sides of the individual beds as well. Install edging strips and wood-chip, gravel, or brick paths after you dig the beds but before planting.

Plant Your Herbs

Following the planting diagram on page 145, start planting in spring as soon as the soil has thawed and is dry enough to dig without clumping up. Sow the calendula seed where you want the plants to grow. It's important to keep seeded areas moist. Water lightly every day until the seedlings appear. When seedlings are a few inches tall, thin them to leave one or two plants in each spot. Snip off unwanted seedlings at ground level with scissors; pulling them out may disturb the roots of the remaining seedlings.

Set out the anise hyssop, hyssop, lavender, mint, sage, southernwood, sweet woodruff, thyme, and yarrow plants as you get them. If the plants were growing in a greenhouse when you bought them, make sure you harden them off before planting. (See "Handling Hardening Off" on page 10.) Wait until after all danger of frost has passed to plant your rosemary and scented geraniums.

Set out the rose as soon as it arrives. It will probably be bareroot (with only packing material around the roots). Remove the packing material, snip off any damaged roots, and soak the roots in a bucket of water overnight. The next day, dig a hole big enough to hold all the roots without bending them. Replace some soil in the middle of the hole to form a cone. Set the rose on top of the cone, with the roots spread out evenly over the sides of the cone. If needed, adjust the height of the cone so the crown of the rose plant (where the roots join the stem) will be even with the soil surface. Replace the soil around the roots, firm it with your hands, and water thoroughly.

Potpourri Garden

BEAUTIFUL
EASY POTPOURRI

Enjoy the aromas of your herbs all year long by capturing their scents in potpourri. It's easy to make—simply take a glass or ceramic bowl, and toss in a handful or so each of whatever dried aromatic herbs you have on hand. Don't forget to mix in some dried flower petals for color.

To make the scent last as long as possible, add a fixative—a material that prevents the aromatic oils from evaporating and holds the fragrance in the potpourri. Common fixatives include orris root, ground and dried rosemary, tonka beans, and vetiver root. They are usually available from craft stores or through mail-order craft suppliers. Essential oils, available from the same sources, are also useful. Just a few drops of these concentrated versions of natural herb scents will intensify the scent of your potpourri.

Potpourri looks pretty displayed in open bowls, but it will lose its fragrance quickly; refresh the scent as needed with a few drops of essential oil. To save your potpourri for special occasions, store it in a glass jar with a lid. Or crumble finished potpourri into little fabric bags, commonly called sachets. Hang them in your closet or lay them in a drawer to scent your clothes. Sachets also make great gifts!

1 It's a snap to make a simple sachet bag for your potpourri. Cut a piece of fabric about 10 inches long and 4 inches wide. With the right side down, fold a ½-inch flap from each end toward the wrong side of the fabric. Stitch straight across ¼ inch from the ends.

2 Fold the strip of fabric in half with the right sides together. Stitch the two raw sides ¼ inch from the edges.

3 Turn the bag so the right sides are out, fill with crumbled potpourri, and close with a ribbon bow.

season 3

June,
July, and August _____

| J | F | M | A | M | J | J | A | S | O | N | D |

Minimize Garden Chores

Mulching is a great way to reduce maintenance in your potpourri garden. It helps to keep the soil moist, so you'll need to water less often. It blocks light from reaching the soil, so fewer weed seeds will sprout, and those that do will be easier to pull out. As mulch breaks down, it will release a small but steady supply of nutrients to feed your herbs. As an added bonus, it will keep soil from splashing up on plants, so you won't have to wash harvested herbs to clean off the clinging dirt. Wait until the soil has warmed up in late spring or early summer to mulch your garden. Weed thoroughly, then spread a 1-inch layer of compost between the plants. Top that with another inch of shredded bark or chopped leaves. This double-layered mulch will provide a small but steady supply of nutrients for your plants, while also keeping the soil moist and discouraging weeds from sprouting.

If you don't get at least ½ inch of rain each week, pull away a bit of mulch and use a trowel to check the soil underneath every few days. When the top 2 to 3 inches are dry, water thoroughly to soak the soil.

Through the growing season, pinch off spent blooms of calendulas and

hyssop to promote bushier growth and more flowers. Also remove spent flowers on anise hyssop to discourage self-sowing.

Enjoy Your Herbs

You can start harvesting your herbs lightly the first summer; just don't take more than a third of the foliage the first year. The plants will be most aromatic if you gather them in early morning, just as the dew has dried off. Harvest rosemary, scented geranium, and sweet woodruff leaves any time during the growing season. Gather anise hyssop, hyssop, lavender, mint, sage, southernwood, and thyme, just as the flowers open. Collect calendulas and rose petals just before the flowers are fully open. Harvest yarrow when the flower clusters are fully colored but before they start to turn brown.

Hang leafy stems of anise hyssop, hyssop, lavender, mint, rosemary, sage, southernwood, sweet woodruff, and yarrow in bunches to dry, or strip the fresh leaves off the stems first. Place the rose and calendula petals, scented geranium leaves, and thyme sprigs on sheets of paper to dry, or lay them on a screen (such as a screen door panel) raised on bricks to allow good air circulation on all sides. A warm, dark, airy place is ideal for fast drying. When herbs are ready (they'll feel completely dry and crumble easily), you can make your potpourri, or store the ingredients in airtight containers until you need them.

Potpourri
Garden

Bring Tender Plants Indoors

In mid- to late September, dig up your scented geranium plants—and your rosemary, if you live north of Zone 8—and plant them in pots. Or, if you don't have room for the whole plants, take cuttings in late summer or early fall, and keep the rooted cuttings indoors for the winter.

Grow your indoor herbs in pots at least 4 inches in diameter. If you have the room for them, containers 6 inches across or bigger are even better. Use well-drained potting soil, such as the kinds formulated for growing cacti, or blend 1 part regular potting soil with 1 part sand and 1 part peat moss. After potting dug-up herbs, water them thoroughly and set them in a shady spot for a few days. Before bringing plants indoors, inspect them carefully for signs of insect pests. If you do notice pest problems, spray with insecticidal soap according to the directions on the label. Move potted rosemary and scented geranium plants indoors before frost.

Your indoor herbs will need at least 5 hours of direct sun each day for good growth. If you can't provide this much natural light, supplement or replace it with fluorescent lights. Hang the lights 6 to 8 inches above the tops of your herbs, and leave them on 14 to 16 hours a day. It's handy to hook your lights up to an inexpensive timer so you won't have to worry about turning the lights on and off manually every day.

Space your potted herbs so they don't touch, to allow good air circulation around their leaves. Allow the soil surface to dry out between waterings. Feed your herbs once a month with half-strength fish emulsion or seaweed extract to keep them vigorous.

If you notice signs of pest damage, such as stippled or distorted leaves, rinse the plant tops with warm water every few days. If pests continue to be a problem, you could spray with insecticidal soap, according to the label directions. Only spray herbs you don't plan to eat.

Prepare Your Garden for Winter

Toward the end of the season, leave a few calendula flowers unpicked so they can ripen and drop their seeds. After the first heavy frost, pull out the remains of the calendulas, and toss them into your compost pile. In early winter, when the ground is frozen, cut the tops of the anise hyssop, mint, sweet woodruff, and yarrow to the ground.

If you live in Zone 5 or north, it's smart to give your plants a protective winter mulch. After the ground freezes, spread several inches of loose straw over the beds, or use boughs from a Christmas tree after the holidays. These mulches will protect your perennial herbs from thawing and freezing damage.

Keeping your garden going

Once your potpourri plants are established, they'll keep getting better year after year with minimal care. In late winter, prune the rose to remove any dead wood. Each spring, after the soil thaws and your perennials begin producing new growth, remove any protective winter mulch. If you don't see any self-sown calendula seedlings by mid-spring, replant with purchased seed.

Wait until mid- to late spring to prune the remaining herbs. On the sage and thyme, cut off winter-damaged tips and trim lightly to shape the plants. Cut lavender back by about one-third. Trim the hyssop plant back to about 8 inches tall. Prune off one-half to two-thirds of the southernwood's top growth. Wait until all danger of frost has passed to set out the rosemary and scented geraniums you've over-wintered indoors.

Each year, renew the compost-and-bark or leaf mulch layers in late spring to early summer. Trim the rose lightly after flowering to shape the shrub. If the perennial herbs look crowded or begin to flower poorly, divide them in spring or fall. Replant a few of the vigorous outer sections and compost the rest.

Over time, shrubby herbs such as hyssop, lavender, sage, and thyme can develop woody stems, leaving the base of the plant looking bare. If this happens, mound 3 to 5 inches of sandy soil over the base of the stems in spring. When the stems have rooted (by fall or the next spring), dig out the old plant, and replant the rooted stems where you want new plants.

A Kitchen
Herb Garden

If you enjoy cooking with garden-fresh herbs,
you'll love this beautiful easy kitchen garden.
It's chock-full of leafy, flowering, and seed-
producing herbs to liven up all of your recipes,
from soups and salads to breads and desserts.

The key to a successful kitchen garden
is finding the right site—as close to your
house as possible. The more convenient the garden
is to reach, the more likely you are to use it.
And with a wealth of sweet and savory herbs
at your fingertips, you'll find plenty of inspiration
to turn a dish into a masterpiece!

A Kitchen Herb Garden

$\mathcal{T}$his kitchen garden is packed with edible herbs, from old friends like parsley and basil to some you may not have tried: anise, chervil, lovage, and sorrel. They'll add fabulous flavor and color to even the most ordinary meal.

158

1 Dill
2 Parsley
3 Chervil
4 Basil
5 Anise
6 Fennel
7 Tarragon
8 Sorrel
9 Thyme
10 Wild strawberry
11 Marjoram
12 Greek oregano
13 Lovage
14 Lemon balm
15 Sage
16 Caraway
17 Summer savory
18 Garlic
19 Coriander
20 Rosemary
21 Chives

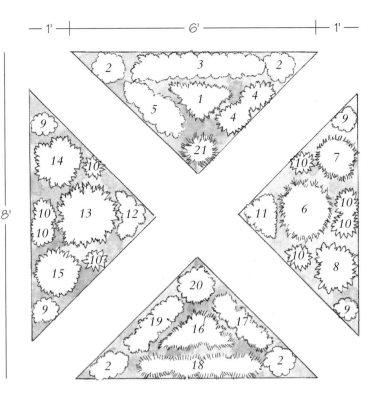

Kitchen Garden

Plants to Buy

These herbs are easiest to start from purchased plants. You'll get faster and often more reliable results.

- ❧ BASIL (2 PLANTS)
- ❧ CHIVES (1 PLANT)
- ❧ GREEK OREGANO (1 PLANT)
- ❧ LEMON BALM (1 PLANT)
- ❧ LOVAGE (1 PLANT)
- ❧ MARJORAM (1 PLANT)
- ❧ PARSLEY (4 PLANTS)
- ❧ ROSEMARY (1 PLANT)
- ❧ SAGE (1 PLANT)
- ❧ SORREL (1 PLANT)
- ❧ TARRAGON (1 PLANT)
- ❧ THYME (4 PLANTS)
- ❧ WILD STRAWBERRY (8 PLANTS)

Seeds to Buy

It's simple to raise these herbs from seed. Sow the seed directly into the garden, right where you want the plants to grow.

- ❧ ANISE (1 PACKET)
- ❧ CARAWAY (1 PACKET)
- ❧ CHERVIL (1 PACKET)
- ❧ CORIANDER (1 PACKET)
- ❧ DILL (1 PACKET)
- ❧ FENNEL (1 PACKET)
- ❧ SUMMER SAVORY (1 PACKET)

Bulbs to Buy

Purchase these bulbs as soon as they are available, and plant them right away to keep them from drying out.

- ❧ GARLIC (1 OR 2 HEADS)

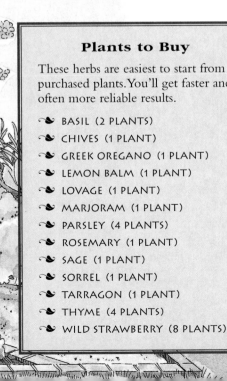

The Plant Guide

A Kitchen Herb Garden

his beautiful easy garden features a wide selection of flavorful herbs. You can use their leaves, seed, flowers, or fruits in a wide variety of delicious recipes. To include as many herbs as possible, the plan calls for only one each of most of the herbs. Even one plant can provide an ample supply of seeds, foliage, and flowers for most cooks. If you know that you're especially fond of a particular herb, however, you could always include more of that one in place of another herb you seldom or never use.

The layout of this garden is simple but elegant. It is basically a square measuring 8 feet on each side, with cross paths that divide the space into four equal-size triangles. The paths make it easy for you to reach all of your herbs without stretching far, so harvesting is a snap. If you like, you could add a feature in the middle of the garden where the paths intersect—perhaps a sundial, a birdbath, or a pretty pot filled with mint or some other herbs.

Seeds

Sow these fast-growing herbs directly in the garden in spring. They will produce generous quantities of tasty leaves and seeds for cooking. After the first year, you may not have to plant these herbs again. They will often self-sow if you allow a few flowers to ripen and drop their seeds.

ANISE
Pimpinella anisum

Anise grows in airy clumps, with lacy, licorice-scented leaves on slender stems topped with clusters of small white flowers in late summer. The flowers are followed by ridged, gray-brown seeds. Use the tender young leaves in salads; add the seeds to breads, cakes, cookies, vegetables, or eggs. Sow this tender annual herb after all danger of frost has passed; thin seedlings to stand 18 inches apart. Anise grows 12 to 18 inches tall. Buy one packet.

CARAWAY
Carum carvi

Caraway usually grows as a biennial, producing feathery leaves during the first year and seed-bearing flowers the second spring. You can use the leaves in salads, but the tangy brown seeds are the real reason to grow caraway. They are a favorite in breads, stews, and cabbage dishes. Sow in early spring, or in fall for an earlier harvest next year. Thin seedlings to stand 6 to 8 inches apart. Plants reach 1 to 2 feet tall in bloom. Buy one packet.

CHERVIL
Anthriscus cerefolium

A must for French potato salad, chervil's ferny, bright green leaves have a flavor somewhere between

Key

TEA

CRAFT

COOKING

parsley and licorice. This is one of those herbs you really need on hand for fresh use because it quickly loses its delicate flavor when dried. Sow this annual or biennial herb directly in the garden in early spring. Thin seedlings to stand about 10 inches apart. Plants grow to 2 feet tall. Buy one packet.

CORIANDER
Coriandrum sativum

The fresh green leaves of this annual herb are the secret ingredient of genuine salsa. In addition to Mexican cooking, they're an important seasoning in Indian, Chinese, and Portuguese cooking. (The fresh leaves are often called cilantro or Chinese parsley.) When the flowers mature, harvest the citrus-flavored coriander seeds for baking or for flavoring sauces and marinades. Sow outdoors in late spring. Thin seedlings to leave 6 to 8 inches between plants. Plants reach 2 to 3 feet tall in bloom. Buy one packet.

DILL
Anethum graveolens

Dill leaves, stalks, and seeds are an important flavoring in making pickled cucumbers and tomatoes. The fresh leaves also complement salmon, pasta, and potato salads. 'Dukat' produces more leaves than regular dill before flowering and setting seed. Sow seed in early to midspring. Thin seedlings to stand 6 to 8 inches apart. Plants reach 2 to 3 feet tall in bloom. Buy one packet.

FENNEL
Foeniculum vulgare

Fennel's feathery, licorice-flavored leaves are wonderful in salads, herb butters, fish dishes, and salad dressings. You can also use the stems (eat them like celery) and the seeds (add them to desserts and breads). Sow seed in spring or fall where you want the plants to grow. Thin to leave one plant. Fennel grows 3 to 5 feet tall. Zones 5 to 9. Buy one packet.

SUMMER SAVORY
Satureja hortensis

Fresh or dried, the narrow green leaves of this annual herb are a perfect complement to any bean dish. They are also great in herb butters, flavored vinegars, and chicken soup. Sow in the garden around the last frost date. (Or, for an earlier harvest, start seeds indoors four to six weeks before your last frost date.) Thin to stand 6 to 8 inches apart. Plants grow 12 to 18 inches tall. Buy one packet.

Plants

Buy plants of the following herbs, or grow your own from divisions, cuttings, or seed sown indoors in pots.

BASIL
Ocimum basilicum

Basil is an essential ingredient in French, Italian, and Thai cooking. It's a perfect partner to fresh or cooked tomatoes in salads and sauces. Try it with other vegetables, too, and with

Kitchen Garden

pasta. This annual herb is easy to grow from seed, but it is very sensitive to frost, so you'd need to start it indoors about six weeks before your last frost date. It's just as practical to buy already-started plants, since you only need a couple. Set them about 1 foot apart. They usually grow about 1 foot tall. Buy two plants.

CHIVES
Allium schoenoprasum

The mild onion-flavored foliage of this perennial herb is a great addition to almost any savory dish. In June, chives also produces pretty pink or lavender flowers that you can add to salads for both flavor and color. Chives self-sows prolifically if you don't remove the spent flowers. The plants reach 12 to 14 inches tall in bloom. Zones 3 to 9. Buy one plant.

GREEK OREGANO
Origanum heracleoticum

Greek oregano leaves have the strong flavor that's a key taste in pizza sauce. It's also a tasty addition to roasted meats. Rub and sniff the leaves before buying, so you're sure to get the aromatic, flavorful Greek oregano and not the bland common oregano. Plants usually grow about 1 foot tall. Zones 5 to 9. Buy one plant.

LEMON BALM
Melissa officinalis

Lemon balm's bright green leaves have a strong lemon scent and a citrus flavor. Add whole or chopped leaves to green salads or fruit salads. They

also taste great as a tea, either alone or blended with other herbs or black tea. The fresh leaves are most flavorful. Plants grow 1 to 2 feet tall. Zones 5 to 9. Buy one plant.

LOVAGE
Levisticum officinale

Lovage looks much like a giant celery plant, with large, long-stalked, green leaves that also taste like celery. Since lovage is much easier to grow, it's a natural substitute for celery leaves, stems, and seeds in soups, stews, and salads. Cut off the bloom stalks to encourage plants to produce more leaves and discourage self-sowing. In full bloom, lovage can reach 6 feet tall. Zones 3 to 8. Buy one plant.

MARJORAM
Origanum majorana

Marjoram, also commonly called sweet marjoram, is closely related to Greek oregano, but its leaves have a milder, sweeter flavor. Add fresh or dried marjoram to vegetables, eggs, salads, soups, herb butters, and stuffings. Marjoram is usually grown as an annual. Plants reach 1 foot tall in bloom. Buy one plant.

PARSLEY
Petroselinum crispum

The vitamin-rich leaves of this biennial herb are either frilly (in curly parsley) or flat (in flat-leaved or Italian parsley). I think the flavor of the flat-leaved type is better, but both are a welcome addition to almost any dish but desserts. For a steady supply

162

Key

TEA

CRAFT

COOKING

of top-quality leaves, treat parsley as an annual: Pull out plants at the end of the first year, and set out new ones each spring. The leafy clumps are usually 8 to 12 inches tall. Zones 5 to 9. Buy four plants.

ROSEMARY
Rosmarinus officinalis

Rosemary is one of the classic cooking herbs, prized for its pungent, needlelike leaves. The strong flavor complements roasted meats, cream sauces, marinades, eggs, cheese, and tomato dishes. The fresh flowers add color and flavor to green salads. In Zones 8 to 10, rosemary can live outdoors through the winter, and it grows as a shrub to 6 feet tall. North of Zone 8, treat it as an annual and buy a new plant each year, or bring your clump indoors for the winter. It will seldom reach more than 3 feet tall. Buy one plant.

SAGE
Salvia officinalis

Sage is a traditional favorite for stuffing and meat dishes. It is also a wonderful addition to cream sauces for pasta. Common culinary sage has gray-green leaves, but if you'd like extra color, try planting 'Purpurea', with purple-green leaves, 'Icterina', with gold-banded green leaves, or 'Tricolor', with green leaves that are splashed with cream, pink, and purple. 'Berggarten' has particularly broad silvery green leaves. Plants grow 1 to 2 feet tall. Zones 4 to 9. Buy one plant.

SORREL
Rumex acetosa

The tangy leaves of garden sorrel add zest to salads, stir-fries, and hot or cold soups. They lose flavor quickly, so wait until the last few minutes of cooking to add them. French sorrel (*R. scutatus*) is similar but has a milder flavor. Pinch off developing flower stems to encourage more leafy growth. The leafy clumps usually grow 12 to 18 inches tall. Zones 5 to 9. Buy one plant.

TARRAGON
Artemisia dracunculus

French tarragon is an essential ingredient for tarragon vinegar and Hollandaise sauce. Its licorice-flavored leaves also complement chicken dishes, salads, cream soups, and tomato sauces. Be sure to buy the tasty French tarragon rather than bitter Russian tarragon. Plants grow 2 to 3 feet tall. Zones 4 to 8. Buy one plant.

THYME
Thymus vulgaris

Common or English thyme offers aromatic, gray-green leaves that are tiny but flavorful. Add fresh or dried thyme to soups, stews, stuffings, vegetables, cheese, and egg dishes. It is also wonderful in a marinade for steak. For a variety of flavors, grow other thymes as well, such as lemon thyme (*T.* × *citriodorus*) and caraway thyme (*T. herba-barona*). Plants usually grow 6 to 12 inches tall. Zones 4 to 9. Buy four plants.

Kitchen Garden

a *garden* in your kitchen

*Y*ou don't have to give up the flavor of fresh herbs just because the calendar says it's winter! Several of the classic culinary herbs also make great houseplants.

Good choices for indoor growing include basil, chives, garlic chives, marjoram, mints, oregano, parsley, rosemary, sage, and winter savory. You could start new plants from seed or cuttings, or bring your garden plants indoors.

If you'll be bringing plants indoors, dig them up in early to midfall, so they'll have a chance to adjust to their new containers. Use pots at least 4 inches in diameter; 6 inches or bigger is better if you'll have the space for them indoors.

Use well-drained potting soil, such as the kinds formulated for growing cacti, or blend 1 part regular potting soil with 1 part sand and 1 part peat moss. Water newly potted plants thoroughly and set them in a shady spot for a few days.

Before bringing plants indoors, inspect them carefully, and spray with insecticidal soap if needed

to control any pests. Move almost all potted herbs indoors before frost. The exceptions are chives and garlic chives: Leave them outdoors through a few frosts, until the tops have died back.

Indoor herbs need at least 5 hours of direct sun each day for good growth. If you can't provide this much natural light, supplement or replace it with fluorescent lights. Hang the lights 6 to 8 inches above the tops of your herbs, and leave them on 14 to 16 hours a day. Space plants so they don't touch to allow good air circulation around the leaves.

Let the soil surface dry out between waterings. Feed your herbs once a month with half-strength fish emulsion or seaweed extract. If you notice signs of pest damage, such as stippled or distorted leaves, try rinsing the plant tops with warm water every few days. If pests continue to be a problem, discard infested herbs: You don't want to spray herbs you'll eat with any pest control.

Through the winter, simply pinch or snip off the fresh leaves as you need them, and enjoy your beautiful easy indoor herb garden!

WILD STRAWBERRY
Fragaria vesca

Also known as alpine strawberry or *fraises des bois,* wild strawberry grows in compact clumps of bright green leaves. Through summer, its small white flowers mature into the sweetest red berries you'll ever taste. Sprinkle the fruits into fruit salad or use them as a colorful and flavorful garnish for special desserts. Plants grow 6 to 10 inches tall. Zones 5 to 9. Buy eight plants, and set them 8 inches apart.

Bulbs

Purchase these bulbs from your local garden center or through a mail-order nursery catalog. Those sold in grocery stores are usually adapted for commercial production and may not grow well in your area. Each bulb or head is made up of several individual cloves.

Kitchen Garden

GARLIC
Allium sativum

Garlic tastes great in just about any dish but dessert. (There are recipes for garlic desserts, too, but I'm not ready to try one!) Add chopped raw cloves to soups, stews, and sauces, or roast them and spread the softened cloves onto bread. The fresh greens are great in pesto sauces or stir-fries. For best growth, plant in fall for harvest the following summer. Plants grow to 2 feet tall. Zones 5 to 9. Buy one or two heads to get 8 to 12 cloves.

The Seasonal Guide

A Kitchen Herb Garden

season 1

January and February

| J | F | M | A | M | J | J | A | S | O | N | D |

Select a Site

Winter is a great time to start planning your new kitchen garden, so you can have everything ready when the weather says it's time to start digging. There are two things to consider when choosing the site: the amount of sunlight and how close the site is to your house. For good growth, your herbs need at least six hours of full sun a day. You'll also need a spot as close as possible to a doorway, so it will be easy for you to dash outside and snip fresh herbs while you are cooking.

The square shape of this garden allows it to fit easily into a corner or along a wall or fence. And the attractive layout means that your kitchen herb garden can be beautiful as well as productive. Since you'll usually only be snipping a few sprigs here and there, the plants will keep their good looks through the season. If you do lots of cooking and plan to harvest heavily, consider growing extra plants of your favorite culinary herbs in your vegetable garden or another sunny, out-of-the-way spot on your property. That way, you will have all the fresh herbs you need for your special cooking projects.

Buy Seeds and Plants

Most of these herbs will be easy to find at your local nursery or garden center in spring. But if you like to be prepared ahead of time, this is a good time to place your orders with mail-order suppliers. Most vegetable and flower gardening catalogs will offer these common herbs, either as seeds or plants. It's also fun to check out herb specialty catalogs. Mail-order companies that specialize in culinary herbs and vegetables may offer special selections with flavors and colors that are particularly popular with gourmet gardeners. Catalogs that sell "heirloom" plants and seeds are also worth investigating; many of these old-time favorite herbs have long proven their worth in the kitchen as well as the garden. You'll find addresses for some of my favorite mail-order catalogs in "Plants and Supplies" on page 262.

A few of the beautiful easy culinary herbs in this garden, including basil, chives, and wild strawberry, are relatively easy to start from seed sown indoors in late winter to early spring. I've recommended buying them as plants because you only need a few of each for this garden. Sometimes it's actually less expensive to buy one plant than a whole packet of seed. But if you enjoy growing your own herb plants from seed, consider starting some of these indoors. Set the plants out after all danger of frost has passed.

season 2

*March,
April, and May*

Prepare the Site

Before grabbing your digging tools, wait until your soil is completely thawed and dry enough to dig without clumping. (If spring tends to be cold and rainy in your area, consider preparing the planting site in fall, so you'll be all ready to plant when warmer weather arrives.)

Start by outlining the 8-foot square of the garden and the cross paths with stakes and string or with a sprinkling of lime or flour. If you are creating this garden out of an existing lawn area, you could leave the paths in grass. Or, for lower maintenance, replace all the grass with wood chips, gravel, or bricks. If you choose a wood-chip, gravel, or brick path, remove all the grass from the garden site. Otherwise, just clear it off the individual planting areas.

Test the soil to check the pH. Add lime or sulfur, if needed, to raise or lower the pH so it is around neutral (7.0).

Using a spading fork, loosen the soil in each of the triangular beds to a depth of 8 inches. Then spread a 1- to 2-inch layer of compost, composted manure, or other organic material over the beds, and dig that into the top 6 inches of soil. Rake to smooth the soil surface.

Install plastic, brick, or metal edging strips around the perimeter of the entire garden to keep grass from creeping into the beds. If you'll have grass paths through the garden, put in edging strips along the inner sides of the individual beds as well. Install the edging strips and wood-chip, gravel, or brick paths after you dig the beds, but before planting.

Plant Your Herbs

Following the planting diagram on page 159, start planting in early spring. Sow the seeds of caraway, chervil, dill, and fennel where you want the plants to grow. Wait until late spring—around your last frost date—to sow anise, coriander, and summer savory. For good germination, keep seeded areas moist; water lightly every day until seedlings appear. When seedlings are a few inches tall, thin them to their recommended spacing. Snip off unwanted seedlings with scissors.

Set out the chives, Greek oregano, lemon balm, lovage, parsley, sage, sorrel, tarragon, thyme, and wild strawberry plants as you get them. If the plants were growing in a greenhouse when you bought them, harden them off before planting. (See "Handling Hardening Off" on page 10.) Wait until all danger of frost has passed to set out your basil, marjoram, and rosemary plants.

For the first year, you have two options with your garlic. One is to plant as early as possible in spring to get a crop in late summer. Or you could fill the spot with some annual herb, such as dill, until early to midfall, which is the ideal planting time for garlic.

*Kitchen
Garden*

season 3
June,
July, and August

J F M A M **J** **J** **A** S O N D

Minimize Garden Chores

Mulching is a great way to reduce maintenance in your kitchen garden. It helps to keep the soil moist, so you'll need to water less often. As an added bonus, it will keep soil from splashing up on plants, so you won't have to wash harvested herbs to remove the clinging dirt.

Wait until the soil has warmed up in late spring or early summer to mulch your garden. Weed thoroughly, then spread a 1-inch layer of compost between the plants. Top that with another inch of shredded bark or chopped leaves. If you don't get at least ½ inch of rain each week, pull away a bit of mulch and use a trowel to check the soil underneath every few days. When the top 2 to 3 inches are dry, water thoroughly to soak the soil.

Enjoy Your Herbs

You can start harvesting most of your herbs by midsummer of the first year. Pinch or snip off fresh leaves and flowers as you need them. Pick wild strawberry fruits when they are rich red all around. Dig up garlic bulbs when most of the topgrowth has turned brown.

Seeds of anise, caraway, coriander, dill, and fennel usually ripen in late summer to early fall. As soon as all the seeds have darkened (but before they drop), snip the seedheads into a paper bag, or cut the stems, tie them together, and hang them upside down over a tray or bag to catch the seeds.

168

Stretch your space by growing herbs in pots. They'll look great and be within easy reach for harvesting.

season 4

September and October

J F M A M J J A **S O** N D

Prepare Your Garden for Winter

Pull out anise, caraway, coriander, and dill plants after you've collected the seed, and toss them in your compost pile. If you live north of Zone 8, dig up your rosemary in mid- to late September, and plant it in a pot of well-drained potting soil. Or, if you don't have room for the whole plant, take cuttings in late summer or early fall. Keep the rooted cuttings indoors for the winter.

Light frost will generally blacken the basil and marjoram, but chervil, parsley, and summer savory may last through a few frosts; pull them all out before the ground freezes. In early winter, cut the topgrowth of chives, fennel, Greek oregano, lemon balm, lovage, sorrel, tarragon, and wild strawberry close to the ground.

North of Zone 6, apply a winter mulch to prevent damage from thawing and refreezing during spells of mild winter weather. Wait until the ground has frozen to mulch; otherwise, you'll invite mice, voles, and other critters to make their nests in your garden. Spread several inches of loose straw over the beds, or use boughs from a Christmas tree after the holidays. 🌀

Keeping your garden going

*E*ach spring, after the soil thaws and your perennials begin to push up their new growth, remove any protective winter mulch. Look for self-sown seedlings of anise, caraway, chervil, coriander, and dill. Replant those that don't appear by midspring.

Wait until mid- to late spring to prune the sage and thyme; cut off winter-damaged tips and trim lightly to shape the plants. Wait until all danger of frost has passed to set out the rosemary you over-wintered indoors.

In late spring to early summer, weed thoroughly and then renew the compost-and-bark or leaf mulch layers. Divide crowded perennial clumps as needed in spring or fall. Replant a few of the vigorous outer sections, and compost the rest or share them with friends.

Kitchen Garden

A Flowering Herbal Border Garden

Who says herbs have to be just plain green? Many herbs can hold their own in any flower garden with bright blooms and beautiful foliage. As an added bonus, you can harvest your handsome herbs for cooking or crafts, so they're practical as well as pretty.

This garden looks like a traditional perennial border, but it's packed with over a dozen herbs that offer either showy flowers or attractive foliage—or both. Once you see how beautiful herbs can be, you'll find many other ways to work them into your flower gardens!

A Flowering Herbal Border Garden

Create a colorful perennial garden with a mix of herbs for all-season interest. This garden is bursting with bright blooms and colorful foliage.

Seeds to Buy

It's simple to raise this herb from seed. Sow the seed directly into the garden, right where you want the plants to grow.

🌱 BRONZE FENNEL (1 PACKET)

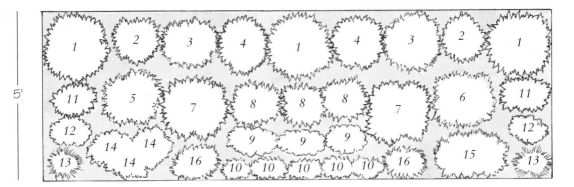

5'

1 Joe-Pye weed
2 Bee balm
3 Bronze fennel
4 Marsh mallow
5 Yarrow
6 Tansy
7 Anise hyssop
8 Purple coneflower

9 Rue
10 Lavender
11 Meadowsweet
12 Feverfew
13 Chives
14 Sage
15 Southernwood
16 Hyssop

N

Border
Garden

Plants to Buy

These herbs are easiest to start from purchased plants. You'll get faster and often more reliable results.

- ANISE HYSSOP (2 PLANTS)
- BEE BALM (2 PLANTS)
- CHIVES (2 PLANTS)
- FEVERFEW (2 PLANTS)
- HYSSOP (2 PLANTS)
- JOE-PYE WEED (3 PLANTS)
- LAVENDER (5 PLANTS)
- MARSH MALLOW (2 PLANTS)
- MEADOWSWEET (2 PLANTS)
- PURPLE CONEFLOWER (3 PLANTS)
- RUE (3 PLANTS)
- SAGE (3 PLANTS)
- SOUTHERNWOOD (1 PLANT)
- TANSY (1 PLANT)
- YARROW (1 PLANT)

The Plant Guide

A Flowering Herbal Border Garden

This garden is a great compromise for gardeners with limited space because it does double-duty as an herb garden *and* a perennial border. The herbs I've included are some of the most beautiful and easy plants you can grow for flowers and foliage. The colors are mostly in the pink, lavender, and blue range, with silver, bronze, or green leaves. White and yellow blooms add splashes of color off and on through the growing season.

The size of this flowering herb border is 15 feet long by 5 feet wide. If you don't have room for the full length, you could cut the design in half to make it 7 to 8 feet long. The border shape will fit perfectly along a fence, wall, driveway, or deck. Just be sure to leave a little space between the back of the border and the structure, so you'll be able to reach the plants in the back without stepping on loosened soil.

Seeds

Sow this fast-growing herb directly in the garden. After the first year, you may not have to plant again; bronze fennel will often self-sow.

BRONZE FENNEL
Foeniculum vulgare 'Purpureum'

Fennel's tall stems and feathery leaves make it a beautiful backdrop for more colorful flowers. Bronze fennel is particularly prized for ornamental gardens, with reddish brown leaves that turn more chocolate brown as they age. The flattened heads of tiny yellow flowers bloom in mid- to late summer and are a colorful complement to the dark foliage. In catalogs, you may see this listed under the name 'Smokey'. Sow in spring or fall. Thin seedlings to leave one plant in each spot. Plants grow 3 to 5 feet tall. Zones 5 to 9. Buy 1 packet.

Plants

Buy plants of the following herbs, or grow your own from divisions, cuttings, or seed sown indoors in pots.

ANISE HYSSOP
Agastache foeniculum

This perennial herb grows in bushy clumps, with upright, branching stems topped with spikes of lavender-blue flowers in mid- to late summer. Both the leaves and flowers are fragrant when fresh or dried, so they're a great addition to potpourri. It will self-sow prolifically, so pinch off most of the flowerheads before the small, black seeds mature and drop. Plants grow to 3 feet tall. Zones 4 to 9. Buy two plants.

BEE BALM
Monarda didyma

The summer flowers of this spreading herb are usually red, but you can also

find cultivars with pink, purple, or white blooms. 'Marshall's Delight' is a good choice for this garden because its pink flowers will complement the other colors. It also resists powdery mildew, a fungal disease that causes gray patches on leaves. In mid- to late spring, pinch out up to a half of the stems at ground level to thin out crowded clumps. Plants grow to 3 feet tall. Zones 4 to 9. Buy two plants.

CHIVES
Allium schoenoprasum

In June, this perennial herb produces pretty pink or lavender flowers that you can add to salads for both flavor and color. The clumps of grasslike green leaves are attractive all season, and they have a mild onion flavor that many cooks prize. Chives will self-sow prolifically if you don't pinch or cut off the spent flowers. Clumps reach 12 to 14 inches tall in bloom. Zones 3 to 9. Buy two plants.

FEVERFEW
Tanacetum parthenium

Feverfew may look delicate, but it's a sturdy, easy-to-grow herb that blooms from early summer to early fall. The white-petaled, yellow-centered flowers look just like tiny daisies. Pinching off the spent flowers can extend the bloom season, and it will reduce the number of self-sown seedlings. You can also cut the whole plant to the ground after bloom for a flush of new growth. Feverfew usually grows to 2 feet tall. Zones 4 to 9. Buy two plants.

HYSSOP
Hyssopus officinalis

Hyssop forms shrubby clumps of narrow, dark green, aromatic leaves. The leafy stems are topped with whorls of blue flowers from summer to early fall. You may also find 'Alba', with white flowers, or 'Rosea', with pink flowers. Regularly clipping off the flowering tips will encourage plants to produce lower, bushier growth and more flowers. Plants normally reach 2½ to 3 feet tall if unclipped. Zones 3 to 9. Buy two plants.

JOE-PYE WEED
Eupatorium purpureum

Tall Joe-Pye is the glory of the late summer garden. Its domed clusters of rosy pink to light purple flowers tower over shorter herbs, with sturdy stalks in multistemmed clumps. The flowers will attract butterflies as well as lots of attention from garden visitors. 'Atropurpureum' also offers deep purple-red stems. 'Album' has white flowers. Plants are slow to emerge in spring, so place markers by the clumps. Stems reach 6 to 8 feet tall in bloom. Zones 3 to 8. Buy three plants.

LAVENDER
Lavandula angustifolia

Lavender is as pretty to look at as it is heavenly to smell, and it keeps its distinctive fragrance when dried. In midsummer English lavender produces spikes of purple-blue flowers

Border Garden

on slender stalks over shrubby clumps of narrow, silvery leaves. 'Munstead' and 'Hidcote' are more compact, growing only 12 to 18 inches tall, with dark purple flowers. Either of these is a good choice for the front of the border. Good drainage is a must for healthy lavender. Plants vary in height. Zones 5 to 8. Buy five plants, and space them about 10 inches apart.

MARSH MALLOW
Althaea officinalis

Marsh mallow is a beautiful herb that produces attractive pink or white, hollyhock-like flowers for most of the summer. The broad, oval to heart-shaped, gray-green leaves are velvety soft. Marsh mallow grows 3 to 4 feet tall. Zones 3 to 8. Buy two plants.

MEADOWSWEET
Filipendula ulmaria

Also known as queen-of-the-meadow, this graceful perennial herb produces frothy clusters of creamy white flowers in mid- to late summer. The large, dark green leaves grow in creeping clumps; divide plants every two to three years to control their spread. Plants can reach 3 to 4 feet tall in bloom, although they may be shorter if the soil is dry. Zones 3 to 9. Buy two plants.

PURPLE CONEFLOWER
Echinacea purpurea

Purple coneflower produces clumps of sturdy stems topped with large, rosy pink, daisylike flowers with raised, orange-brown centers. Plants

bloom from midsummer into fall, especially if you snip off the dead flowers in summer. The blooms of 'Crimson Star' are a particularly deep rose-pink. You may also find cultivars with white flowers, such as 'White Swan'. Plants may self-sow. Purple coneflower grows 3 to 4 feet tall. Zones 3 to 9. Buy three plants, and space them about 18 inches apart.

RUE
Ruta graveolens

Even if it didn't bloom, rue would be worth growing for its foliage alone. The bright blue-green leaves are deeply divided, giving the whole plant a delicate, lacy look. In mid-summer, the clumps are accented with clusters of bright yellow-green flowers. Good drainage is essential for healthy growth. Plants usually reach 2 feet tall. Zones 5 to 9. Buy three plants for this garden, and space them about 1 foot apart.

SAGE
Salvia officinalis

Common culinary sage grows in shrubby clumps, with oblong, gray-green leaves accented by spikes of purple-blue flowers in mid- to late summer. 'Berggarten' has broader, more silvery leaves. If you'd like extra color, try planting 'Purpurea', with purple-green leaves, 'Icterina', with gold-banded green leaves, or 'Tricolor', with green leaves that are splashed with cream, pink, and purple. You can also find cultivars with white or pink flowers. Plants

Create an attractive edging for your border by weaving flexible young woody stems between short pegs you've pounded into the ground.

grow 1 to 2 feet tall. Zones 4 to 9. Buy three plants, and space them about 1 foot apart.

SOUTHERNWOOD
Artemisia abrotanum

Southernwood's shrubby mounds of finely cut, gray-green leaves add a unique texture to this garden. The plants do bloom in late summer, but the tiny greenish yellow flowers are barely noticeable. For a stronger silver effect, you could grow wormwood instead. Both plants are great for dried arrangements and wreaths, too. Southernwood grows to about 3 feet tall. Zones 4 to 9. Buy one plant.

TANSY
Tanacetum vulgare

Tansy's ferny, bright green foliage complements its flattened heads of buttonlike, bright yellow summer flowers. The long-lasting blooms look great in both fresh and dried bouquets. Tansy roots spread quickly, so it's smart to plant the clumps in a large, bottomless bucket sunk into the soil. You can also divide the clumps every year or two to control their spread. Tansy grows to 3 feet tall in bloom. Zones 4 to 9. Buy one plant.

YARROW
Achillea millefolium

Common yarrow produces flattened clusters of red, pink, or white flowers on slender stems clad in feathery green foliage. These summer flowers are great for fresh or dried arrangements. If you prefer yellow flowers, you could substitute another species or hybrid. Plants vary in height but are usually around 2 feet tall. Zones 3 to 8. Buy one plant.

The Seasonal Guide

A Flowering Herbal Border Garden

season 1

January and February

`J F M A M J J A S O N D`

Select a Site

Winter is a great time to start thinking about your new flowering herb border, so you'll have the site picked out when the weather is right for digging. For best growth and most prolific flowering, choose an open spot that will get at least six hours of sun a day through the growing season. This rectangular border would look great against a fence or wall or along a driveway. Average, well-drained soil will suit most of these herbs just fine.

Buy Seeds and Plants

Although your local nursery or garden center will probably carry most of these herbs for sale in spring, this is a good time to place your orders if you prefer to shop by mail. Marsh mallow is somewhat unusual, so it's smart to order ahead of time from a specialty herb catalog, so you'll be sure to have the plant when you need it. (If you can't find the plant for sale, buy the seed and sow it directly in the garden in spring.) Mail-order catalogs will likely also offer a wider selection of different herb cultivars than your local sources. Check the pictures and descriptions if you want a particular flower or leaf color. You'll find addresses for some of my favorite mail-order catalogs in "Plants and Supplies" on page 262.

season 2

March, April, and May

`J F M A M J J A S O N D`

Prepare the Site

Your soil is ready to dig when it is completely thawed and dry enough to crumble easily in your hand. If you know that your soil is slow to thaw in spring, you could prepare the site in fall, so you can plant as soon as the weather is right.

Outline the 15-foot-long, 5-foot-wide rectangle on the ground with stakes and string or with a sprinkling of lime or flour. Remove any rocks and debris, and strip off the existing vegetation with a spade or rented sod cutter. Test the soil to check the pH. Add lime

or sulfur, if needed, to raise or lower the pH so it is around neutral (7.0).

Use a spading fork or rotary tiller to loosen the top 8 inches of soil. Then spread a 1- to 2-inch layer of compost, composted manure, or other organic material over the beds, and dig that into the top 6 inches of soil. Rake to smooth the soil surface. Install plastic, brick, or metal edging strips on all sides of the border to keep grass from creeping into the garden.

Plant Your Herbs

Following the planting diagram on page 173, start planting in early spring as soon as the beds are ready. Sow the bronze fennel where you want the plants to grow; just sprinkle a few seeds in each of the two spots. Water lightly every day until the sprouts appear. When seedlings are a few inches tall, thin them to leave one or two of the strongest sprouts in each spot. Snip off unwanted seedlings at ground level with scissors; pulling them out may disturb the roots of the remaining seedlings.

Set out the other plants as you get them. If they were growing in a greenhouse when you bought them, make sure you harden them off before planting. (See "Handling Hardening Off" on page 10.) Place the potted plants on the soil according to the planting diagram. Adjust spacings as needed, then dig and plant. Water thoroughly after planting.

It's usual for perennial gardens to look a little sparse for the first year or two. Don't be tempted to simply set your plants closer together because they will quickly become a crowded mess once they fill in. If you want a fuller look right away, tuck annual herbs into the spaces between the perennials for the first few years.

For this garden, good choices for filler herbs include green or purple basil, yellow calendulas, or yellow or pink nasturtiums. Parsley—either the curly or flat-leaved type—also makes a great filler for flower gardens. Its tidy clumping habit, dark green color, and attractive foliage make it an excellent partner for more colorful flowers. Set out new plants each spring for the first year or two, until the perennials fill in.

Border Garden

PERSONALIZING YOUR BEAUTIFUL EASY HERB GARDEN

The garden designs in this chapter are a great place to start in creating your new herb gardens. But don't feel that you have to copy them exactly. Part of the fun of gardening is expressing yourself with different garden layouts and plants that fit your site, your personal preferences, and your needs.

For instance, the flowering herbal border garden in this section is designed as a rectangle. But, you could adapt it to fit along a curving fence. If you don't have room for the whole border, you could plant just a section of it. Or, if you have a large space to fill, repeat the plan to create a longer border.

Another way to customize a design is to add a path through or around the garden. Wood-chip, gravel, or grass paths are natural choices for an informal garden. Brick paths offer more solid footing and a more formal look. You can soften their formality by letting herbs spill onto the bricks.

Add a personal touch to a garden path by planting some of your favorite creeping herbs between the bricks. Lay bricks or pavers in a bed of sand rather than in mortar. Then remove a few of the bricks or blocks to create planting pockets. Fill the holes with a mix of sand and soil, then plant a variety of creeping thymes. The thymes will release their unforgettable aromas when you step on them.

season 3

June,
July, and August ——————

Minimize Garden Chores

In late spring or early summer, weed thoroughly, then spread 1 inch of compost between the plants. Top that with another inch of shredded bark or chopped leaves.

If you don't get at least ½ inch of rain each week, use a trowel to check soil dryness every few days. When the top 2 to 3 inches are dry, water thoroughly to soak the soil. While most of the herbs in this garden can withstand some drought, those along the back—especially the Joe-Pye weed, marsh mallow, and meadowsweet—will thrive with some extra moisture. You can meet their needs without soaking the rest of your herbs by running a soaker hose along the back of the border, about 1 foot in from the back edge. During dry spells, attach your garden hose to the end of the soaker hose, and let it run for a few hours until the soil is moist.

Through the growing season, pinch off spent blooms of bee balm and hyssop to promote bushier growth. Also remove spent flowers on anise hyssop, chives, and fennel to discourage self-sowing.

Enjoy Your Herbs

Unlike most herb gardens, this one is primarily for looks rather than for culinary or craft use. But you can, of course, pick the foliage and flowers for fresh bouquets or arrangements. Colorful yarrow, bee balm, feverfew, lavender, and purple coneflower will bring the beauty and fragrance of your outdoor garden into your home.

Gather herb flowers and foliage in early morning, if possible; evening is the second-best time. Use sharp pruners, scissors, or knives to cut the stems cleanly. Make your cuts just above a leaf or leaf pair. Immediately place the cut ends in a bucket of tepid water. When you bring them indoors, cut the stems' bases again, while they are still under water. Cut at a 45-degree angle to allow the stems to take up more water. Also pull or trim off any leaves that would be under the waterline in your finished arrangement.

To thoroughly condition the cut material, which will help it last as long as possible, place the containers of flowers and foliage in a basement or other cool, humid place for six to eight hours, or overnight. When you are ready to arrange them, recut the stems under water to the desired length.

For informal arrangements, you can just insert a loose mix of herb flowers and foliage in a vase, jar, or crock of water. For a more formal look, use a piece of floral foam that you've soaked in water. The foam will give you much more control over the placement of the flowers and leaves. It will also let you use a wider variety of containers, such as baskets or decorative tins; simply set the foam in a waterproof bowl or tray set inside the ornamental

Border Garden

container. Foam works best with herbs that have relatively stiff stems, such as dill and bee balm; softer stems, such as those of chives, may bend if you try to insert them into the foam.

To create a pleasing arrangement, use stems of various lengths to give depth. It helps to start with spiky flowers, such as anise hyssop, to create the outline of the arrangement. Next, fill in with more rounded flowers, such as bee balm, tansy, or yarrow. Finally, add filler materials, such as the lacy flowers of fennel.

When creating fresh arrangements, don't overlook the value of including foliage as well as flowers. In fact, you can create interesting arrangements from nothing but herb leaves, such as silvery lavender or southernwood with ferny blue rue or feathery bronze fennel. Leaves also make an excellent comple-ment to colorful flowers, contributing color and texture as well as fragrance.

Besides the leafy herbs included in this garden, check out your other herb plantings to gather foliage for your arrangements. Parsley, for instance, makes a good filler behind brightly col-ored blooms. Other useful foliage herbs include dusky purple sage, white-and-green pineapple mint, and spiky rose-mary, just to name a few.

To keep your cut flowers looking good, add a commercial preservative to the water in the arrangement container. Or make your own preservative by adding one or two drops of bleach and 1 teaspoon of sugar to each quart of water. Adding a small piece of charcoal will also help to keep the water fresh. Keep the container filled with water; add more daily, if needed.

season 4
September and October

| J | F | M | A | M | J | J | A | **S** | **O** | N | D |

Prepare Your Garden for Winter

This flowering herb border will con-tinue to look good well into fall, with the Joe-Pye weed, the last of the cone-flowers, and a few other scattered blooms. Once a few heavy frosts have called an end to the growing season, cut the tops of anise hyssop, bee balm, bronze fennel, chives, feverfew, Joe-Pye weed, marsh mallow, purple coneflower, tansy, and yarrow to the ground. Toss the tops into your compost pile.

It's smart to give your plants a protec-tive winter mulch, especially if you live north of Zone 6. After the ground has frozen, spread several inches of loose straw over the beds, or use boughs from a Christmas tree after the holidays. These mulches will protect your perennial herbs from damage caused by thawing and freezing during spells of mild winter weather.

Keeping your garden going

As the perennials fill in, this beautiful easy herb border will keep getting better each year, with just a little help from you. Each spring, after the soil thaws and your perennials begin to push their way up out of the ground, remove any winter protection.

Wait until mid- to late spring to prune the lavender, rue, and sage. Cut off winter-damaged tips and trim lightly to shape the rue and sage plants; cut the lavender back by about one-third. Trim the hyssop plant back to about 8 inches tall. Prune off one-half to two-thirds of the southernwood's top growth.

Each year, renew the compost-and-bark or leaf mulch layers in late spring to early summer. Divide perennial clumps every three to four years, or more often if they look crowded or begin to flower poorly. Replant a few of the vigorous outer sections and compost the rest, or share them with friends. Hyssop, lavender, rue, and sage plants can get spindly after a few years. Replace them every three years or so with plants you've grown from seed or cuttings.

Over time, shrubby herbs such as hyssop, lavender, rue, and sage can develop woody stems, leaving the base of the plant looking bare. If this happens, mound 3 to 5 inches of sandy soil over the base of the stems in spring. During the summer, water as needed to keep the mound moist. When the stem bases have rooted into the mound (usually by fall or the next spring), cut them off, dig out the old plant, and replant with the rooted stems.

Border Garden

An Herbal
Tea Garden

There's nothing like a hot cup of herbal tea to soothe the stresses of a long day. Besides tasting great, it's an excellent excuse to take a little break, stroll through your garden, or settle down on a comfortable bench to admire the beauty and fragrance of your herbs close up.

Whether you prefer the tangy taste of rose hips, the refreshing zing of peppermint, the spicy flavor of sage, or the mild, fruity flavor of chamomile, you can find all the fixings you need for the perfect pot of herbal tea in this beautiful easy garden.

An Herbal Tea Garden

Treat yourself to a cup of tea from your homegrown herbs! Take it out to the garden, so you can enjoy the beauty of your herbs as well as their flavors. Many herb teas are good for you as well as good-tasting. Enjoy!

Plants to Buy

These herbs are easiest to start from purchased plants. You'll get faster and often more reliable results.

- ANISE HYSSOP (1 PLANT)
- BEE BALM (1 PLANT)
- CATNIP (1 PLANT)
- HOREHOUND (2 PLANTS)
- HYSSOP (1 PLANT)
- LEMON BALM (3 PLANTS)
- MINT (4 PLANTS)
- ROMAN CHAMOMILE (4 PLANTS)
- RUGOSA ROSE (1 PLANT)
- SAGE (1 PLANT)
- SCENTED GERANIUM (2 PLANTS)
- THYME (6 PLANTS)
- WILD STRAWBERRY (2 PLANTS)

1 *Rugosa rose*
2 *Bee balm*
3 *Catnip*
4 *Roman chamomile*
5 *Wild strawberry*
6 *Scented geranium*
7 *Hyssop*
8 *Anise hyssop*
9 *Lemon balm*
10 *Mint*
11 *Horehound*
12 *Sage*
13 *Thyme*

N

10'

5'

2'

Tea Garden

Bench

ROCK

The Plant Guide

An Herbal Tea Garden

This garden includes a wide variety of great tea herbs, prized for their leaves, flowers, or fruits. With this selection at your fingertips, you can blend an herbal brew to suit any mood. Base your tea on just one herb to enjoy the full flavor, or blend several mild-flavored herbs for a special treat. If you enjoy a stronger flavor, blend one or more of your favorite herbs with black tea for a potent brew.

This garden offers a somewhat unusual layout—basically a 10-foot-diameter circle with a central path. Except for the scented geraniums, these herbs are all perennials, so you'll enjoy the beauty and bounty of your herbal tea garden for years to come. And as you'd expect in a book on beautiful easy herbs, they'll need minimal care.

Plants

Buy plants of the following herbs, or grow your own from divisions, cuttings, or seed sown indoors in pots.

ANISE HYSSOP
Agastache foeniculum

This pretty perennial herb grows in bushy clumps, with upright, branching stems topped with spikes of lavender-blue flowers in mid- to late summer. The fresh or dried leaves and flowers make a mild, lightly sweet tea with a light licorice flavor. Anise hyssop will self-sow prolifically, so pinch off most of the flowerheads before the small black seeds mature and drop. Plants grow to 3 feet tall. Zones 4 to 9. Buy one plant.

BEE BALM
Monarda didyma

The aromatic leaves of this spreading perennial are old-time favorites for making a pleasant citrus-flavored tea. In fact, bee balm was once used by colonists as a substitute for the

Anise hyssop, mints, and other tea herbs are beautiful and fragrant, so you'll enjoy them in the garden as well as in your tea!

Key

TEA

CRAFT

COOKING

British-taxed black tea. Red flowers are most common, but cultivars with pink, purple, or white flowers are also available. In mid- to late spring, pinch out up to half of the stems at ground level to thin out crowded clumps. Plants grow to 3 feet tall. Zones 4 to 9. Buy one plant.

CATNIP
Nepeta cataria

Catnip forms fast-spreading clumps of fuzzy, green foliage and brushy spikes of small white to pinkish flowers. Its minty leaves make a soothing tea that can be useful for relieving coughs, especially when sweetened with a bit of honey. Plants will spread quickly, so divide them each spring and replant just a few sections, or grow them in bottomless pots sunk into the soil. Catnip grows to 3 feet tall. Buy one plant.

HOREHOUND
Marrubium vulgare

Horehound drops, the old-fashioned candy used to soothe coughs and sore throats, are made from the soft gray leaves of this perennial herb. You can make a throat- and cough-soothing tea from the fresh or dried leaves; sweeten it with honey to taste. Horehound grows quickly from transplants, but it's also easy to raise from seed sown either indoors or directly in the garden in early spring. In fact, plants will often self-sow if you don't harvest the tops before flowering. Horehound grows 2 to 3 feet tall. Zones 4 to 9. Buy two plants.

HYSSOP
Hyssopus officinalis

Hyssop forms shrubby clumps of narrow, dark green, aromatic leaves with blue flowers from summer to early fall. The fresh or dried leaves make a rather strong-flavored tea that can help quiet coughs. Mixing hyssop with other herbs or with sugar and lemon will improve the flavor. Plants normally reach 2½ to 3 feet tall. Zones 3 to 9. Buy one plant.

LEMON BALM
Melissa officinalis

Lemon balm's bright green leaves have a strong lemon scent and a pleasant citrus flavor. They taste great as a tea, either alone or blended with other herbs or black tea. The fresh leaves are most flavorful. Cut stems close to the ground when plants begin to bloom to encourage a flush of new leafy growth. Plants grow 1 to 2 feet tall. Zones 5 to 9. Buy three plants, and space them 12 to 18 inches apart.

MINTS
Mentha spp.

Mints come in dozens of different scents and flavors, from apple and grapefruit to the more familiar peppermint and spearmint. Try a few different kinds to see which you like best. Peppermint is a traditional favorite for a stomach-soothing hot tea; it also holds its flavor well as an iced tea. All mints can spread vigorously, especially in moist soil, so plant

If you plan to hang your herbs for drying, gather them into small bundles as you harvest. This will save you time later on and reduce the chance of damaging the herbs by repeated handling.

them in a bottomless pot or bucket sunk into the soil. Different mints vary in height, but they usually reach about 2 feet tall. Zones 5 to 9. Buy four plants, and space them 12 to 18 inches apart.

ROMAN CHAMOMILE
Chamaemelum nobile

Roman chamomile is a low-growing perennial herb with small, daisylike white flowers over carpets of ferny, bright green, sweetly scented leaves. The fresh or dried flowers make a mild, lightly fruity, calming tea. Annual German chamomile can be used the same way. If you are sensitive to the pollen of ragweed or other chrysanthemum relatives, however, use caution when drinking

chamomile tea; it may cause an allergic reaction. Plants grow to about 6 inches tall. Zones 3 to 8. Buy four plants, and plant them in two groups, spaced 1 foot apart within the pairs.

RUGOSA ROSE
Rosa rugosa

This cold-hardy shrub rose produces fragrant pink, red, or white flowers, with a large flush of bloom in early summer and continued scattered bloom into fall. The flowers are followed by large, red fruits (called hips) that are high in vitamin C. These hips make a tangy tea. Rugosa rose doesn't need much pruning—just a little light trimming after bloom to shape the plant. A mature plant will reach 4 to 5 feet tall. Zones 3 to 8. Buy one plant.

Key

TEA

CRAFT

COOKING

SAGE
Salvia officinalis

The fresh or dried leaves of culinary sage make a warming, aromatic tea that can soothe upset stomachs and sore throats. Common sage has gray-green leaves, but if you'd like extra color, try planting 'Purpurea', with purple-green leaves. Plants grow 1 to 2 feet tall. Zones 4 to 9. Buy one plant.

SCENTED GERANIUMS
Pelargonium spp.

Scented geraniums come in dozens of leaf forms and fragrances, including apple, coconut, ginger, lemon, peppermint, and rose—just to name a few! Some of them, including rose and peppermint, make pleasant teas.

Gather rose hips for drying when they are plump and fully colored. Snip them off the plant with sharp pruning shears, and lay the hips on a screen to dry.

You can also use the leaves to make flavored sugars to sweeten other herbal teas; see "Scented Geraniums" on page 63 for instructions. Scented geraniums are only hardy outdoors in frost-free regions, but you can grow them anywhere as annuals. They also make wonderful houseplants. Heights vary, depending on the species and cultivar. Buy two plants.

THYMES
Thymus spp.

Although these aromatic herbs are most commonly used for cooking, the fresh or dried leaves and flowering tops are also useful for tea. Common or English thyme (*T. vulgaris*) makes a warm, pungent tea that can help quiet a cough or soothe an upset stomach. Lemon thyme *(T. × citriodorus)* has a citrus flavor. Bushy types grow 6 to 12 inches tall; creeping types may only be 1 to 2 inches tall. Zones 4 to 9. Buy six plants, and space them 6 to 12 inches apart.

WILD STRAWBERRY
Fragaria vesca

Also known as alpine strawberry or *fraises des bois*, wild strawberry grows in compact clumps of bright green leaves. Through summer, its small white flowers mature into the sweetest red berries you'll ever taste. You can also dry the leaves for a mild, soothing tea. Plants grow 6 to 10 inches tall. Zones 5 to 9. Buy two plants.

The Seasonal Guide

An Herbal Tea Garden

season 1

January and February _____

J	F	M	A	M	J	J	A	S	O	N	D

Select a Site

Winter is a great time to stake out a site for your herbal tea garden, so you'll be ready to dig and plant when spring arrives. You'll need an area big enough for a 10-foot-diameter circle. Look for a spot that gets at least six hours of sun a day during the growing season. Average, well-drained soil will be just fine for these herbs. This garden is pretty enough to look good in a highly visible part of your yard.

Buy Plants

You'll be able to find most, if not all, of these tea herbs at your local nursery or garden center in spring. But if you like to plan ahead, or if you want to be sure you'll get a particular leaf or flower color, this is a good time to sit down with your favorite mail-order catalogs. Most flower and vegetable gardening catalogs will sell a good selection of these herbs, but it's fun to branch out and look at herb specialty catalogs, too. If you are searching for a specific cultivar of bee balm or rugosa rose, look for mail-order suppliers that specialize in perennials and shrubs. You'll find addresses for some of my favorite mail-order catalogs in "Plants and Supplies" on page 262.

season 2

March, April, and May _____

J	F	M	A	M	J	J	A	S	O	N	D

Prepare the Site

Before grabbing your spade, wait until your soil is completely thawed and dry enough to dig without turning into muddy clumps. If you want to get an extra-early start in the spring, you could instead prepare the site in fall, so everything will be ready for planting as soon as warmer weather returns.

To draw the outline of the 10-foot-diameter circle, insert a sturdy stake in the center of the site. Tie one end of a rope to the stake, then measure out 5 feet of rope from the stake. Holding the free end of the rope taut, walk around the circle and outline the garden with a sprinkling of lime or flour. To mark off

Every tea garden needs a bench, a cozy spot where you can sit and enjoy your home-brewed herbal tea.

the central path, draw a line across the center of the circle. On one side of the line, draw a parallel line 2 feet away. On the other side of the line, outline a rectangle about 2 feet deep and 3 feet wide to create a spot for the bench.

If you are creating this garden out of an existing lawn area, you could leave the central path and bench area in grass. Or, for lower maintenance, replace all the grass with wood chips, gravel, or bricks. If you choose a wood-chip, gravel, or brick path, use a spade to remove all the grass from the garden site; otherwise, just clear it off the individual planting areas.

Test the soil to check the pH. Add lime or sulfur, if needed, to adjust the pH so it is around neutral (7.0).

Use a spading fork or rotary tiller to loosen the top 8 inches of soil in each planting area. Then spread a 1- to 2-inch layer of compost or other organic material over the beds, and dig that into the top 6 inches of soil. Rake to smooth the soil surface. Install plastic, brick, or metal edging strips around the outside of the circle to keep grass from creeping into the garden. If you're leaving the central path and bench area in grass, also outline them with edging strips.

Add three stepping stones: one on either side of the bench area and one in the center of the bed in front of the bench area. And don't forget to add a bench—roughly 18 inches wide and 2 feet long—either at this point, or after planting. (If your bench has different dimensions, adjust the size of the bench area accordingly.)

BREWING HERBAL TEA

To brew the perfect pot of tea, just follow these few simple steps.

1 Bring a kettle of fresh, cool water to a rolling boil.

2 Pour a half cup or so of the water into a nonmetal teapot (such as china or earthenware). Swirl the water around to rinse and warm the pot; dump it out.

3 Add 1 tablespoon of fresh or 1 teaspoon of dried herbs for each cup you'll be serving, along with 1 extra tablespoon of fresh or 1 extra teaspoon of dried herbs "for the pot."

4 Pour the boiling water over the herbs. Cover and let steep for about five minutes.

5 Taste to check the strength frequently, until the flavor is pleasing to you; let it sit longer, if needed. Then strain out the herbs. Serve with sugar, honey, and lemon or orange slices, as desired.

Iced herbal tea is just as easy. Follow the above steps, but use 2 tablespoons of fresh or 2 teaspoons of dried herbs for each cup of water. Chill before serving.

Hot or iced, herbal teas are worth drinking for their flavor alone. Several of the tea herbs featured in this garden also offer medicinal properties, such as quieting coughs or soothing upset stomachs. These herbs are generally considered safe for otherwise healthy, nonpregnant, non-nursing women, so you can enjoy a cup or two as you wish. To be on the safe side, however, don't rely on home-brewed herbal teas to cure chronic problems. Always consult your doctor first, and discontinue use if you notice any side effects.

Plant Your Herbs

Following the planting diagram on page 187, start planting in spring as soon as the soil has thawed and is dry enough to dig without clumping. Set out the anise hyssop, bee balm, catnip, horehound, hyssop, lemon balm, mint, Roman chamomile, sage, thyme, and wild strawberry plants as you get them. If the plants were growing in a greenhouse when you bought them, make sure you harden them off before planting. (See "Handling Hardening Off" on page 10.) If you don't plan to divide your catnip and mint plants every year or two, control their spread by planting them in bottomless pots or buckets sunk into the soil. Leave the top inch of the containers above the soil level to discourage roots from sneaking out over the top.

Also set out your rose as soon as you get it. If it is growing in a container, plant it as you would the perennials. If you bought it by mail, it will probably be bareroot (with only packing material around the roots). Remove the packing material, snip off any damaged roots, and soak the roots in a bucket of water overnight. The next day, dig a hole big enough to hold all the roots without bending them. Replace some soil in the middle of the hole to form a cone. Set the rose on top of the cone, with the roots spread out evenly over the sides of the cone. If needed, adjust the height of the cone so the crown (where the roots join the stem) will be even with the soil surface. Replace the soil around the roots, and water thoroughly.

Wait until after all danger of frost has passed to plant scented geraniums.

*Tea
Garden*

season 3
*June,
July, and August*

J	F	M	A	M	J	J	A	S	O	N	D

Minimize Garden Chores

Mulching is a great way to minimize maintenance in your herbal tea garden. It helps to keep the soil moist, so you'll water less often. It blocks light from reaching the soil, so fewer weed seeds will sprout. As it breaks down, it will release a small but steady supply of nutri-ents to feed your herbs. As an added bonus, it will keep soil from splashing up on plants, so you won't have to wash harvested herbs to remove the clinging dirt.

Wait until the soil has warmed up in late spring or early summer to mulch your garden. Weed thoroughly, then spread a 1-inch layer of compost between the plants. Top that with another inch of shredded bark or chopped leaves. If you don't get at least 1/2 inch of rain each week, pull away a bit of mulch, and use a trowel to check the soil underneath every few days. When the top 2 to 3 inches are dry, water thoroughly to soak the soil.

Enjoy Your Herbs

You can harvest lightly from your tea herbs the first summer; just don't take more than a third of the foliage the first year. To get the best flavor, gather them in early morning, just as the dew has dried off. For fresh use, pick the leaves and flowers as needed. For drying, gather bee balm, horehound, hyssop, lemon balm, mint, sage, and scented geraniums just before the flowers open. Harvest Roman chamomile blooms and thyme sprigs just as the flowers open fully. Gather anise hyssop and catnip in mid- to late summer, when the plants are in full bloom. Pick strawberry leaves in early summer for drying; gather the fruits when they are all red for fresh use. Wait until fall to gather ripe rose hips for drying.

Hang leafy stems of anise hyssop, catnip, horehound, hyssop, mint, and sage in bunches to dry, or strip the fresh leaves off the stems first. Place bee balm and lemon balm leaves, Roman chamomile flowers, rose hips, scented geranium and strawberry leaves, and thyme sprigs on a screen (such as a screen door panel). Raise the screen on bricks to allow good air circulation on all sides. A warm, dark, airy place is ideal for fast drying. You can also dry herbs in a microwave; refer to "Easy Microwave Drying" on page 79. When herbs feel completely dry—after a week or two— store them in airtight containers.

season 4
September and October

| J | F | M | A | M | J | J | A | **S** | **O** | N | D |

Prepare Your Garden for Winter

In mid- to late September, dig and pot up your scented geraniums. Or, if you don't have room for the whole plants, take cuttings in late summer or early fall, and keep the rooted cuttings indoors for the winter.

In early winter, when the ground is frozen, cut the tops of anise hyssop, bee balm, catnip, horehound, lemon balm, mint, and wild strawberry to the ground. Toss the clippings into your compost pile.

After the ground is frozen, consider giving your garden a protective winter mulch, especially if you live north of Zone 6. Spread several inches of loose straw over the beds, or use boughs from a Christmas tree after the holidays. These mulches will protect your perennial herbs from damage caused by thawing and freezing during spells of mild winter weather.

Keeping your garden going

*T*his beautiful easy tea garden is based on dependable perennial herbs, so it will look good for years with minimal care. In late winter, prune the rose to remove any dead wood. Each spring, after the soil thaws and your perennials begin to nudge their way up out of the ground, remove any winter mulches.

Wait until mid- to late spring to prune the remaining woody-stemmed herbs. On the sage and thyme, cut off winter-damaged tips, and trim lightly to shape the plants. Trim the hyssop plant back to about 8 inches tall. Wait until all danger of frost has passed to set out the scented geraniums you've overwintered indoors.

Each year, renew the compost-and-bark or leaf mulch layers in late spring to early summer.

Trim the rose lightly after flowering to shape the shrub. If your perennial herbs look crowded or begin to flower poorly, divide them in spring or fall. Replant a few of the vigorous outer sections and compost the rest, or share with friends.

Over time, shrubby herbs such as hyssop, sage, and thyme can develop woody stems, leaving the base of the plant looking bare. If this happens, mound 3 to 5 inches of sandy soil over the base of the stems in spring. During the summer, water as needed to keep the mound moist. If heavy rain washes the mound away, add more soil to keep the stem bases covered. When the stem bases have rooted into the mound (usually by fall or the next spring), cut them off, dig out the old plant, and replant with the rooted stems.

Container
Herb Gardens

You don't need a large garden to enjoy
the flavor and fragrance of homegrown herbs.
Many beautiful easy herbs adapt well to
life in containers, so you can grow a variety
of herbs in a small space.

Use potted herbs as you would other
container plants—to brighten a balcony, decorate
a deck, or perk up a porch. They'll need a bit more
care than their garden counterparts to stay in top
shape. But once you experience the charm
and convenience of container herb gardens,
you'll never want to be without them.

Container
Herb Gardens

A collection of container herbs will keep flavor and fragrance at your fingertips all season long.

Seeds to Buy

It's simple to raise this herb from seed. Sow the seed directly into the container, right where you want the plants to grow.

🌶 NASTURTIUM (1 PACKET)

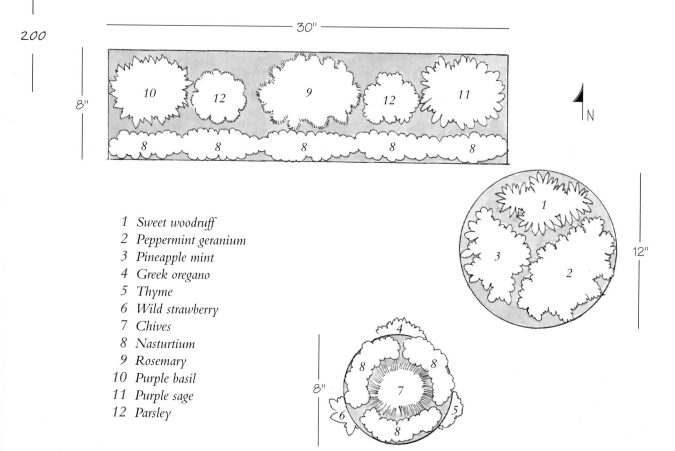

1 Sweet woodruff
2 Peppermint geranium
3 Pineapple mint
4 Greek oregano
5 Thyme
6 Wild strawberry
7 Chives
8 Nasturtium
9 Rosemary
10 Purple basil
11 Purple sage
12 Parsley

Plants to Buy

These herbs are easiest to start from purchased plants.

- ❧ CHIVES (1 PLANT)
- ❧ GREEK OREGANO (1 PLANT)
- ❧ PARSLEY (2 PLANTS)
- ❧ PEPPERMINT GERANIUM (1 PLANT)
- ❧ PINEAPPLE MINT (1 PLANT)
- ❧ PURPLE BASIL (1 PLANT)
- ❧ PURPLE SAGE (1 PLANT)
- ❧ ROSEMARY (1 PLANT)
- ❧ THYME (1 PLANT)
- ❧ WILD STRAWBERRY (1 PLANT)
- ❧ SWEET WOODRUFF (1 PLANT)

Container Gardens

The Plant Guide

The possible combinations of container herb plantings are practically unlimited. The only real key to good-looking pots and planters is combining herbs with different heights, habits, and leaf shapes and colors so the plants look good together all season—even when they're not in flower. Of course, you'll also want to group herbs that share similar light and moisture needs. But beyond that, you can simply rely on your own creativity.

To get you started, this section includes instructions for three different container herb gardens. The first garden is a simple but beautiful hanging basket with a mix of fragrant and colorful cascading herbs. The second is a strawberry pot—a terracotta container with planting pockets on the sides as well as the top. This kind of container is a traditional favorite for growing compact herbs, such as thymes. And the third garden is a windowbox planting, with a variety of herbs that are both attractive and tasty.

Seeds

Sow this fast-growing annual directly in the pots after planting your other herbs.

NASTURTIUM
Tropaeolum majus

Nasturtiums do double duty in container gardens, producing unusual circular leaves and brightly colored flowers, both of which are edible as well as eye-catching. Plants bloom from midsummer to frost, in white or shades of red, pink, orange, and yellow. The fresh leaves have a peppery flavor that spices up salads, and the flowers make a great garnish. Look for the vining types if you want them to cascade over the edge of your container. Bush types grow to about 10 inches tall in pots. Vining types may trail several feet, but pinching will keep them shorter and fuller. Buy one packet.

Plants

Buy plants of the following herbs, or grow your own from divisions, cuttings, or seed sown indoors in pots.

Containers are a great way to control spreading herbs like this variegated lemon balm (Melissa officinalis 'Variegata').

Key

TEA

CRAFT

COOKING

CHIVES
Allium schoenoprasum

Chives grows in grasslike clumps, with mild onion-flavored foliage that's a great addition to almost any savory dish. In early summer, this perennial herb also produces pretty pink or lavender flowers; add them to salads for both flavor and color. Pick fresh flowers and leaves as needed; cut them off 1 or 2 inches above the base. Clumps usually grow 1 foot tall in pots. Zones 3 to 9. Buy one plant.

GREEK OREGANO
Origanum heracleoticum

Greek oregano leaves have the strong flavor that's a key flavor in pizza sauce. It's also a tasty addition to roasted meats. Rub and sniff the leaves before buying, so you're sure to get the aromatic, flavorful Greek oregano and not the bland common oregano. Pinch off leaves as needed for fresh use. Plants usually grow about 1 foot tall. Zones 5 to 9. Buy one plant.

PARSLEY
Petroselinum crispum

Parsley's neat clumping habit and dark green foliage make it an excellent filler for container plantings. The vitamin-rich leaves of this biennial herb are either frilly (in curly parsley) or flat (in flat-leaved or Italian parsley). Both are a welcome addition to almost any dish but desserts. The leafy clumps are usually 8 to 12 inches tall. Buy two plants.

PEPPERMINT GERANIUM
Pelargonium tomentosum

The broad, fuzzy leaves of peppermint geranium just beg to be petted. And when you rub the soft, velvety foliage, you'll release the refreshing peppermint scent. The trailing habit of this plant makes it a perfect choice for hanging baskets. Scented geraniums are only hardy outdoors in frost-free regions, but you can grow them anywhere as annuals. They also make wonderful houseplants. Peppermint geranium usually only grows 1 foot tall but can trail 2 feet or more. Buy one plant.

PINEAPPLE MINT
Mentha suaveolens 'Variegata'

Pineapple mint is a particularly pretty choice for containers, with fruity mint-scented, light green leaves prominently edged in white. The main stems tend to sprawl or cascade, but they send up vertical sideshoots that give the plant a bushy, full look. Pinch back overly long or straggly-looking shoots to promote branching. In a basket, pineapple mint will probably grow 8 to 10 inches tall. Zones 5 to 9. Buy one plant.

PURPLE BASIL
Ocimum basilicum cultivar

This annual herb is a classic ingredient in Italian, French, and Thai cooking. But it's pretty as well as useful, especially if you plant the kinds with dark purple leaves. Try

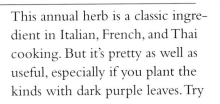

Container Gardens

'Red Rubin' or 'Dark Opal', with smooth leaves, or 'Purple Ruffles', with crinkled leaves. This annual herb is very sensitive to frost, so wait until all danger of frost has passed before setting it out. Plants grow 12 to 18 inches tall. Buy one plant.

PURPLE SAGE
Salvia officinalis 'Purpurea'

Common culinary sage grows in shrubby clumps of oblong, aromatic leaves, accented by spikes of purple-blue flowers in mid- to late summer. 'Purpurea', with purplish green leaves, looks especially good in a container with purple basil. Use the fresh or dried leaves of either kind to liven up stuffing or roasted meats. Plants grow about 1 foot tall. Zones 4 to 9. Buy one plant.

ROSEMARY
Rosmarinus officinalis

Rosemary is one of the classic cooking herbs, prized for its pungent, needlelike leaves. The fresh flowers also add color and flavor to green salads. North of Zone 8, treat it as an annual, and buy a new plant each year or bring your potted clump indoors for the winter. It will seldom reach more than 1 to 2 feet tall in a container. Buy one plant.

THYMES
Thymus spp.

Thymes are a great choice for container gardens because they have a compact, shrubby, or creeping habit. You can also use their aromatic leaves for cooking or potpourri. Common or English thyme (*T. vulgaris*) has a bushy form, with a piny, woodsy fragrance. Lemon thyme *(T. × citriodorus)* has a citrus scent and flavor. Creeping thymes, such as mother-of-thyme (*T. serpyllum*), look great cascading over the edge of a pot or planter. Choose any of these or one of the dozens of other kinds for your strawberry jar. Most thymes grow 6 to 12 inches tall. Zones 4 to 9. Buy one plant.

WILD STRAWBERRY
Fragaria vesca

Also known as alpine strawberry or *fraises des bois,* wild strawberry grows in compact clumps of bright green leaves. Through summer, its small white flowers mature into the sweetest red berries you'll ever taste. Sprinkle the fruits into fruit salad or use them as a garnish for special desserts. Plants grow 6 to 10 inches tall. Zones 5 to 9. Buy one plant.

SWEET WOODRUFF
Galium odoratum

Sweet woodruff has a creeping, sprawling habit that's shown off beautifully in a hanging basket. All season long, you'll admire the bright green new leaves against the darker green older foliage. The small, white, late spring flowers are an added bonus. To keep plants looking good, pinch off straggly shoots; dry these pieces and add them to potpourri. (They release a sweet scent when dried.) Plants grow about 8 inches tall. Zones 4 to 8. Buy one plant.

Key

TEA

CRAFT

COOKING

The Seasonal Guide

Container Herb Gardens

season 1

January and February _____

| J | F | M | A | M | J | J | A | S | O | N | D |

Choose Your Containers

To recreate this exact garden, you'll need three containers: a hanging basket, a strawberry jar, and a windowbox. Buy a hanging basket with a 12-inch diameter across the top. Look for a strawberry jar 12 to 18 inches tall, with a top opening about 8 inches across and three side pockets. For the windowbox, choose a plastic or fiberglass planter about 30 inches long, 8 inches wide, and 6 to 8 inches deep. For display, you

could slip this liner into a more decorative wooden windowbox. Make sure your windowbox planter has drainage holes in the bottom.

Buy Seeds and Plants

Most, if not all, of these herbs will be easy to find at your local nursery or garden center in spring. But if you want to plan ahead, winter is a good time to pre-order your container herb plants and seeds from mail-order catalogs. The one exception is purple basil: Unless you will be growing your own plant from seed, wait until late spring to buy this from a local garden center. You'll find addresses for some of my favorite mail-order catalogs in "Plants and Supplies" on page 262.

Container Gardens

season 2

March, April, and May _____

| J | F | M | A | M | J | J | A | S | O | N | D |

Prepare the Containers

Wait until mid- to late spring, around the time of your last frost date, to prepare and plant your containers. Make a planting mix by mixing equal parts pot-

ting soil and compost in a large tub or wheelbarrow. Add 1 to 2 cups of natural organic fertilizer for each container you will be planting, and stir to blend well. This mixture will be loose enough to hold ample moisture while letting the excess drain away. It will also supply nutrients to feed your plants through the season.

Add water and knead it into the mixture until the mix feels evenly moist, but not wet. (When you squeeze a handful,

TRAINING AN HERB TREE

If you're looking for something special to accent your porch or patio garden, why not try your hand at training an herb "tree"? It's easy to do, and the results look fantastic.

An herb tree, also known as a standard, is a simple type of topiary. Standards have a single stem or trunk topped with a round head of clipped foliage.

To train your own standard, simply follow the steps below I've chosen rosemary for this example, but many other woody or thick-stemmed herbs also work well, including hyssop, lavender, myrtle, and scented geraniums.

1 Choose a young, single-stemmed, unbranched rosemary plant. Plant it in a 4-inch pot. Insert a thin wooden or bamboo stake next to the plant. Clip off the top of the stake where you want the middle of the finished top to be.

2 As the stem grows, loosely tie it to the stake at 4-inch intervals with soft string or plastic-coated wire ties. Pinch off sideshoots as they form along the trunk of the standard. (Leave the foliage that's growing directly from the stem.) When the shoot top gets near where you want the head to be, pinch the upper sideshoots to promote branching. Don't pinch out the tip of the main shoot until it is about 1 inch below the desired height.

3 Keep pinching out the tips of the upper sideshoots as needed to develop a dense, leafy head. Once the top is bushy, you can pinch or cut off the leaves growing from the main stem to expose the trunk. Trim your standard as needed once or twice a season to keep the desired shape. Check the ties every few months, and loosen them if needed to keep them from cutting into the trunk.

A collection of potted herbs will spice up your steps. For seasonal color, add a few pots of flowering annuals or perennials.

it should stick together lightly, but you shouldn't be able to squeeze out the water.) Fill the basket and windowbox with the moist mix to within 1 inch of the rim. Fill the strawberry jar up to the level of the lowest opening.

Plant Your Herbs

If your herbs were growing in a greenhouse when you bought them, make sure you harden them off before planting. (See "Handling Hardening Off" on page 10.) Water them thoroughly so their soil is completely moist. To remove them from their containers, slide one hand over the top of the pot, with the stems between your fingers. Turn the pot over so it is resting on your hand, then use your other hand to pull off the pot. Use your fingers to loosen any matted or circling roots, then set the plant in place, according to the planting diagrams on page 200.

Hanging Basket: Plant the peppermint geranium, pineapple mint, and sweet woodruff at evenly spaced intervals around the basket. Set the plants near the middle, so the center of the basket will still look full when your herbs start to trail outward. For each herb, scoop out a handful or two of mix, then set in the plant. Adjust the depth of the hole so the top of the rootball is about 1 inch below the rim of the basket. When you have placed all three herbs, add or remove mix as needed so the final surface is 1 inch below the basket rim. Water thoroughly until water starts to run out of the bottom.

Strawberry Jar: A finished strawberry jar can be pretty heavy, so it's best to plant it in its permanent location. A sunny spot—with at least six hours of sun a day—is ideal.

Choose the Greek oregano, thyme, or wild strawberry for the lowest pocket.

Slide the roots of the chosen herb into the pocket from the outside, so the rootball is resting on the potting mix. Add more mix to the container, up to the level of the next pocket. Repeat the planting and filling process until you've planted all the side pockets. Then add more mix, to within 1 inch of the rim of the top opening. Push aside or scoop out a handful of mix, and set the clump of chives in the center. Fill in again with mix so the top is 1 inch below the rim. Plant two or three nasturtium seeds in each of three spots evenly spaced around the chives. Water thoroughly but gently to avoid washing mix out of the pockets.

Once the seeds have sprouted, thin the seedlings to leave one plant in each of the three spots. Snip off the unwanted seedlings with scissors; pulling them out may damage the remaining plants.

Windowbox: Scoop out a handful or two of mix to make room for the rosemary in the middle of the back half of the box. Adjust the depth of the hole so the top of the rootball is about 1 inch below the box rim, then fill in around the roots with mix. Use the same technique to plant the basil and sage at the ends and the parsley between the ends and the rosemary. Add or remove mix as needed so the final level is 1 inch below the box rim. Then sow nasturtium seeds in a row along the front of the box, 2 to 3 inches back from the front edge. Space the seeds about 3 inches apart and about 1 inch deep. Water thoroughly until water starts to run out of the drainage holes.

Set your planter in its holder, sited in a spot with at least six hours of full sun a day. When the seedlings emerge, thin them out to leave five plants evenly spaced along the front half of the box.

season 3

June, July, and August

| J | F | M | A | M | **J** | **J** | **A** | S | O | N | D |

Minimize Garden Chores

While the compost-enriched potting mix will hold some moisture, you'll still need to water regularly. Allow the surface of the mix in the strawberry jar and windowbox to get dry to the touch, but keep the hanging basket evenly moist.

During hot, windy weather, you may need to water as often as once a day. To perk up a dried-out basket, soak it in a tub of water for a few hours, then hang it in a shady, sheltered spot overnight before moving it back to its normal location.

The compost and fertilizer you included in the container mix will go a long way toward meeting your herbs' nutrient needs. To give them an extra boost, water them with fish emulsion, mixed at half the recommended strength, every two weeks from mid-summer to early fall.

Enjoy Your Herbs

While you'll grow these container gardens primarily for their looks, you can also harvest lightly from them. Simply pinch off leaves and flowers as you need them for fresh use. Wait to pick the alpine strawberries until they are fully red. And take every opportunity to brush or rub the aromatic herbs to enjoy their sweet and spicy scents.

season 4
September and October

| J | F | M | A | M | J | J | A | **S** | **O** | N | D |

Prepare Your Pots for Winter

These container herb gardens will look great up to the first frost. If you have very limited gardening space, you may just want to dump all the plants and mix into your compost pile at the end of the season and start fresh next year. If you want to keep as many of the herbs as possible, separate them in early to mid-fall, before the first frost. Pull out and compost the basil, nasturtiums, and parsley. Plant the peppermint geranium and rosemary in pots to grow indoors over the winter. Then plant the remaining perennial herbs in an empty corner of your vegetable garden or another out-of-the-way spot for the winter. 🌑

Keeping your garden going

*I*f you've dumped out your container herbs in fall, simply brush out any remaining mix, and store the containers indoors for the winter. In spring, start again as for a new garden.

If you've separated your container plants to save them, bring the peppermint geranium and rosemary indoors before the first frost. Grow them on a sunny windowsill or under fluorescent lights through the winter. Protect the herbs in the garden with a mulch of straw or evergreen boughs after the soil freezes. Remove the mulch when new growth emerges in spring. After all danger of frost has passed, gradually move the geranium and rosemary outdoors. When you are ready to replant your containers, purchase new basil and parsley plants and nasturtium seeds, and dig up the perennial herbs.

Container Gardens

A Bird, Bee, and Butterfly Garden

Just about anything you plant can attract birds and butterflies to your garden by supplying shelter and nesting sites. But if you really want to make your yard a haven for birds and butterflies, herbs are an excellent choice because they provide food as well as shelter.

Herbs that attract birds, bees, and butterflies are also beautiful, so you'll enjoy looking at this garden as much as at the delightful creatures that visit. And when you add a water source as a garden feature, you'll be providing one-stop shopping for all these creatures' needs!

A Bird, Bee, and Butterfly Garden

Bring the beauty of hummingbirds, songbirds, and butterflies to your backyard with these colorful pollen-producing and nectar-rich herbs.

Seeds to Buy

It's simple to raise these herbs from seed. Sow the seed directly into the garden, right where you want the plants to grow.

- ❧ BORAGE (1 PACKET)
- ❧ FENNEL (1 PACKET)

1 Anise hyssop
2 Joe-Pye weed
3 Purple coneflower
4 Fennel
5 Yarrow
6 Tansy
7 Feverfew
8 Catnip
9 Borage
10 Bee balm
11 Lemon balm
12 Sage
13 Marjoram
14 Creeping thyme
15 Parsley

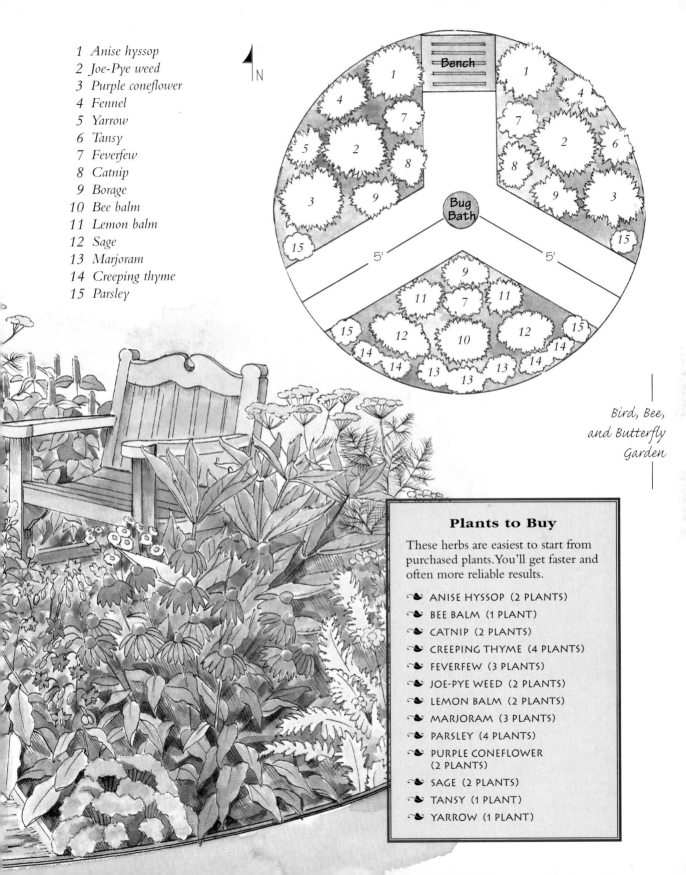

N

Bench

Bug
Bath

5'   5'

*Bird, Bee,
and Butterfly
Garden*

Plants to Buy

These herbs are easiest to start from purchased plants. You'll get faster and often more reliable results.

- ANISE HYSSOP (2 PLANTS)
- BEE BALM (1 PLANT)
- CATNIP (2 PLANTS)
- CREEPING THYME (4 PLANTS)
- FEVERFEW (3 PLANTS)
- JOE-PYE WEED (2 PLANTS)
- LEMON BALM (2 PLANTS)
- MARJORAM (3 PLANTS)
- PARSLEY (4 PLANTS)
- PURPLE CONEFLOWER (2 PLANTS)
- SAGE (2 PLANTS)
- TANSY (1 PLANT)
- YARROW (1 PLANT)

The Plant Guide

A Bird, Bee, and Butterfly Garden

To attract birds, bees, and butter-flies to your garden, you need to provide three simple things: shelter, food, and water. The herbs included in this garden will meet the first two needs; the water source you supply will meet the third.

So why are herbs so good at at-tracting bees and butterflies? If you've ever looked closely at your herbs, you've seen that their blooms are very often clusters of many tiny flowers. This is most obvious in plants like dill, mints, thymes, and yarrow. But if you look carefully at herbs with daisylike flowers, such as purple coneflower and feverfew, you'll see that the yellow centers are ac-tually many tiny, tubular flowers. The small flowers of all these herbs provide pollen and nectar that even the smallest insects can reach.

And what about birds? Well, when you plant herbs to attract insects to your garden, you provide a ready source of food for insect-eating birds. Many birds also relish the seeds of purple cone-flowers, fennel, and other herbs for winter food.

This gorgeous garden includes over a dozen easy-care herbs in a 10-foot-wide circle divided into three equal-size beds. I've also added a birdbath to provide water for your wildlife, along with a bench for you to sit on and enjoy watching your beautiful birds, bees, and butterflies.

Seeds

Sow these fast-growing herbs directly in the garden in spring. After the first year, you may not have to plant again; these herbs will often self-sow.

BORAGE
Borago officinalis

Bees are attracted to borage's pretty blue flowers that bloom midsummer through fall and make a pleasant-tasting honey from them. This easy-to-grow annual also produces cucumber-flavored leaves that you can add to salads. Borage grows 2 to 3 feet tall. Thin seedlings to leave one plant in each spot on the garden plan. Buy one packet.

FENNEL
Foeniculum vulgare

Fennel's lacy yellow flowerheads will attract a wide range of beneficial in-sects to your garden in mid- to late summer. As a plus, the feathery, licorice-flavored leaves are wonderful in salads, herb butters, fish dishes, and salad dressings. You can also use the stems (eat them like celery) and the seeds (add them to desserts and breads). Bronze fennel (*F. vulgare* 'Purpureum') has chocolate brown leaves. Fennel grows 3 to 5 feet tall. Thin seedlings to leave one plant in each spot on the garden plan. Zones 5 to 9. Buy one packet.

214

Key

TEA

CRAFT

COOKING

Plants

Buy plants of the following herbs, or grow your own from divisions, cuttings, or seed sown indoors in pots.

ANISE HYSSOP
Agastache foeniculum

This pretty perennial herb grows in bushy clumps, with upright, branching stems topped with spikes of lavender-blue flowers in mid- to late summer. The blooms are irresistible to bees and many other insects. Anise hyssop will self-sow prolifically, so pinch off most of the flowerheads before the small, black seeds mature and drop. Plants grow to 3 feet tall. Zones 4 to 9. Buy two plants.

BEE BALM
Monarda didyma

Bee balm's bright red flowers are enticing to both bees and hummingbirds. You can use the leaves to make a pleasant citrusy tea. In mid- to late spring, pinch out up to half of the stems at ground level to thin out crowded clumps and encourage good air circulation around the remaining stems. Plants grow to 3 feet tall. Zones 4 to 9. Buy one plant.

CATNIP
Nepeta cataria

Catnip forms fast-spreading clumps of fuzzy, green foliage. In summer, the brushy spikes of small white to pinkish flowers are covered with butterflies, bees, and many other beneficial insects. Catnip will spread quickly, so divide the clumps each

Joe-Pye weed is one of the premier butterfly plants, creating a gorgeous focal point in the summer garden.

spring and replant just a few sections, or grow them in bottomless pots sunk into the soil. Plants grow to 3 feet tall. Buy two plants.

CREEPING THYME
Thymus serpyllum

Creeping thyme's low carpets of tiny, aromatic leaves provide shelter for many ground-dwelling beneficial insects, such as ground beetles. In summer, the leaves are practically smothered in pink, red, or white flowers that attract bees and other beneficials. You could also plant some of the bushier thymes, such as English thyme (*T. vulgaris*) or lemon thyme (*T.* × *citriodorus*), for a variety of aromas and leaf colors. Heights range from less than 1 inch up to 12 inches. Zones 4 to 9. Buy four plants, and set them out in two groups, spaced 1 foot apart within the pairs.

Bird, Bee, and Butterfly Garden

FEVERFEW
Tanacetum parthenium

Feverfew may look delicate, but it's a sturdy, easy-to-grow herb that blooms from early summer to early fall. The white-petaled, yellow-centered flowers look just like tiny daisies and attract a variety of insects. Pinching off the spent flowers can extend the bloom season as well as reduce the number of self-sown seedlings. Feverfew usually grows to 2 feet tall. Zones 4 to 9. Buy three plants.

JOE-PYE WEED
Eupatorium purpureum

Tall Joe-Pye is the glory of the late summer garden. Its domed clusters of rosy pink to light purple flowers tower over shorter herbs, with sturdy stalks in multistemmed clumps. The flowers will attract bees and butterflies as well as lots of attention from garden visitors. 'Album' has white flowers. Stems reach 6 to 8 feet tall in bloom. Zones 3 to 8. Buy two plants.

LEMON BALM
Melissa officinalis

The tiny white flowers of this perennial herb are very enticing to bees. You'll also enjoy lemon balm for the strong lemon scent and a pleasant citrus flavor of its leaves. Add whole or chopped leaves to green salads or fruit salads. They also taste great as a tea, either alone or blended with other herbs or black tea. Plants grow 1 to 2 feet tall. Zones 5 to 9. Buy two plants.

MARJORAM
Origanum majorana

Marjoram, also commonly called sweet marjoram, is closely related to Greek oregano, but its leaves have a milder flavor. In summer, the clusters of purplish pink flowers are practically covered with butterflies, bees, and other beneficials. Marjoram is usually grown as an annual. Plants reach 1 foot tall in bloom. Buy three plants.

PARSLEY
Petroselinum crispum

The vitamin-rich leaves of this biennial herb are either frilly (in curly parsley) or flat (in flat-leaved or Italian parsley). Both kinds are a favorite food source for the colorful larvae of black swallowtail and yellow swallowtail butterflies. The tiny second-year flowers will attract a wide range of insects. Parsley usually reaches about 18 inches tall in bloom. Buy four plants.

PURPLE CONEFLOWER
Echinacea purpurea

Purple coneflower produces clumps of sturdy stems topped with large, rosy pink, daisylike flowers with orange-brown centers. The flowers are popular with both bees and butterflies. Plants bloom from midsummer into fall, especially if you snip off the dead flowers in summer. Stop deadheading in late summer to leave seedheads for winter bird food. Purple coneflower grows 3 to 4 feet tall. Zones 3 to 9. Buy two plants.

216

Key

TEA

CRAFT

COOKING

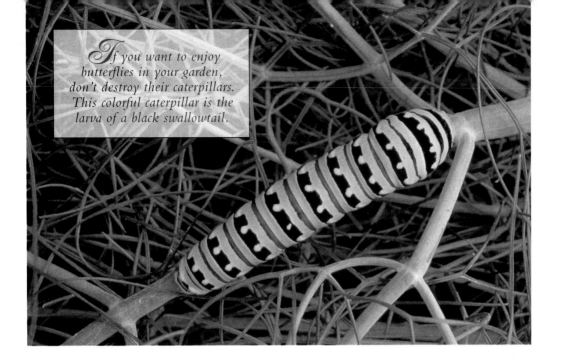

If you want to enjoy butterflies in your garden, don't destroy their caterpillars. This colorful caterpillar is the larva of a black swallowtail.

SAGE
Salvia officinalis

Common culinary sage grows in shrubby clumps of gray-green, aromatic leaves. Its loose spikes of purple-blue summer flowers attract many bees. If you want to add extra color to your garden, try planting 'Purpurea', with purple-green leaves or 'Icterina', with gold-banded green leaves. Plants grow 1 to 2 feet tall. Zones 4 to 9. Buy two plants.

TANSY
Tanacetum vulgare

For centuries, gardeners have planted tansy by their doors to keep ants, flies, and mosquitoes at bay. While their reputation for repelling some insects has stood the test of time, tansy's buttonlike yellow flowers are very attractive to others, including many butterflies and bees. Tansy roots spread quickly, so it's smart to plant the clumps in a large, bottomless bucket sunk into the soil. You can also divide the clumps every year or two, as needed, to control their spread. Tansy grows to 3 feet tall in bloom. Zones 4 to 9. Buy one plant.

YARROWS
Achillea spp.

Common yarrow (*A. millefolium*) produces flattened clusters of red, pink, or white flowers on slender stems clad in feathery green foliage. If you prefer yellow flowers, you could substitute another species or hybrid, such as fernleaf yarrow (*A. filipendulina*) or the hybrid 'Moonshine'. All yarrows produce the flattened heads of tiny flowers that are enticing to many different insects. Plants vary in height but are usually around 2 feet tall. Zones 3 to 8. Buy one plant.

The Seasonal Guide

A Bird, Bee, and Butterfly Garden

season 1

January and February

| J | F | M | A | M | J | J | A | S | O | N | D |

Select a Site

Winter is a great time to start planning your new bird, bee, and butterfly garden. You'll need an area big enough to hold a circle 10 feet across. Look for a site that gets at least six hours of full sun through the growing season. Average, well-drained garden soil will work fine for all these herbs.

If possible, choose a site where you can see the garden from a window or deck. That way, you'll be able to look out and enjoy the beautiful birds and butterflies, even if you don't have time to walk out and sit on the garden bench.

While this garden contains many beautiful and useful herbs, keep in mind that its primary purpose is to provide food and shelter for wildlife. This means, for instance, that caterpillars (the larval form of butterflies and moths) may be feeding on some of your herbs, chewing holes in the leaves. While it's a small price to pay for the pleasure you'll get from the adults, it's something to think about when choosing a site for the garden. Consider siting this garden where it can be enjoyed from a distance rather than close up.

Buy Seeds and Plants

You should have no trouble finding all of these herbs at your local garden center or nursery in spring. But if you like to plan ahead, this is a good excuse to spend some time with your favorite mail-order seed, plant, and garden supply catalogs.

Most places that sell vegetables or flowers will also carry these herbs, and it's always fun to look at specialty herb catalogs. Some garden-supply companies even sell beneficial insects, such as green lacewings, ladybugs, predatory (non-stinging) wasps, and praying mantis egg cases, which you can release in your garden to supplement the native populations of these creatures. You'll find addresses for some of my favorite mail-order catalogs in "Plants and Supplies" on page 262.

Bee balm attracts more than bees—it's also a favorite with hummingbirds and hummingbird moths.

Prepare the Site

Start preparing your new garden site in early spring as soon as your soil is completely thawed and dry enough to dig without turning into muddy clumps. Or, if you want to get an extra-early start in the spring, you could instead prepare the site in fall, so everything will be ready for planting as soon as warm weather returns.

To draw the outline of the 10-foot-diameter circle, insert a sturdy stake in the center of the site. Tie one end of a rope to the stake, then measure out 5 feet of rope from the stake. Holding the free end of the rope taut, walk around the circle, and outline the garden with a sprinkling of lime or flour. To mark off the paths, start by drawing a line from the center of the circle out to one edge. To draw the remaining two paths, measure an angle roughly 120 degrees on each side of the first line, and mark those two lines. You'll end up with a Y-pattern that divides the circle into three equal wedges. Measure out 1 foot to each side of each line to outline the paths (basically making a thicker Y).

If you are creating this garden out of an existing lawn area, you could leave the paths in grass. Or, for lower maintenance, replace all the grass with wood chips or gravel. Any of these three materials will provide shelter for beneficial ground-dwelling insects. If you choose a wood-chip, gravel, or brick path, use a spade to remove all the grass from the garden site; otherwise, just clear it off the individual planting areas.

Test the soil to check the pH. Add lime or sulfur, if needed, to raise or lower the pH so that it is around neutral (7.0).

Use a spading fork or rotary tiller to loosen the top 8 inches of soil in each planting area. Then spread a 1- to 2-inch layer of compost, composted manure, or other organic material over the beds, and dig that into the top 6 inches of soil. Rake to smooth the soil surface. Install plastic, brick, or metal edging strips around the outside of the circle to keep grass from creeping into the garden. If you're leaving the paths in grass, also outline them with edging strips.

Don't forget to add a small bench at the end of one of the paths, so you'll have a place to sit and watch the visiting wildlife. And at the junction of the three paths, add a birdbath—or ideally a "bug bath," as explained in "Give Your Bugs a Bath" on page 220—to provide a water source for thirsty creatures.

Plant Your Herbs

Following the planting diagram on page 213, start planting in spring as soon as the soil has thawed and is dry enough to

Bird, Bee, and Butterfly Garden

GIVE YOUR BUGS A BATH

Yes, even bugs enjoy a bath now and then—or at least a drink of water. If you live in a rainy or humid area, puddles or dew may provide all the moisture your bees, butterflies, and other beneficials need. During dry spells, or all season long, if you wish, you can provide supplemental water by creating a "bug bath."

A bug bath is simply a shallow container, such as a birdbath or a large plant saucer, with water and a few small rocks to provide perches where tiny insects can land and drink. You can set the container on a pedestal, such as a regular birdbath, or place it on the ground. Change the water every few days to discourage mosquitoes. Refill the bath as often as needed to keep the water partly covering the rocks.

Make a simple "bug bath" for butterflies by adding a few rocks to a birdbath or shallow pan partly filled with water.

dig without clumping. Sow borage and fennel in early spring. Set out the anise hyssop, bee balm, catnip, creeping thyme, feverfew, Joe-Pye weed, lemon balm, parsley, purple coneflower, sage, tansy, and yarrow plants as you get them. If the plants were growing in a greenhouse when you bought them, make sure you harden them off before planting. (See "Handling Hardening Off" on page 10.) If you don't plan to divide your catnip plants every year or two, control their spread by planting them in bottomless pots or buckets sunk into the soil. Leave the top inch of the containers above the soil level to discourage roots from sneaking out over the top. Wait until after all danger of frost has passed to set out your marjoram plant.

season 3

June, July, and August ————————————

| J | F | M | A | M | J | J | A | S | O | N | D |

Bird, Bee, and Butterfly Garden

Minimize Garden Chores

Mulching is an excellent way to reduce maintenance in your bird, bee, and butterfly garden. It helps to keep the soil moist, so you'll water less often. It also blocks light from reaching the soil, so fewer weed seeds will sprout, and those that do will be easier to pull out. As it breaks down, the mulch will release a small but steady supply of nutrients to feed your herbs. As an added bonus, it will keep soil from splashing up on plants, so you won't have to look at muddy or soil-encrusted leaves and flowers.

Late spring or early summer, when the soil has warmed up, is the ideal time to mulch your garden. Weed thoroughly, then spread a 1-inch layer of compost between the plants. Cover the compost with 1 inch of shredded bark or chopped leaves.

If you don't get at least $1/2$ inch of rain each week, pull away a bit of mulch, and use a trowel to check the soil underneath every few days. When the top 2 to 3 inches are dry, water thoroughly to soak the soil. While you are out watering, remember to fill the bird- or bug bath; it may need refilling every day during hot weather.

Enjoy Your Herbs

Birds, bees, and butterflies will do most of the harvesting in this herb garden, enjoying the ample supply of pollen and nectar. But you can still snip a few leaves or flowers here and there as needed. Anise hyssop, bee balm, catnip, and lemon balm all make pleasant teas; borage, fennel, marjoram, parsley, and sage are popular culinary herbs.

Most of these herbs are also pretty enough to hold their own in any bouquet or fresh arrangement. They'll bring the beauty and fragrance of your outdoor garden into your home. Gather herb flowers and foliage in early morning, if possible; evening is the second best time. Use sharp pruners, scissors, or knives to cut the stems cleanly. Make your cuts just above a leaf or leaf pair. Immediately place the cut ends in a bucket of tepid water. When you bring them indoors, cut the stem bases again, while they are still under water. Also pull or trim off any leaves that would be under the waterline in your finished arrangement.

To keep your cut flowers looking good, add a commercial perservative to the water in the arrangement container.

Or make your own preservative by adding one or two drops of bleach and 1 teaspoon of sugar to each quart of water. Adding a small piece of charcoal will also help to keep the water fresh. Keep the container filled with water; add more daily, if needed.

For informal arrangements, you can just insert a mix of herb flowers and foliage in a vase, jar, or crock of water. For a more formal look, use a piece of floral foam that you've soaked in water. The foam will give you much more control over the placement of the flowers and leaves. It will also let you use a wider variety of containers, such as baskets; simply set the foam in a waterproof bowl or tray set inside the decorative container.

222

season 4
September
and October _____

| J | F | M | A | M | J | J | A | **S** | **O** | N | D |

Prepare Your Garden for Winter

While the weather stays warm, you can continue enjoying your herbs, either outdoors in the garden or indoors in cooking and crafts. If your fennel seeds didn't mature earlier in the season, they will be ready for harvest now. Gather herb seeds when they turn dark but before they drop. Brush the seeds directly from the plant into a bowl, or cut off

the whole seedheads, store them in paper bags, and rub the seeds off later.

After the first frost, pull out the borage and marjoram, and toss their remains in the compost pile. Don't be in a hurry to cut down the remaining herbs, though; many will bear seeds that will attract birds to your garden through the winter.

While leaving the topgrowth will provide some winter protection, you may want to add some extra mulch if you live north of Zone 6. After the ground is frozen, mulch with several inches of loose straw, or use boughs from a Christmas tree after the holidays. This will protect your perennial herbs from damage caused by thawing and freezing during spells of mild winter weather. 🌀

Keeping your garden going

*T*his beautiful easy herb garden will thrive for years with just a little care from you. Wait until later in winter to cut down the remaining topgrowth of the anise hyssop, bee balm, catnip, fennel, feverfew, Joe-Pye weed, lemon balm, purple coneflower, tansy, and yarrow. (Wait to cut back the sage until it starts producing new growth; then trim the plant to shape.)

When your perennial herbs start to push up new growth in spring, remove the winter mulch. If you don't see self-sown borage seedlings by midspring, replant with new seed. If you allowed seed-producing herbs to mature in the garden last fall, you may need to weed out unwanted seedlings.

Midspring is also a good time to tuck in a few new parsley plants, wherever there's a little extra space. That way, you'll always have some first-year plants for their leaves and some second-year plants for their flowers. (Parsley will die after flowering but sometimes self-sows.) Wait until all danger of frost has passed to set out new marjoram plants.

Each year, renew the compost-and-bark or leaf mulch layers in late spring to early summer. If your perennial herbs look crowded or begin to flower poorly, dig up and divide the clumps in spring or fall. Discard the dead centers, and replant one or two of the vigorous outer sections from each clump. Share the remaining sections of the divided clumps with gardening friends, use them to start new gardens, or toss them into your compost pile.

Bird, Bee, and Butterfly Garden

A Mediterranean Herb Garden

Many of our favorite herbs—including lavender, rosemary, sage, and thyme—grow wild in the Mediterranean regions of Spain, France, Italy, and Greece. This dry, sunny area produces rugged herbs that are intensely fragrant and very tasty. The flavors of the foods in this region are usually based on the herbs that grow there.

You can bring the flavors and fragrances of the Mediterranean to your own backyard with this beautiful easy herb garden. The secret to success is choosing a site with good drainage. These herbs don't like soggy soil!

A Mediterranean Herb Garden

Enjoy the warm scents and flavors of the Mediterranean with this easy-care herb garden. You'll be able to make your own garden-fresh pesto, spaghetti sauce, and other savory dishes, make delightfully fragrant potpourri, and even grow your own saffron!

Plants to Buy

These herbs are easiest to start from purchased plants. You'll get faster and often more reliable results.

- BUSH BASIL (4 PLANTS)
- GREEK OREGANO (2 PLANTS)
- LAVENDER (5 PLANTS)
- PARSLEY (8 PLANTS)
- PURPLE SAGE (3 PLANTS)
- ROSEMARY (3 PLANTS)
- SCENTED GERANIUM (1 PLANT)
- THYME (6 PLANTS)

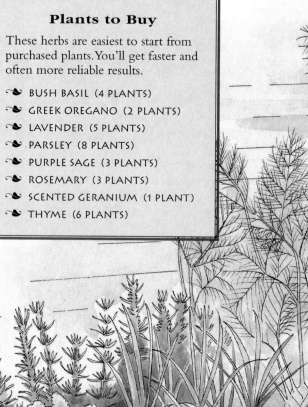

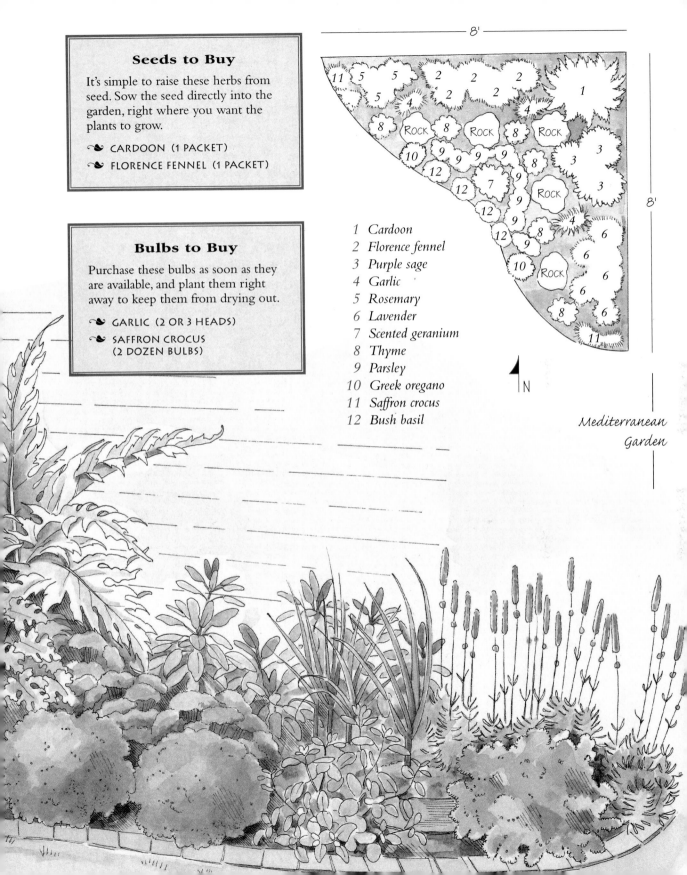

Seeds to Buy

It's simple to raise these herbs from seed. Sow the seed directly into the garden, right where you want the plants to grow.

- ❧ CARDOON (1 PACKET)
- ❧ FLORENCE FENNEL (1 PACKET)

Bulbs to Buy

Purchase these bulbs as soon as they are available, and plant them right away to keep them from drying out.

- ❧ GARLIC (2 OR 3 HEADS)
- ❧ SAFFRON CROCUS (2 DOZEN BULBS)

8'

8'

1 Cardoon
2 Florence fennel
3 Purple sage
4 Garlic
5 Rosemary
6 Lavender
7 Scented geranium
8 Thyme
9 Parsley
10 Greek oregano
11 Saffron crocus
12 Bush basil

N

Mediterranean Garden

The Plant Guide

A Mediterranean Herb Garden

This garden includes a variety of culinary, edible, and fragrance herbs that are popular in the Mediterranean region. They will grow in other climates, too, as long as you're careful to provide excellent drainage and plenty of sunshine.

The triangular shape of this garden makes it perfect for a sunny corner, perhaps beside your house, deck, or garage. A south-facing spot is ideal, since these annuals, perennials, and bulbs will thrive with the extra warmth.

Seeds

Sow these fast-growing herbs directly in the garden in early to midsummer for a fall harvest.

CARDOON
Cynara cardunculus

This tall, thistlelike perennial herb is prized for its edible leaf stalks. Cut off the flat part of the leaves, and chop the stalks into soups and stews or steam them. Cardoon is also beautiful enough to grow just for its looks, with its huge clumps of arching, toothed, grayish green leaves. Plants reach 4 to 6 feet tall in bloom. Thin seedlings to leave one plant. Buy one packet.

FLORENCE FENNEL
Foeniculum vulgare var. *azoricum*

Florence fennel, also known as sweet fennel or finocchio, produces feathery green leaves with thickened stems that form a bulblike base. Harvest the bulb by cutting just below the swollen area. Chop the bulb, and add it to salads or soups. Florence fennel grows as an annual in most areas. Sow in midsummer for fall harvest. Plants usually reach 3 to 4 feet tall. For this garden, you'll want five plants, spaced about 1 foot apart. Buy one packet.

Plants

Buy plants of the following herbs, or grow your own from divisions, cuttings, or seed sown indoors in pots.

BUSH BASIL
Ocimum basilicum

Although native to India, Africa, and Asia, basil has come to be synonymous with the flavors of the Mediterranean. This annual herb is a perfect partner to fresh or cooked tomatoes in salads and sauces. Try it with other vegetables, too, and with pasta. The compact habit of bush basil makes it a great edging plant. 'Spicy Globe' is an especially dense, bushy selection. Bush basil usually grows 8 to 10 inches tall. Buy four plants.

GREEK OREGANO
Origanum heracleoticum

Oregano is the foundation flavor of Italian tomato sauces and Greek moussaka. Rub and sniff the leaves

Key

TEA

CRAFT

COOKING

before buying, so you're sure to get the aromatic, flavorful Greek oregano and not the bland common oregano. Plants usually grow about 1 foot tall. Zones 5 to 9. Buy two plants.

LAVENDER
Lavandula angustifolia

This Mediterranean native is as pretty to look at as it is heavenly to smell. It produces spikes of purple-blue flowers on slender stalks over shrubby clumps of narrow, silvery leaves. 'Munstead' and 'Hidcote' are more compact, growing only 12 to 18 inches tall, with dark purple flowers. Zones 5 to 8. Buy five plants.

PARSLEY
Petroselinum crispum

Finely minced fresh parsley brightens the flavor and appearance of dozens of shellfish and vegetables dishes in the Mediterranean. The leaves of this biennial herb are either frilly (in curly parsley) or flat (in flat-leaved or Italian parsley). I find that the flavor of the flat-leaved type is better, but both are a welcome addition to al-most any dish. For a steady supply of leaves, treat parsley as an annual: Pull out plants at the end of the first year, and set out new ones each spring. The leafy clumps are usually 8 to 12 inches tall. Buy eight plants.

PURPLE SAGE
Salvia officinalis 'Purpurea'

Common culinary sage grows in shrubby clumps of oblong, aromatic leaves, accented by spikes of purple-

blue flowers in mid- to late summer. 'Purpurea', with purplish green leaves, makes an especially pretty partner for purple-flowered lavender. Use the fresh or dried leaves of either kind to liven up stuffing or roasted meats. Plants grow about 1 foot tall. Zones 4 to 9. Buy three plants.

ROSEMARY
Rosmarinus officinalis

Rosemary grows like a shrub in the Mediterranean. It is a key flavoring for grilled or roasted lamb. The strong flavor also complements cream sauces, marinades, eggs, cheese, and tomato dishes. In Zones 8 to 10, rose-mary can live outdoors through the winter, and it grows to 6 feet tall. North of Zone 8, treat it as an annual and buy new plants each year, or bring them indoors for the winter. They will seldom reach more than 3 feet tall. Buy three plants.

SCENTED GERANIUM
Pelargonium spp.

Scented geraniums are popular potted plants for patios and balconies in the Mediterranean. They come in dozens of leaf forms and fragrances, including lemon, peppermint, and rose—just to name a few! And they grow as well in the garden as in pots. Scented geraniums are only hardy outdoors in frost-free regions, but you can grow them anywhere as annuals. They also make won-derful houseplants. Heights vary. Buy one plant.

Mediterranean Garden

THYMES
Thymus spp.

Thyme is a Mediterranean native that thrives in well-drained, sandy soil in full sun. Common or English thyme (*T. vulgaris*) has a bushy form and a piney, woodsy fragrance. Lemon thyme *(T. × citriodorus)* has a citrus scent and flavor. Choose either of these or one of the dozens of others. Most thymes grow 6 to 12 inches tall. Zones 4 to 9. Buy six plants.

Bulbs

Purchase these bulbs as soon as they are available, and plant them right away to prevent them from drying out.

GARLIC
Allium sativum

Garlic is great in just about any dish but dessert! (There are recipes for garlic desserts, too, but I'm not ready to try one!) Add chopped raw cloves to soups, stews, and sauces, or roast them and spread the softened cloves onto bread. The fresh greens are great in pesto sauces or stir-fries. For best growth, plant in fall for harvest the following summer. Purchase these bulbs from your local garden center or through a mail-order nursery catalog. Those sold in grocery stores are usually adapted for commercial production and may not grow well in your area. Each bulb, or head, is made up of several individual cloves. Plants grow to 2 feet tall. Zones 5 to 9. Buy two or three heads, and plant four to six cloves in each spot.

SAFFRON CROCUS
Crocus sativus

Saffron crocus looks very much like its spring-blooming crocus relatives, except that it always blooms in early fall. The pointed, lavender-pink petals surround three thin, branching structures, called stigmata or threads. These are the parts you harvest to produce the unique flavoring used in paella and bouillabaisse. Be sure to get the bulbs of saffron crocus and not the poisonous autumn crocus (*Colchicum* spp.). Plants grow 6 to 8 inches tall. Zones 6 to 9. Buy two dozen bulbs.

Mulching with gravel helps protect lavender and other Mediterranean herbs that will rot without good drainage.

230

Key

TEA

CRAFT

COOKING

The Seasonal Guide

A Mediterranean Herb Garden

season 1

January and February

J	F	M	A	M	J	J	A	S	O	N	D

Select a Site

A successful Mediterranean herb garden starts with the right site. Winter is a good time to start looking for the perfect planting spot. Choose a site that will get at least six hours of full sun a day. Excellent drainage is also very important; a site with loose, sandy, or gravelly soil is ideal. This garden is perfectly shaped to fit into a corner setting, ideally sheltered by two walls. A spot near the house is particularly convenient for easy harvesting.

Buy Seeds and Plants

You'll find many, although probably not all, of these Mediterranean herbs for sale at your local garden center or nursery in spring. It's smart to order cardoon and Florence fennel seed now from a mail-order catalog, so you'll be sure to have it by planting time. You will probably have to wait until midsummer to find saffron crocus in bulb catalogs. You'll find addresses for some of my favorite mail-order catalogs in "Plants and Supplies" on page 262.

Mediterranean Garden

season 2

March, April, and May

J	F	M	A	M	J	J	A	S	O	N	D

Prepare the Site

Start digging in early spring as soon as your soil is completely thawed and dry enough to crumble instead of clump. Mark the outline of the garden—basically two straight 8-foot sides joined by a curved line—on the ground with stakes and string or with a sprinkling of lime or flour. If you are siting the garden against a wall or fence, leave 12 to 18 inches between the garden and the structure, so you'll be able to walk all around the garden for easy maintenance. Remove any rocks and debris, and strip off the existing vegetation with a spade or rented sod cutter. Test the soil to check the pH. Add lime or sulfur, if needed, to adjust the pH so it is neutral or slightly alkaline (7.0 to 7.2).

Use a spading fork or rotary tiller to loosen the top 8 inches of

a simple SPAGHETTI garden

Once you've tried homemade tomato sauce, it can be hard to go back to the bottled stuff. Planting a "spaghetti garden" is a fun and practical way to have all the needed ingredients on hand when you get the urge to cook.

Of course, every spaghetti garden needs at least a few tomato plants. Paste tomatoes are particularly good for making sauce because they have thicker walls and smaller seed cavities than most tomatoes. Basil is also a key ingredient for a great sauce.

Besides these two basics, add other vegetables and Mediterranean herbs according to your space and tastes. Consider including garlic, Greek oregano, rosemary, onions, and thyme in your planting. I always grow both sweet bell and hot peppers to add to my spaghetti sauce. And I've found that diced zucchini makes a great sauce thickener when you're in the mood for a meatless sauce!

Buy a box of your favorite pasta, and you have the makings for a great spaghetti dinner!

soil in each planting area. Then spread a 1- to 2-inch layer of compost, composted manure, or other organic material over the beds, and dig that into the top 6 inches of soil. Rake to smooth the soil surface. Install plastic, brick, or metal edging strips along the curved front edge to keep grass from creeping into the garden. If you're leaving the paths along the straight sides in grass, also line the straight edges with edging strips.

Add five stepping stones in a rough semicircle to create a path through the middle of the garden.

Plant Your Herbs

Start planting in spring, as soon as the beds are ready, following the planting diagram on page 227. Set out Greek oregano, lavender, parsley, purple sage, and thyme plants as you get them. If the plants were growing in a greenhouse when you bought them, harden them off before planting. (See "Handling Hardening Off" on page 10.) Sow car-

doon seed one to two weeks before your last frost date. Thin the seedlings to leave one plant. Wait until after all danger of frost has passed to set out basil, rosemary, and scented geranium plants.

Wait until midsummer to sow the Florence fennel seed. Pull back the mulch in the planting area, and scratch the soil lightly with a hand fork. Scatter the seed over the loosened soil, firm it in, then water gently. Water daily until the seedlings appear. When seedlings are a few inches tall, thin them to about 1 foot apart. Snip off unwanted seedlings at ground level with scissors. Pull the mulch layers back around the remaining seedlings.

The first year, you have two options with your garlic. One is to plant as early as possible in spring to get a crop in late summer. Or you could fill the spot with some annual herb, such as dill, until early to midfall, the ideal planting time. You'll have to wait until the following summer for your harvest, but you'll get a better harvest of large bulbs that way.

Mediterranean Garden

season *3*

June, July, and August ⎯⎯⎯⎯⎯⎯

| J | F | M | A | M | **J** | **J** | **A** | S | O | N | D |

Minimize Garden Chores

Wait until the soil has warmed up in late spring or early summer to mulch your

Mediterranean garden. Weed thoroughly, then spread a ½-inch layer of compost between the plants. Top that with another ½ inch of shredded bark or chopped leaves. If you live in a humid or rainy climate, you may choose to mulch with a 1-inch layer of gravel instead of the compost and bark or leaves. This will help ensure good drainage

around the bases of the plants.

If you don't get at least ½ inch of rain each week, pull away a bit of mulch and use a trowel to check the soil underneath every few days. When the top 2 to 3 inches are dry, water thoroughly to soak the soil.

Enjoy Your Herbs

While this garden is pretty enough to grow just for looks, it also contains many useful herbs. Pinch or snip off fresh leaves of bush basil, Florence fennel, Greek oregano, parsley, purple sage, rosemary, scented geranium, and thyme as you need them.

Wait until fall to harvest cardoon and the bulbs of Florence fennel. Blanch cardoon stems about a month before the average date of your first fall frost, by wrapping the bottom two-thirds of the plant with cardboard or heavy paper. The blanched stems will be ready to eat in three to four weeks. To harvest Florence fennel bulbs, use a knife to cut just below the swollen leaf bases.

season 4
September and October

| J | F | M | A | M | J | J | A | **S** | **O** | N | D |

Plant Garlic and Saffron

Garlic grows best when you plant it in early fall, so its roots get established before winter sets in. Separate the heads of garlic into individual cloves. Plant the cloves 2 inches deep and 4 to 6 inches apart. Keep them lightly watered. The following spring, the plants will emerge and mature for a midsummer harvest.

Plant your saffron crocus corms in late summer or mid- to late fall, whenever you get them. Set them 3 to 4 inches deep and 4 to 6 inches apart.

Dig up garlic bulbs when most of the topgrowth has turned brown. Collect the red saffron threads when the flowers open. Dry them for a few days on a sheet of paper away from breezes. Store the dried threads in an airtight jar.

Prepare Your Garden for Winter

Dig up your scented geranium—and your rosemary, if you live north of Zone 8—in mid- to late September, and plant them in pots of well-drained potting soil. Or, if you don't have room for whole plants, take cuttings in late summer or early fall, and keep the rooted cuttings indoors for the winter.

Pull out basil and parsley before the ground freezes. In early winter, cut the topgrowth of cardoon, Florence fennel, and Greek oregano close to the ground.

North of Zone 6, apply a loose winter mulch after the ground has frozen to prevent damage from thawing and refreezing during spells of mild winter weather.

Keeping your garden going

Just a little regular maintenance will keep your Mediterranean garden looking its best through the years. Each spring, after the soil thaws and your perennials begin to produce new growth, remove any protective winter mulch.

Wait until mid- to late spring to prune the purple sage and thyme; cut off winter-damaged tips, and trim lightly to shape the plants. This is also a good time to cut back lavender plants by one-third to promote bushy growth. Wait until all danger of frost has passed to set out the rosemary and scented geranium you overwintered indoors. Also set out new parsley and basil plants after the last frost date.

In late spring to early summer, weed thoroughly and then renew the compost-and-bark or leaf mulch layers. If you don't see regrowth on the Florence fennel, replant with new seed in midsummer. Dig up and divide crowded perennial clumps as needed in spring or fall. Replant a few of the vigorous outer sections; discard the dead sections. Use the rest to start new plantings, or compost them.

Over time, shrubby herbs such as lavender, purple sage, and thyme can develop woody stems, leaving the base of the plant looking bare. If this happens, mound 3 to 5 inches of sandy soil over the base of the stems in spring. During the summer, water as needed to keep the mound moist. When the stem bases have rooted into the mound (usually by fall or the next spring), cut them off, dig out the old plant, and replant with the rooted stems.

A Formal
Herb Garden

While herbs look great in informal gardens, they also feel right at home in a formal herb garden. This classic herb garden can add a touch of elegance to any property. Its symmetrical beds are edged with low hedges of clipped or naturally compact herbs. And since each bed includes similar, but not identical, herbs, the garden has a sense of balance without being boring.

Of course, a formal garden wouldn't be complete without some sort of accent piece. A sundial is a traditional favorite, but you could use a birdbath or planter instead.

A Formal
Herb Garden

*Add a touch of elegance to your
yard with this traditional formal herb
garden. The colorful flowers and fragrant
herbs will make it a favorite spot for
family and guests.*

Plants to Buy

These herbs are easiest to start from purchased plants. You'll get faster and more reliable results.

- BASIL (8 PLANTS)
- BEE BALM (2 PLANTS)
- BURNET (2 PLANTS)
- CHIVES (4 PLANTS)
- HYSSOP (14 PLANTS)
- LAVENDER (14 PLANTS)
- LEMON BALM (4 PLANTS)
- PARSLEY (8 PLANTS)
- PURPLE CONEFLOWER
  (2 PLANTS)
- ROSE GERANIUM
  (2 PLANTS)
- RUE (2 PLANTS)
- SAGE (2 PLANTS)
- THYME (8 PLANTS)

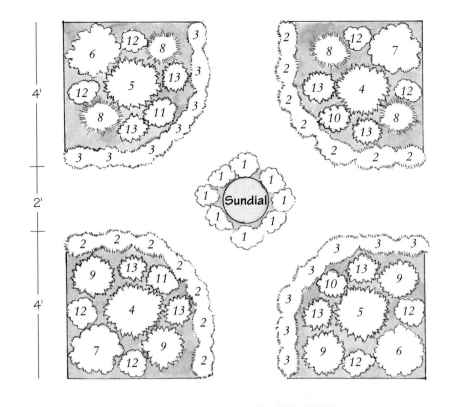

4'

2'

4'

Sundial

N

Formal
Garden

1 Thyme
2 Hyssop
3 Lavender
4 Bee balm
5 Purple coneflower
6 Rue
7 Burnet
8 Chives
9 Lemon balm
10 Rose geranium
11 Sage
12 Parsley
13 Basil

The Plant Guide

A Formal Herb Garden

Since a formal garden is more for show than for harvest, it's important to plant herbs that will look good throughout most of the growing season. To get this long season of interest, this garden includes many herbs with attractive foliage, such as burnet, chives, and rue. Their flowers will come and go, but the leaves will stay attractive from spring to fall.

Of course, you aren't just limited to leaves; flowering herbs can also have a place in the formal garden. But you'll want to stick to just a few colors so the planting doesn't look too "busy." I've based this beautiful easy garden on pinks and blues, accented by a few touches of white and yellow at certain times of the year.

Plants

Buy plants of the following herbs, or grow your own from divisions, cuttings, or seed sown indoors in pots.

BASIL
Ocimum basilicum

While you may think of basil mostly as a cooking herb, it's also pretty enough for a formal garden. The common sweet basil has broad, bright green leaves on upright, bushy plants. 'Spicy Globe' forms perfect mounds of tiny green leaves. 'Red Rubin' and 'Dark Opal' produce shiny, dark purple foliage on bushy plants. Many other species and cultivars are also available. This annual herb is easy to grow from seed, but it is very sensitive to frost, so you'd need to start it indoors about six weeks before your last frost date if you want to grow your own. Basil plants usually grow about 1 foot tall. Buy eight plants.

BEE BALM
Monarda didyma

The summer flowers of this spreading perennial herb are usually red, but you can also find cultivars with pink, purple, or white blooms. 'Marshall's Delight' is a good choice for this garden because its pink flowers will complement the other colors. It also resists powdery mildew, a fungal disease that causes gray patches on leaves. In mid- to late spring, pinch out up to a half of the stems at ground level to thin out crowded clumps. Plants grow to 3 feet tall. Zones 4 to 9. Buy two plants.

BURNET
Poterium sanguisorba

This dainty-looking perennial herb forms mounds of ferny, pale green leaves accented with long-stemmed, pinkish flowers in summer. Pinching off the spent flowers can promote fresh leafy growth and discourage self-sowing. Plants reach 1 foot tall. Zones 4 to 9. Buy two plants.

CHIVES
Allium schoenoprasum

In June, this perennial herb produces pretty pink or lavender flowers that you can add to salads for both flavor and color. The clumps of grasslike green leaves are attractive all season, and they have a mild onion flavor. It's easy to start chives from seed: Fill four 4-inch pots with potting soil and scatter seed evenly over the surface of each pot. When seedlings are 3 to 4 inches tall, transplant the contents of each pot as a clump. After bloom, cut off the spent flowers to prevent rampant reseeding. Clumps reach 12 to 14 inches tall in bloom. Zones 3 to 9. Buy four plants.

HYSSOP
Hyssopus officinalis

Hyssop forms shrubby clumps of narrow, dark green, aromatic leaves. It tolerates regular clipping well and makes a great low hedge for edging garden beds. Trim hyssop plants lightly the first year to develop a boxy hedge shape. In following years, shear as needed during the growing season to keep plants about 1 foot tall. If you want to save money, buy just a few hyssop plants the first year, and take cuttings from them to start those you need for the edgings. Zones 3 to 9. Buy 14 plants.

LAVENDER
Lavandula angustifolia

Aromatic English lavender produces spikes of purple-blue flowers on slender stalks over shrubby clumps of narrow, silvery leaves. 'Munstead' and 'Hidcote' are compact selections, growing only 12 to 18 inches tall, with dark purple flowers. To save money, you could start your own plants from seed; try 'Lady', which has a fairly uniform, compact habit and medium purple flowers. Plants grow 8 to 10 inches tall. 'Lady' usually blooms within four months of sowing and in following years as well. Zones 5 to 8. Buy 14 plants.

LEMON BALM
Melissa officinalis

Lemon balm grows in low, leafy mounds of bright green, lemon-scented leaves. After bloom, cut off all the stems 1 to 2 inches above the ground to get a flush of new leafy growth. Mulching with a few handfuls of compost or watering with fish emulsion can promote speedier regrowth. Plants grow 1 to 2 feet tall. Zones 5 to 9. Buy four plants.

PARSLEY
Petroselinum crispum

Parsley's dark green foliage looks great all season long. Try the finely crinkled leaves of curly parsley or the flat, ferny leaves of Italian parsley. For the best-looking leaves, treat this biennial herb as an annual: Pull out plants at the end of the first year, and set out new ones each spring. The leafy clumps are usually 8 to 12 inches tall. Buy eight plants.

Formal Garden

PURPLE CONEFLOWER
Echinacea purpurea

Purple coneflower produces clumps of sturdy stems topped with large, rosy pink, daisylike flowers from midsummer into fall. Plants tend to self-sow readily, so it's best to cut off spent flowers, back to the uppermost leaf; this can also extend the bloom season. The cultivar 'Magnus' holds its petals straight out, rather than re-flexed, making the flowers look larger. The blooms of 'Crimson Star' are a particularly deep rose-pink. Purple coneflower grows 3 to 4 feet tall. Zones 3 to 9. Buy two plants.

ROSE GERANIUM
Pelargonium graveolens

Rose geranium forms bushy clumps of fragrant leaves accented with pink flowers. For a little extra variety, you could try 'Grey Lady Plymouth', with more finely cut leaves edged in white. Scented geraniums are only hardy outdoors in frost-free regions, but you can grow them anywhere as annuals. They also make wonderful houseplants, so you can bring your favorites indoors to grow on a sunny windowsill through the winter. Rose geranium usually grows 1 to 2 feet tall. Buy two plants.

RUE
Ruta graveolens

Even if it didn't bloom, rue would be worth growing for its foliage alone. The bright blue-green leaves are deeply divided, giving the whole plant a delicate, lacy look. In midsummer, the clumps are accented with clusters of bright yellow-green flowers. Good drainage is essential for healthy growth. Plants usually reach 2 feet tall. Zones 5 to 9. Buy two plants.

SAGE
Salvia officinalis

Go for the traditional gray-green leaves of common culinary sage, or try the broader, silvery leaves of the cultivar 'Berggarten'. 'Icterina' has green-and-yellow leaves, which would be a beautiful complement if you've chosen to include variegated lemon thyme around the center sundial. You could also try the dusky purple foliage of 'Purpurea' or the festive purple, pink, and white leaves of 'Tricolor'. Plants reach 1 to 2 feet tall. Zones 4 to 9. Buy two plants.

THYMES
Thymus spp.

Thymes have tiny, aromatic leaves and a compact, shrubby or creeping habit. Common or English thyme (*T. vulgaris*) has a bushy form and a piney, woodsy fragrance. Lemon thyme (*T. × citriodorus*) has a citrus scent and flavor; its cultivar 'Variegatus' has gold-edged green leaves. Creeping thymes, such as mother-of-thyme (*T. serpyllum*), have colorful pink, red, or white flowers. These are just a few of the dozens of thyme species and cultivars that are available. Most thymes grow 6 to 12 inches tall. Zones 4 to 9. Buy eight plants.

242

Key

TEA

CRAFT

COOKING

The Seasonal Guide

A Formal Herb Garden

season *1*

January and February _____

J	F	M	A	M	J	J	A	S	O	N	D

Select a Site

Winter's a great time to start thinking about where you want to put your formal herb garden. Choose a site that gets at least six hours of sun a day through the growing season. Average, well-drained garden soil will suit these herbs just fine. This garden is so beautiful that you'll want to site it close to your house or deck so you will see it often. It would also make a great accent in the middle of an open lawn area.

Buy Plants

You could find many, if not all, of these herbs for sale in spring at your local nursery or garden center. But if you like to plan ahead, this a good time to pull out your mail-order catalogs and place your orders. If you want a particular color of bee balm or purple coneflower, look in catalogs that specialize in perennials. Most mail-order suppliers will ship your herbs at the right planting time for your area. The only exception to mail-order is basil plants; they generally don't ship well, so it's best to wait and buy them locally or to send for the seeds and start you own plants indoors. You'll find addresses for some of my favorite mail-order catalogs in "Plants and Supplies" on page 262.

Formal Garden

season *2*

March, April, and May _____

J	F	M	A	M	J	J	A	S	O	N	D

Prepare the Site

Before you dig, make sure that the soil is no longer frozen, and that it's dry enough to dig without making muddy clumps. (If you prefer, you could prepare the site for this garden in fall and plant the following spring.)

When you are ready to dig, mark off the outline of the whole garden and the smaller interior beds with stakes and string, or with a sprinkling of lime or flour. If you are siting the garden in a corner or along a fence or wall, leave a 12- to 18-inch path around the outside of the garden, so you can reach all sides of the beds for maintenance.

garden OR knot?

If you're looking for an ultra-formal planting, a knot garden might be the perfect thing for you. A knot garden is simply a geometric pattern of interlocking lines "drawn" in low, clipped herb hedges. Using herbs with different foliage colors adds extra interest to the pattern. You can also add contrast by using one mulch or a combination of light and dark mulches to accent the different parts of the pattern.

Choose a pattern, and pick the plants and mulches that you find most appealing. A few traditional plant favorites include germander (*Teucrium chamaedrys*), hyssop, lavender, lavender cottons (*Santolina* spp.), and rue. Other good options include rosemary, sages, southernwood, thymes, and winter savory. (Figure on one plant per foot for small herbs and one plant every 2 feet for large herbs.) Dark-colored mulches, such as cocoa bean hulls, complement silvery and blue leaves; dark green foliage looks great against light-colored gravel or shredded bark.

Knot gardens are definitely not low maintenance. You'll need to shear the plants several times a year to keep them neat and compact, and rake the mulches to remove dropped leaves and other debris. You'll also need to keep extra sheared plants as "spares" to fill in spaces in case some plants in the pattern die.

Sundials can be simple or more elaborate like this one. Choose a style that suits your garden.

If you are creating this garden out of an existing lawn area, you could leave the central walkway as a grass path. For easier maintenance, however, brick and gravel are both good choices. If you choose a brick or gravel path, remove all existing vegetation from the whole garden site; otherwise, just strip the grass off the five individual planting areas. Test the soil to check the pH. Add lime or sulfur, if needed, to adjust the pH so it is around neutral (7.0).

Loosen the soil in each of the five beds to a depth of 8 inches. It will probably be easiest to do this with a spading fork because a tiller could be hard to manage in the odd-shaped beds. Then spread a 1- to 2-inch layer of compost, composted manure, or other organic material over the beds, and dig that into the top 6 inches of soil. Rake to smooth the soil surface.

Install plastic, brick, or metal edging strips around the outside of the entire garden. If you'll have a grass path through the garden, put in edging strips along the inner sides of the individual beds as well. Install edging strips and gravel or brick paths after you dig the beds, but before planting.

Plant Your Herbs

Following the planting diagram on page 239, start planting in early spring as soon as the beds are ready. Set out the other plants as you get them (except for the basil and scented geranium—wait until after the last frost date to plant these out). If your plants were growing in a greenhouse when you bought them, harden them off before planting. (See "Handling Hardening Off" on page 10.) Place the potted plants on the soil according to the diagram. Adjust spacings as needed, then dig and plant. Water thoroughly after planting.

season 3

June,
July, and August _____

| J | F | M | A | M | **J** | **J** | **A** | S | O | N | D |

Minimize Garden Chores

If you don't get at least ½ inch of rain each week, pull away a bit of mulch and use a trowel to check the soil underneath every few days. When the top 2 to 3 inches are dry, water thoroughly.

In late spring or early summer, weed thoroughly, then spread 1 inch of compost between the plants. Top that with another inch of shredded bark or chopped leaves. This will discourage more weeds from sprouting.

Through the growing season, pinch off spent blooms of bee balm and purple coneflower to promote bushier growth and more flowers. Also remove spent flowers on chives to discourage self-sowing. Clip or pinch the hyssop and lavender "hedges" as often as needed to keep them compact.

Enjoy Your Herbs

This beautiful easy formal garden is more for pleasure than for harvesting, but many of these herbs are as useful as they are pretty. Bee balm and lemon balm, for instance, are wonderful for tea, and basil, parsley, sage, and thyme are classic cooking herbs. Simply pinch or snip off leaves as needed for fresh use. Lavender and rose geranium are perfect for potpourri, but don't harvest more than a few shoots at a time; you want the plants to look lush and full in your garden.

season 4

September
and October _____

| J | F | M | A | M | J | J | A | **S** | **O** | N | D |

Prepare Your Garden for Winter

Dig up your scented geranium in mid- to late September, and plant it in a pot of well-drained potting soil. Let it adjust outdoors before bringing it inside. Or, if you don't have room for the whole plant, take cuttings in late summer or early fall, and keep the rooted cuttings indoors for the winter.

Once a few frosts have called an end to the growing season, pull out the basil and parsley plants. Cut the tops of bee balm, burnet, chives, lemon balm, and purple coneflower to the ground.

It's smart to give your plants a protective winter mulch, especially if you live north of Zone 6. After the ground has frozen, spread several inches of loose straw over the beds, or use boughs from a Christmas tree after the holidays.

Keeping your garden going

A little regular maintenance will keep your formal herb garden looking great for years to come. When your perennial herbs start producing new growth in spring, remove any protective winter mulch. After all danger of frost has passed, set out new basil and parsley plants. This is also a good time to move your rose geranium plant back outdoors.

Wait until mid- to late spring to prune the sage and thyme; cut off winter-damaged tips, and trim lightly to shape the plants. This is also a good time to cut back lavender plants by one-third to promote bushy new growth. Trim the hyssop plants back to about 8 inches tall.

Each year, renew the compost-and-bark or leaf mulch layers in late spring to early summer.

If your perennial herbs look crowded or begin to flower poorly, dig up and divide the clumps in spring or fall. Discard the dead centers, and replant one or two of the vigorous outer sections from each clump. Share the remaining sections with gardening friends, use them to start new gardens, or toss them into your compost pile.

After a few years, hyssop, lavender, and rue may get woody and die out. It's smart to keep a few extra rue plants on hand—perhaps in the corner of your vegetable garden—so you can replace older plants as they die off. Plan to replace the whole hyssop and lavender edgings every four to five years to keep them looking good. Start new hyssop and lavender plants from cuttings or seed the year before replanting.

An Herbal
Salad Garden

A crisp, cool green salad is a refreshing addition to any summer supper. It can even be a meal in itself! With an herbal salad garden, you'll have everything you need for great green salads. Once you've experienced the superior flavor of just-picked herbs, you'll never want to be without them.

This salad garden is simply four 3-foot square beds, so it's easy to prepare, plant, and maintain. I've suggested an L-shaped layout, but you could easily adjust the pattern and the number of beds to fit your needs and your space.

An Herbal Salad Garden

This simple herb garden will provide a steady supply of salad fixings from early summer to frost.

Plants to Buy

These herbs are easiest to start from purchased plants. You'll get faster and often more reliable results.

- BURNET (1 PLANT)
- CHIVES (2 PLANTS)
- HORSERADISH (1 PLANT)
- PARSLEY (2 PLANTS)
- SORREL (1 PLANT)

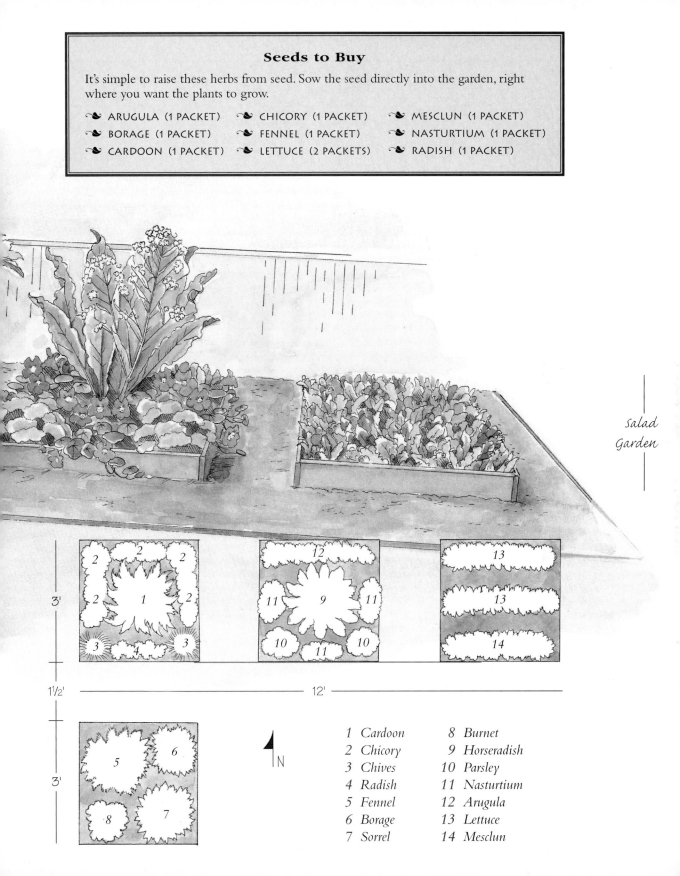

Seeds to Buy

It's simple to raise these herbs from seed. Sow the seed directly into the garden, right where you want the plants to grow.

🌱 ARUGULA (1 PACKET)   🌱 CHICORY (1 PACKET)   🌱 MESCLUN (1 PACKET)

🌱 BORAGE (1 PACKET)   🌱 FENNEL (1 PACKET)   🌱 NASTURTIUM (1 PACKET)

🌱 CARDOON (1 PACKET)   🌱 LETTUCE (2 PACKETS)   🌱 RADISH (1 PACKET)

salad Garden

3'

1½'

12'

3'

N

1 Cardoon   8 Burnet
2 Chicory   9 Horseradish
3 Chives   10 Parsley
4 Radish   11 Nasturtium
5 Fennel   12 Arugula
6 Borage   13 Lettuce
7 Sorrel   14 Mesclun

The Plant Guide

Many of the herbal greens—including arugula, chicory, nasturtium, and sorrel—are slightly bitter or spicy. But what a flavor they bring to a salad when you mix them with sweet lettuce. This garden yields many other flavors as well, such as cucumber-flavored borage and burnet, oniony chives, and licorice-like fennel. Lightly steamed cardoon stems provide an interesting crunch, while borage, chives, and nasturtium flowers add bright spots of edible color!

The seeds and plants I've suggested for this garden are a good starting place, but feel free to tailor your salad garden to suit your taste. For instance, you might prefer to raise onions instead of radishes, or to grow a bush cucumber in place of horseradish. And since you will be replanting the annual crops each year, you can experiment with different cultivars to find which work best for you.

Seeds

Sow these fast-growing herbs and vegetables directly in the garden in spring.

ARUGULA
Eruca vesicaria subsp. *sativa*

The peppery-tasting green leaves of this annual herb add spark to salads. They also taste great in pasta dishes and stir-fries. Regularly harvesting the tender, young leaves will encourage the plant to keep producing new growth. When plants bloom, you can also harvest the flowers and stems for your salads. Arugula grows 12 to 16 inches tall. Buy one packet.

BORAGE
Borago officinalis

This easy-to-grow annual produces broad green leaves that add a cucumber flavor when chopped into salads. The edible, bright blue flowers also add color to green salads. Borage self-sows freely, so you'll probably only have to plant it once. If the self-sown seedlings aren't where you want them, you can move them to the desired location when they are still small (with one or two pairs of leaves). Borage grows 2 to 3 feet tall and tends to sprawl a bit as it matures. Thin seedlings to leave one plant. Buy one packet.

CARDOON
Cynara cardunculus

A relative of artichoke, this tall, thistlelike perennial herb is prized for its edible leaf stalks. Steam them and dress them with vinaigrette for a great side salad. Cardoon is also beautiful enough to grow just for its looks, with huge, 3- to 4-foot-wide clumps of arching, toothed, grayish green leaves. Plants reach 4 to 6 feet tall in bloom. Thin seedlings to leave one plant. Zones 5 to 9. Buy one packet.

252

Key

TEA

CRAFT

COOKING

CHICORY
Cichorium intybus

The leaves of the many types of chicory are slightly bitter but very delicious. They are extremely popular in Italian salads. Heading types, also called radicchio, produce dense clusters of leaves; cutting or leaf chicories grow in loose clumps. You could also grow witloof chicory, which produces long, thick roots that you harvest and bring indoors for winter "forcing." Chicory grows from 1 to 2 feet tall. Thin seedlings to stand about 1 foot apart. Zones 3 to 9. Buy one packet.

FENNEL
Foeniculum vulgare

Fennel's feathery, licorice-flavored leaves are wonderful in salads, herb butters, fish dishes, and salad dressings. You can also use the stems (eat them like celery) and the seeds (add them to desserts and breads). Fennel grows 3 to 5 feet tall. Thin seedlings to leave one plant. Zones 5 to 9. Buy one packet.

LETTUCE
Lactuca sativa

What would a salad be without crisp, cool lettuce? Make a break from the standard plastic-wrapped iceberg in the grocery store by growing a variety of head and leaf lettuces in your herbal salad garden. Choose at least two different kinds—perhaps one heading type, such as 'Buttercrunch' and one looseleaf type, such as 'Oak Leaf', or one green- and one red-leaved lettuce. Scatter the seeds on the soil surface and rake lightly; don't cover the seed. Thin plants to stand 8 to 12 inches apart. Buy two packets.

MESCLUN
Mixed greens and herbs

Mesclun is simply a mixture of different salad greens all grown together in the garden. Traditional mesclun mixes include arugula, chervil, endive, and lettuce, but many companies also offer other mixes, with ingredients such as chicory, dandelion, mustard, orach, and purslane. Buy a mix that sounds good to you, or blend your own from your favorite greens. Buy one packet.

NASTURTIUM
Tropaeolum majus

Nasturtiums will do double duty in your herbal salad garden because you can harvest both the leaves and the flowers. The fresh leaves have a peppery flavor that spices up salads, and the flowers make a great garnish. Bush types usually grow 10 to 12 inches tall; vining types may trail several feet. Thin seedlings to leave one plant in each spot. Buy one packet.

RADISH
Raphanus sativus

The colorful roots of this easy annual crop add a crisp texture and peppery flavor to salads. Red-skinned radishes

Salad Garden

are most common, but you can also find cultivars with pink or white skin for variety. Radishes grow and pass their prime quickly, so the best approach is to make small successive sowings (around 1 foot of row at a time) every ten days in spring and fall. Thin to stand 2 inches apart. Buy one packet.

Plants

Buy plants of the following herbs, or grow your own from divisions, cuttings, or seed sown indoors in pots.

BURNET
Poterium sanguisorba

This dainty-looking perennial herb forms mounds of ferny, pale green, jagged-edged leaves that taste just like cucumber. Pinch off the pink summer flowers to promote fresh leafy growth and discourage self-sowing. Burnet grows to 12 inches tall. Zones 4 to 9. Buy one plant.

CHIVES
Allium schoenoprasum

The mild onion-flavored foliage of this perennial herb is a great addition to almost any kind of green, pasta, or potato salad. The pretty pink or lavender, early summer flowers are also edible and attractive in salads. Garlic chives (*A. tuberosum*) has more of a garlic flavor. Both kinds of chives will self-sow prolifically if you do not remove the spent flowers. The plants reach 12 to 14 inches tall in bloom. Zones 3 to 9. Buy two plants.

HORSERADISH
Armoracia rusticana

The roots of this perennial herb look very much like a huge white radish with beige skin. Peeled, ground, and mixed with a little vinegar and salt, horseradish is an essential ingredient in making an American-style seafood sauce for cold shrimp and oysters on the half-shell. A little horseradish sauce or just a few of the young, tender leaves can also add zip to green salads. Horseradish grows 2 to 3 feet tall. Zones 5 to 9. Buy one root (or one already-started plant).

PARSLEY
Petroselinum crispum

The vitamin-rich leaves of this biennial herb are either frilly (in curly parsley) or flat (in flat-leaved or Italian parsley). Both are a welcome addition to green, pasta, or potato salads. For a steady supply of leaves, treat parsley as an annual: Pull out plants at the end of the first year and set out new ones each spring. The leafy clumps are usually 8 to 12 inches tall. Buy two plants.

SORREL
Rumex acetosa

The tangy leaves of garden sorrel add zest to green salads as well as to stir-fries and hot or cold soups. French sorrel (*R. scutatus*) has a milder flavor. Pinch off developing flower stems to encourage more leafy growth. The clumps usually grow 12 to 18 inches tall. Zones 5 to 9. Buy one plant.

254

Key

TEA

CRAFT

COOKING

The Seasonal Guide

An Herbal Salad Garden

season 1

January and February

| J | F | M | A | M | J | J | A | S | O | N | D |

Select a Site

Winter is a good time to start thinking about your new salad garden. First, figure out where you are going to put it. Look for a site with full sun—at least six hours of direct sun a day. Average, well-drained soil is ideal, but since you will be building raised beds, it's okay if your soil is on the wet, clayey, or rocky side. These square beds would fit well against a fence or in a corner of your yard.

If possible, site your salad garden near your house, so the plants will be within easy reach for harvesting. But since this garden is primarily for use and not for looks, you might want to screen it with a border of attractive herbs and flowers.

Buy Seeds and Plants

Your local garden center or nursery will probably stock many of the seeds and plants you need for this garden in spring. A few that might be a bit tricky to find include cardoon and mesclun seeds, horseradish roots, and burnet plants. Also keep in mind that local sources will carry a limited selection of vegetable seeds—perhaps two or three kinds of lettuce and one or two radish cultivars. To make sure you get all the herbs and vegetables you need, check out your favorite mail-order plant and seed catalogs, and place your orders now. Mail-order companies that specialize in culinary herbs and vegetables may offer special selections that are particularly popular with gourmet gardeners. You'll find addresses for some of my favorite mail-order catalogs in "Plants and Supplies" on page 262.

Gather Your Materials

These raised beds will be easiest to maintain if you frame their sides with rocks or timbers. A frame will help to hold the soil in place, so your paths will stay clean and the soil will stay loose and free-draining. The frames should be about 6 inches high. If you have lots of large rocks, you could use those to outline the beds. Cinder blocks (also known as cement blocks) are another option.

If you prefer a wood frame, you could use square timbers, which will stay in place by themselves, or else use boards held in place by metal rods driven into the ground. Avoid using pressure-treated or creosoted wood for your raised beds. Naturally rot-resistant woods, such as cedar, are a better choice if you can find them. You could also substitute plastic lumber—recycled plastic formed into boards or timbers.

Salad Garden

season 2

*March,
April, and May*

| J | F | **M** | **A** | **M** | J | J | A | S | O | N | D |

Prepare the Site

Before you dig, make sure that the soil is no longer frozen, and that it's dry enough to dig without making muddy clumps. (If you prefer, you could prepare the site for this garden in fall and plant the following spring.)

When you are ready to dig, mark off the outline of the four beds with stakes and string or with a sprinkling of lime or flour. If you are siting the garden in a corner or along a fence or wall, leave a 12- to 18-inch path around the outside of the garden, so you can easily reach all sides of the beds for planting, mainte- nance, and harvesting.

If you are creating this garden out of an existing lawn area, you could leave the 18-inch gaps between the beds as grass paths. Or, for lower maintenance, replace all the grass around the beds with wood chips, gravel, or pavers. If you choose a wood-chip, gravel, or paver path, remove all existing vegeta- tion from the whole garden site; other- wise, just strip the grass off the individual planting areas.

Loosen the soil in each of the beds to a depth of about 4 inches (or deeper, if you'd like). Then install whatever framing material you've chosen around each bed. Completely fill each frame

with a mixture of 2 parts well-drained topsoil and 1 part compost. Test the soil in each frame to check the pH. Add lime or sulfur, if needed, to adjust the pH so it is around neutral (7.0). Rake each bed to smooth the soil surface.

If you've decided to lay mulch around the beds, surround the outside of the entire garden with plastic or metal edging strips to keep grass from creeping into the paths. Mulch the paths, if desired, and your garden is ready for planting.

Plant Your Herbs

Following the planting diagram on page 251, start planting in early spring as soon as the beds are ready. Sow the seeds of arugula, borage, fennel, and radishes where you want the plants to grow. Wait until about two weeks before your last frost date to plant the cardoon, lettuce, and mesclun seeds. Sow chicory and nasturtium seeds after your last frost date.

For good germination, keep seeded areas moist; water lightly every day until seedlings appear. When seedlings are a few inches tall, thin them to their rec- ommended spacing. Snip off unwanted seedlings at ground level with scissors; pulling them out may disturb the roots of the remaining seedlings.

To extend your harvest of arugula, lettuce, mesclun, and radishes, sow again every two weeks through spring and again in late summer. Tuck these extra sowings in between other crops, or plant them where you've pulled out already- harvested rows.

Raised beds are ideal for easy-care herbal salad gardens. They provide excellent drainage and make planting and harvesting a snap!

Early spring is the time to set out your horseradish, either as a dormant root or an already-growing plant. Horseradish spreads quickly, so plant it in a large bottomless pot or bucket sunk into the center of one bed to contain the roots.

Set out the burnet, chives, parsley, and sorrel plants as you get them. If the plants were growing in a greenhouse when you bought them, make sure you harden them off before planting them out in the garden. (See "Handling Hardening Off" on page 10.)

season 3

June, July, and August

| J | F | M | A | M | **J** | **J** | **A** | S | O | N | D |

Minimize Garden Chores

Mulching is a smart way to reduce maintenance in your herbal salad garden. It helps to keep the soil moist, so you'll need to water less often. It blocks light from reaching the soil, so fewer weed seeds will sprout, and those that do will be easier to pull out. As it breaks down, it will release a small but steady supply of nutrients to feed your herbs and vegetables. And as an added bonus, it will keep soil from splashing up on plants, so you won't have to wash clinging dirt off harvested herbs and vegetables.

mix your own MESCLUN

*P*lant a patch of mesclun, and you have a ready-made tossed salad every time you harvest. Mesclun—basically a bunch of salad greens tossed together in one seed mix—is a great way to grow a variety of flavorful greens in a limited space.

One of the secrets of mesclun's popularity is its versatility. When you grow a variety of different leafy greens like arugula, radicchio, and leaf lettuces, you can make a completely different salad every day, especially when you add fresh herbs. Combining the different colors, flavors, and textures in exciting new combinations will add a touch of adventure to the dinner table.

Many seed catalogs now devote whole sections to gourmet greens, so buy a pack each of any that sound appealing. The exact proportions of ingredients are up to you. As a start, try mixing a whole packet of one or two lettuce cultivars with a half packet each of the other greens. After the first sowing, add more lettuce or more of the other greens to adjust the mix to your particular tastes.

If you eat lots of salad, plan on harvesting 1 foot of row per person per day. (Of course, you'll need less than that if you are growing other kinds of greens from your garden as well.) Pick the leaves while they're still small—just an inch or two long—and take a few from each plant so they'll keep on growing. Keep harvesting as long as the plants keep producing tender new growth. When growth slows or the leaves get too bitter, pull out the plants, and sow a new batch of seed.

Below are some suggestions for homemade mesclun mixes you can try, depending on your tastes.

Traditional mesclun:
Combine arugula, chervil, endive, and your favorite looseleaf lettuce.

Tangy mix:
Blend arugula, chicory (red and green), garden cress, lettuce (red and green), and mustard.

Tart mix:
Use arugula, chicory, dandelion, and endive.

Mild mix:
Combine chervil with corn salad, mizuna, orach, and purslane.

Due to mesclun's growing popularity, seed companies are also starting to offer prepackaged mesclun mixes. These mixes are also fun to experiment with and save you the effort of buying and blending several different kinds of seeds.

Wait until the soil has warmed up in late spring or early summer to mulch your garden. Weed thoroughly, then spread a 1-inch layer of compost between the plants. Top that with another inch of shredded bark or chopped leaves. If you don't get at least $\frac{1}{2}$ inch of rain each week, pull away a bit of mulch and use a trowel to check the soil underneath every few days. When the top 2 to 3 inches are dry, water thoroughly to soak the soil. Keep in mind that raised beds often dry out more quickly than regular gardens, so be prepared to water a bit more often for top yields.

Enjoy Your Herbs

Start harvesting from your salad garden in late spring to early summer. Pick the young, tender leaves of arugula starting when they are 4 to 6 inches long; keep picking until flowerstalks appear, then pull the plants out or allow them to flower and self-sow.

Start picking leaf lettuces and chicories as needed when they are big enough to use; harvest heading lettuces and chicories when the heads feel firm by cutting them off at ground level.

Mesclun is ready when the leaves are 3 to 4 inches tall; use scissors or a knife to cut them $\frac{1}{2}$ inch above the soil. (The plants will then produce new leaves.) Pull radishes when the roots are about 1 inch in diameter.

Pinch or snip off the leaves and/or flowers of borage, burnet, chives, fennel, nasturtium, parsley, and sorrel as needed throughout the growing season.

Salad Garden

You can start harvesting cardoon leaf stalks in midsummer; cut off the flat parts of the leaves before using the stalks. But for the most tender stalks, blanch them before harvesting by wrapping the bottom two-thirds of the plant in heavy paper or cardboard. Apply the wrap about a month before your average first fall frost. Harvest the blanched stems in three to four weeks.

Pot Up Herbs for Winter Harvest

After a whole season of enjoying home-grown salad greens, it's hard to go back to cellophane-wrapped lettuce from the grocery store. With a little advance planning, though, you can perk up winter salads with indoor-grown herbs.

In fall, dig up a plant or two of parsley as well as a clump of chives, and plant them in 6- to 8-inch pots of moist potting soil. After potting dug-up herbs, water them thoroughly, and set them in a shady spot for a few days. Before bringing plants indoors, inspect them carefully for signs of insect pests. If you do notice pest problems. spray with in-secticidal soap according to the directions on the label. Bring parsley plants in before frost. Leave potted chives outside through a few frosts before bringing them inside.

Your indoor herbs will need at least five hours of direct sun each day for good growth. If you can't provide this much natural light, supplement or replace it with fluorescent lights. Harvest as needed.

season 4
September and October

| J | F | M | A | M | J | J | A | **S** | **O** | N | D |

Prepare Your Garden for Winter

After the first few frosts, pull out any remaining arugula, borage, chicory, lettuce, mesclun, nasturtium, parsley, and radish plants. Add them to your compost pile.

You can harvest your horseradish roots now or wait until spring; dig them up (getting as many of the roots as pos-sible), replant one or two, and bring the rest indoors to store in a refrigerator or a cool cellar.

In early winter, cut the remaining topgrowth of burnet, cardoon, chives, fennel, horseradish, and sorrel close to the ground.

North of Zone 6, apply a winter mulch to prevent damage from thawing and refreezing during spells of mild winter weather. Wait until the ground has frozen to mulch; otherwise, you'll invite mice, voles, and other critters to make their nests in your garden. Spread several inches of loose straw over the beds, or use boughs from a Christmas tree after the holidays.

Keeping your garden going

This herbal salad garden includes both annual and perennial herbs and vegetables. It will take a little more work than a purely decorative garden to keep it in top shape, but you'll be rewarded by ample harvests of great-tasting salad ingredients all summer and fall.

In late winter to early spring, remove protective winter mulches as soon as your perennial herbs start sending up new growth.

If you didn't harvest your horseradish in fall, you can do it in spring as soon as the soil is thawed and dry enough to dig. Dig up as much as you can to get as many of the root pieces as possible. (Those you miss will probably sprout new plants!) Break or cut off what you need, set aside one or two pieces for replanting, and share the rest with friends. Before replanting, add a few handfuls of compost to the site, and dig the organic matter into the soil to enrich the growing area.

Spring is also the time to replant your annual herbs and vegetables, including the arugula, chicory, lettuces, mesclun, nasturtiums, parsley, and radishes. Borage usually self-sows, but if you don't notice any seedlings by midspring, replant with new seed.

Each year, renew the compost-and-bark or leaf mulch layers in late spring to early summer. Divide burnet, chives, and sorrel clumps every three or four years, or more often if they look crowded or begin to flower poorly. Replant a few of the vigorous outer sections; compost the rest, or share them with friends.

Plants and Supplies

The Cook's Garden

P.O. Box 535
Londonderry, VT 05148
(802) 824-3400
fax (802) 824-3027

Culinary vegetable and herb seeds, books, garden supplies

Bountiful Gardens

18001 Shafer Ranch Road
Willits, CA 95490-9626
(707) 459-6410
fax (707) 459-6410 **(6 pm - 10 pm)**

Organically grown and open-pollinated herb and vegetable seeds, gardening supplies

The Gourmet Gardener

8650 College Boulevard
Overland Park, KS 66210-1806
(913) 345-0490
fax (913) 451-2443

Herb seeds, books

Caprilands Herb Farm

534 Silver Street
Coventry, CT 06238
(203) 742-7244

More than 300 varieties of herb plants and seeds, tours, lectures, gardens

Le Jardin du Gourmet

P.O. Box 75
St. Johnsbury Center, VT 05863-0075
(800) 659-1446
fax (802) 748-9592

Herb seeds

Companion Plants

7247 N. Coolville Ridge Road
Athens, OH 45701
(614) 592-4643
fax (614) 593-3092

Herbs for all uses—aromatic, culinary, dye, ornamental, repellents

Nichols Garden Nursery

1190 N. Pacific Highway
Albany, OR 97321-4580
(541) 928-9280
fax (541) 967-8406

Herb seeds and plants, garlic and shallot bulbs, books, spices, potpourris, teas, accessories, garden supplies

262

Richters

Goodwood
Ontario, Canada L0C 1A0
(905) 640-6677
fax (905) 640-6641
http://www.richters.com

Herb plants and seeds, garden supplies

Sandy Mush Herb Nursery

316 Surrett Cove Road
Leicester, NC 28748-9622
(704) 683-2014
(Thursday, Friday, and Saturday, 9 am – 5 pm)

More than 600 culinary, tea, decorative, and scented herbs, scented geraniums, flowering perennials, seeds, books, gourmet vegetables

Shepherd's Garden Seeds

30 Irene Street
Torrington, CT 06790
(860) 482-3638
fax (860) 482-0532

Herb seeds, garden supplies

Well-Sweep Herb Farm

205 Mt. Bethel Road
Port Murray, NJ 07865
(908) 852-5390

Herb seeds and plants, books, garden supplies, tours, lectures, gardens

Recommended Reading

Blose, Nora, and Dawn Cusick. *Herb Drying Handbook*. New York: Sterling Publishing Co., 1993.

Bonar, Ann. *The Macmillan Treasury of Herbs: A Complete Guide to the Culitvation and Use of Wild and Domesticated Herbs*. New York: Macmillan Publishing Co., 1985.

Bradley, Fern, ed. *Rodale's Garden Answers: Vegetables, Fruits and Herbs*. Emmaus, PA: Rodale Press, 1995.

Bremness, Lesley. *The Complete Book of Herbs*. New York: Viking Studio Books, 1988.

Buchanan, Rita, ed. *Taylor's Guide to Herbs*. Boston: Houghton Mifflin Co., 1995.

DeBaggio, Thomas. *Growing Herbs from Seed, Cutting & Root*. Loveland, CO: Interweave Press, 1994.

Foster, Gertrude B., and Rosemary F. Louden. *Park's Success with Herbs*. Greenwood, SC: Geo. W. Park Seed Co., 1980.

Foster, Steven. *Herbal Renaissance: Growing, Using and Understanding Herbs in the Modern World*. Salt Lake City, UT: Gibbs-Smith Publisher, 1993.

Gardner, Jo Ann. *The Heirloom Garden: Selecting & Growing Over 300 Old-Fashioned Ornamentals*. Pownal, VT: Storey Communications, 1992.

Grieve, Mrs. M. *A Modern Herbal*. New York: Dover Publications, 1971.

Hoffman, David. *The New Holistic Herbal*. Rockport, MA: Element Books, 1991.

Kowalchik, Claire, and William H. Hylton, eds. *Rodale's Illustrated Encyclopedia of Herbs*. Emmaus, PA: Rodale Press, 1987.

Lathrop, Norma Jean. *Herbs: How to Select, Grow, and Enjoy*. Los Angeles: Price, Stern, Sloan, HP Books, 1981.

McClure, Susan. *The Herb Gardener*. Pownal, VT: Storey/Garden Way Publishing, 1996.

McHoy, Peter, and Pamela Westland. *The Herb Bible*. New York: Barnes and Noble, 1994.

Michalak, Patricia S. *Rodale's Successful Organic Gardening: Herbs*. Emmaus, PA: Rodale Press, 1993.

Oster, Maggie. *Herbal Vinegar*. Pownal, VT: Storey Publishing, 1994.

Oster, Maggie, and Sal Gilbertie. *The Herbal Palate Cookbook*. Pownal, VT: Storey Communications, 1996.

Rose, Jeanne. *Jeanne Rose's Modern Herbal*. New York: Perigee Books, Berkley Publishing Group, 1987.

Shaudys, Phyllis V. *Herbal Treasures: Inspiring Month-by-Month Projects for Gardening, Cooking and Crafts*. Pownal, VT: Storey Communications, 1990.

————. *The Pleasure of Herbs: A Month-by-Month Guide to Growing, Using and Enjoying Herbs*. Pownal, VT: Storey Communications, 1986.

Simmons, Adelma Grenier. *Herb Gardening in Five Seasons*. New York: Hawthorn Books, 1964.

Smith, Miranda. *Your Backyard Herb Garden*. Emmaus, PA: Rodale Press, 1996.

Tierra, Michael. *The Way of Herbs*. New York: Pocket Books, 1980.

Tyler, Varro E. *The Honest Herbal: A Sensible Guide to the Use of Herbs & Related Remedies*. 3rd ed. Binghamton, NY: The Haworth Press, 1993.

Weiss, Gaea, and Shandor Weiss. *Growing and Using the Healing Herbs*. Emmaus, PA: Rodale Press, 1985.

Wilson, Jim. *Landscaping with Herbs*. Boston: Houghton Mifflin Co., 1995.

Index

Illustration and Photo Credits

Illustrations

Mia Bosna: *traditional, color*
pages 1, 3, 5, 7, 11, 12, 16, 18, 19, 21, 73, 74, 77, 78, 79, 80, 84, 85, 86, 127, 152, 180, 191, 194, 206, 220, 278

Jean Emmons: *traditional, color gardens*
pages 130-131, 144-145, 158-159, 172-173, 186-187, 200-201, 212-213, 226-227, 238-239, 250-251

Jeff George: *traditional, black & white*
pages 23, 24, 26, 28, 29, 32, 33, 35, 36, 37, 38, 40, 41, 43, 49, 50, 52, 53, 56, 57, 58, 59, 60, 62, 63, 65, 66, 67, 69, 70, 89, 92, 99, 103, 106, 113, 116, 125

Dale Mack: *electronic, color*
Trowel icons starting on page 4, north icons starting on page 131, fork icons starting on page 132

Chris Rhoads: *electronic, color*
Icons starting on these pages: 3, 75, 133, 147, 161, 175, 189, 203, 215, 229, 241, 253

Photos

David Cavagnaro
pages 35, 42, 76, 86-87, 140, 156, 217, 226, 248, 258

Rosalind Creasy
pages x, 23, 64, 128, 168, 184, 190, 200, 207, 230

R. Todd Davis
pages 41, 56

© Alan & Linda Detrick
pages 38, 39, 40, 72, 78, 80, 134, 138, 147

John Glover
pages 20-21, 30, 49, 57, 60, 83, 158, 170, 177, 179, 198, 224

**judywhite/
New Leaf Images**
pages 25, 26, 29, 33, 54, 61, 62, 63, 67, 136, 238

© Dency Kane
pages 14, 244, 129, 257

Janet Loughrey
pages 53, 65, 172, 277

Charles Mann
pages 43, 44, 58, 71

Clive Nichols
pages 32, 55, 202

Jerry Pavia
pages 48, 52, 59, 142

Photosynthesis
pages 31, 51

**© photographer/
Positive Images**
pages 193, 218

Rodale Stock Images
Cover, pages iii, iv-v, vi, 2, 22, 24, 27, 28, 36, 37, 47, 50, 68, 69, 70, 75, 82, 126-127, 144, 164, 186, 188, 215, 232, 236, 245, 250

Mark Turner
pages 34, 45, 66, 130

**Kay Wheeler/
Spectrum Images**
pages 46, 210, 212

USDA Plant Hardiness Zone Map

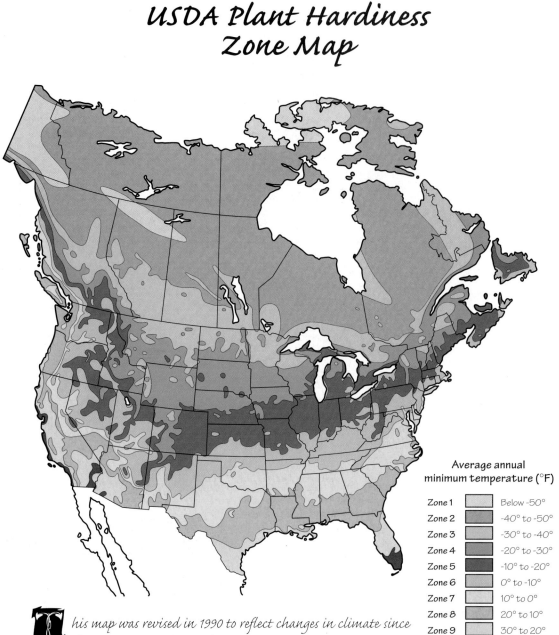

Average annual
minimum temperature (°F)

Zone 1		Below -50°
Zone 2		-40° to -50°
Zone 3		-30° to -40°
Zone 4		-20° to -30°
Zone 5		-10° to -20°
Zone 6		0° to -10°
Zone 7		10° to 0°
Zone 8		20° to 10°
Zone 9		30° to 20°
Zone 10		40° to 30°

This map was revised in 1990 to reflect changes in climate since the original USDA map, done in 1965. It is now recognized as the best estimator of minimum temperatures available. Look at the map to find your area, then match its pattern to the key on the right. When you've found your pattern, the key will tell you what hardiness zone you live in. Remember that the map is a general guide; your particular conditions may vary.